AGRARIAN RADICALISM IN CHINA, 1968–1981

HARVARD EAST ASIAN SERIES 102

The Council on East Asian Studies at Harvard University,
through the Fairbank Center for East Asian Research and
the Japan Institute, administers research projects designed to further
scholarly understanding of China, Japan, Korea, Vietnam,
Inner Asia, and adjacent areas.

AGRARIAN RADICALISM
IN CHINA, 1968–1981

David Zweig

HARVARD UNIVERSITY PRESS
Cambridge, Massachusetts, and London, England
1989

This book is printed on acid-free paper, and its binding materials
have been chosen for strength and durability.

Library of Congress Cataloging-in-Publication Data

Zweig, David.
  Agrarian radicalism in China, 1968–1981 / David Zweig.
    p.   cm.—(Harvard East Asian series; 102)
  Bibliography: p.
  Includes index.
  ISBN 0-674-01175-9 (alk. paper)
  1. Rural development—China. 2. Radicalism—China. 3. Commu-
nism and agriculture—China. 4. China—Social conditions—1949–
1976.
  I. Title. II. Series.
  HN 740.Z9C695 1989   88-21261
  306'.0951—dc19   CIP

To Dan, Bernie, Belma, and Bobby

CONTENTS

TABLES

FIGURES

PREFACE

THE CULTURAL REVOLUTION'S promise to create a revolutionary society free of inequalities and bureaucratic oppression caught the imagination of young people world-wide in the sixties. I was among those who hoped that China had found a way to create a different kind of socialism. As a student in Beijing from 1974 to 1976, I learned how Mao's theory to prevent bureaucratism was supposed to work, but at the same time saw the tension it bred in the lives of most Chinese. I was skeptical then; however, it was Mao's death and the fall of the Gang of Four in 1976 that changed my perception of China along with China's perception of itself. What had once appeared radical now looked retrogressive; what had seemed spontaneous was now seen to be oppressive; noble purposes had been driven by ignoble acts. I knew all this before, but somehow I had hoped that China would succeed where other revolutions had failed.

In response to a comment by Michel Oksenberg during a 1978 seminar at The University of Michigan about rural inequality, I began my decade-long investigations of peasant China. China's vast countryside provided a complex arena for examining how Mao's supporters used his theories during the Cultural Revolution decade (1966–1976) to try and create a new socialist countryside, and how peasants and local cadres reacted to that drive toward rural communism. This book, an outgrowth of that study, also addresses the broader issue of popular resistance to state-directed social change and efforts of postrevolutionary regimes to reassert control over society in order to continue socioeconomic and political transformations.

Like the previous generation of analysts of contemporary China, I began my research by spending three months in Hong Kong in fall 1980, where I interviewed eighteen refugees and emigrés at the Universities Service Center. In Hong Kong it was difficult to find a large population of informants who had lived in the countryside for an extended period of time. The experiences of urban youths who

ix

had settled in the countryside were often limited to a few years of rural residence. Yet other Hong Kong informants proved immensely useful, particularly two people who had participated in work teams sent to the countryside to implement radical policies.

China's opening to the West eventually allowed me the opportunity to go directly to rural China. From December 1980 through July 1981, while a visiting scholar at Nanjing University, I interviewed peasants, team and brigade officials, and commune leaders in three different rural collectives outside Nanjing, Jiangsu Province: a prosperous vegetable brigade in Nanjing's near suburbs, directly under the city's administration, which I visited for about thirty-five days; a comparatively poor, hilly brigade located north of the Yangzi River but still within Nanjing's city limits, where I lived for twenty-seven days in the commune guesthouse; and a large, wealthy, rice-producing brigade with a developed industrial infrastructure, also under the city's administration in a county south of Nanjing, where I lived in the brigade headquarters for fifteen days.

At all times I talked openly with cadres and peasants. In 1981 the radical policies I was studying had been repudiated, so people felt relatively free to inform me of what I believe to be the real events. No doubt the cadres who had implemented these policies were still in power, but when they were not self-critical, other officials provided different interpretations of events that helped clarify the real situation. Except for the first two weeks in my first research site and a few other instances, I carried out all my interviews on a one-to-one basis. In fact, after my second research visit, Jiangsu Province's provincial Foreign Affairs Office criticized Nanjing University for leaving me unaccompanied in this commune. During my third visit, even though I was constantly accompanied by a commune official and a professor, they always left the room during my interviews. In one instance they asked two cadres who wanted to listen to an interview with a peasant in their village to leave the room as well.

The two biggest deficiencies of Hong Kong informants, as compared to informants within the People's Republic of China (PRC), are the partial picture they portray of events and the difficulty in verifying their stories. Only in a few cases have interviewers in Hong Kong been able to study one location and cross-check the stories. For example, Anita Chan, Richard Madsen, and Jonathan Unger, authors of *Chen Village: The Recent History of a Peasant Community in Mao's China* (Berkeley: University of California Press, 1984), interviewed a whole emigré community from one PRC village living in Hong Kong. In another instance, Victor Nee researched a Fujian provincial village after interviewing its villagers in Hong Kong. But generally it is difficult to know if Hong Kong informants are embellishing their stories or even lying. By checking their information with newspaper reports and other interviews we can verify the patterns they describe. But issues—the level of policy initiation, intensity of support for and opposition to policies, and the exact timing of events—are hard to corroborate when the researcher depends on one source of information.

In China, in contrast, one has access to levels of rural cadres and officials unavailable in Hong Kong. Not only did I interview Nanjing officials responsible for agriculture and county officials responsible for field and water conservation projects, but I spent many hours talking to commune and brigade officials who worked under their city and county superiors. At times the officials on the various levels openly criticized each other over events that had transpired five years before. This way of learning about local events can teach one a great deal about local politics and enable one to interpret one's data more confidently. To this extent, one develops a feel for the local political environment.

Another frequent complaint in the 1970s was that Hong Kong refugees and emigrés told only the seedy side of Chinese life. Living in China allowed me to clarify this problem. Even in the late 1970s many people indicated they would have left China if offered the chance, but primarily for economic, not political reasons. And given the conflicts, jealousies, rumor-mongering, and bureaucratic fiat I discovered in rural China, it is clear that Hong Kong informants rarely lied about the complicated nature of rural life. The picture scholars have constructed of rural China over the past twenty to thirty years is basically accurate; if they erred it was to underestimate the problems. Local "emperors" do terrorize certain vilages, lineage conflicts do disrupt policy implementation and local life, and sexual mischief is commonplace in rural China. As the radicals tried to transform rural China in accordance with their vision, they ignored these rural realities. Since rural reality played a major role in defeating Mao and the radicals, it would be foolish for us to ignore it as well.

My field research in Hong Kong and Nanjing was supplemented by unofficial interviews with Chinese college students and urban ("rusticated") youths who had lived in the countryside for five or ten years and were currently living in Beijing or Nanjing. One informant introduced me to another. These youths were extremely insightful about rural life and had lived in areas rarely visited by Hong Kong emigrés. Access to them gave me additional information on events in Shanxi, Shaanxi, Jilin, Shandong, northern and southern Jiangsu, Zhejiang, Anhui, Fujian, Hubei, Hebei, Hunan, Guangxi, Yunnan,

Sichuan, and of course Guangdong provinces. No location had been totally unaffected by the radical program, showing that the impact and pressures to implement various radical policies had been widespread and strong. Yet the local responses varied across localities, which was also true of my three field sites.

Although my interviews in rural China were officially authorized, I must protect the identities of my informants. I doubt that the state will want to track them down, but the possibility exists that higher-level rural officials might take retribution against subordinates who criticized them. In the notes to the text I therefore refer to three general categories of interviews—Hong Kong interview, 1980; Rural Nanjing interview, 1981; and Rusticated youth interview, Beijing or Nanjing, 1980 or 1981—and do not designate a particular person, date, or place. I will gladly supply information for specific citations should any reader want to know more about the circumstances of a particular interview.

Another major source of information was the Chinese press, particularly the *People's Daily*, which during the "rightist revanches" of 1971–1972 and 1979–1980 published much information on local events. In the later period reporters who investigated places that had carried out radical policies corroborated the picture my informants and field research drew. No doubt articles in the controlled press reflected government bias, but they also told their readers when national radical leaders tried to mobilize support for their policies. By comparing the official line of the press with information from interviews on the timing and pattern of implementation, I can address a major issue of this study: the relationship between elite advocacy of radical policies and local implementation.

Also useful was the digest of provincial newspapers compiled by People's University in Beijing, entitled *Zhonggue renmin daxue shubao zilai, baokan ziliao, nongye jingji* (Chinese People's University Materials Room, Material Republished from the Press, Agricultural Economics). A few articles from 1978 were of particular importance. Recent publications such as *Zhongguo nongye dashiji, 1949–1980* (Major Events in Chinese Agriculture; Beijing: Nongye chubanshe, 1982), and *Zhonghua renmin gongheguo jingji dashiji, 1949–1980* (Major Economic Events in the PRC; Beijing: Shehui kexueyuan chubanshe, 1984) have supplied new information on national meetings about which we previously knew very little. The Chinese have also eased access to documents from major meetings through collections such as *Nongcun jingji zhengce huibian, 1978–1981*, vols. 1 and 2, and *1981–1983*, vols. 1 and 2 (Compendium of Agricultural Economic Policies; Beijing: Nongcun duwu chubanshe, 1982). These books have enriched my outline of major policy debates. As a result of this wide variety of sources, I feel comfortable generalizing about the pattern of politics radical policies generated across the entire country.

The list of people who helped me finish this project is long, and I apologize if I have forgotten some who contributed along the way. At the University of Michigan Michel Oksenberg shared his masterly insights on Chinese politics with me. Martin Whyte, a most gentle but acute critic, was of immense help, as was Allen Whiting, whose friendship helped me survive graduate school. Robert Putnam made me think about elite-mass relations, while Norma Diamond and Harriet Mills helped shape my views about China. I give my thanks to Robert Dernberger, Michael Cohen, and Albert Feuerwerker. I acknowledge an intellectual debt to my longtime friends from Michigan: Kirk Beattie, Kevin Kramer, Peter Hauslohner, Nina Halpern, James Tong, Richard Barrett, Merit Janow, Clement Henry, and Yeung Sai-cheung.

At the Universities Service Centre in Hong Kong, Director John Dolfin and my research assistant, who prefers to remain anonymous, were both extremely helpful. My research in China was facilitated by the Department of External Affairs in Ottawa, Canada's Embassy in Beijing, China's Ministry of Education, and the Foreign Affairs Office and Economics Department at Nanjing University. In these places I was helped by Don Waterfall, Mary Sun, Ji Xiaolin, Zhang Rongcun, Chen Guanghua, and Zhou Haisu. I will always owe a special debt to the Nanjing peasants and local leaders who opened their minds and hearts to me. Their continued friendship furnishes me with new insights into the complexities of rural China.

Research support came from the Rackham School of Graduate Studies, the University of Michigan, and the Social Sciences and Humanities Research Council of Canada.

Wherever I have worked, colleagues have supported my efforts to complete this book. The Political Science Department at Florida International University (FIU) under Chairman John Stack gave me a lighter course load, and the College of Arts and Sciences (Dean James A. Mau) funded data analysis carried out by Perin Patel and Li Qiang. Brian Nelson at FIU made excellent comments on chapter 1. Colleagues in Political Science at the University of Waterloo, Ontario, gave me a semester off to finish the first draft. Thanks are due to Dean Robin Banks of the Faculty of Arts for financial assistance, to Ginny Freeman for typographical help, and especially to Brian MacOwan for data analysis, graphics, and text formatting. Another grant from the

Social Sciences and Humanities Research Council of Canada in 1985–86 supported my work at that time.

The Fairbank Center at Harvard University gave me a postdoctoral fellowship in 1984–1985. Benjamin Schwartz, Patrick Maddox, Philip Kuhn, Dwight Perkins, Lucian Pye, William Joseph, and especially Roderick MacFarquhar read parts or all of my study, while Nancy Hearst shared her bibliographic insights with me. I am grateful to Merle Goldman for her encouragement.

Other people who read and made useful comments on my work include Daniel Levine, Jonathan Unger, Edward Friedman, Thomas Bernstein, and James Scott. Thanks are also due to my new colleagues at the Fletcher School of Law and Diplomacy, Tufts University, for intellectual support, and to Dean Jeswald Salacuse and the Hewlett Fund at Fletcher. The roster of helpful people includes Mark Rosenberg, James Heitler, Larry Sullivan, Don Klein, Jeremy Paltiel, Victor Falkenheim, Edwin Winckler, Stanley Rosen, John P. Burns, Morris Mottale, Ross Munro, and Ramon Myers.

An article based upon the material in this book, entitled "Strategies of Policy Implementation: 'Policy Winds' and Brigade Accounting in Rural China, 1968–1978," was published in *World Politics*, 37, no. 2 (January 1985): 267-293. I wish to thank the publisher for permission to use this material, much of which appears in chapters 2 and 5. A second paper appeared in Italian in an edited volume on the occasion of the tenth anniversary of the death of Mao Zedong.

Special thanks are due to Kathleen Hartford and Paul Cohen, who read the entire manuscript, as did Marc Blecher, who was there at the beginning, back in 1980 when I was groping for a theory, and again at the end, when I wrote it up. Their chapter-by-chapter comments helped improve this manuscript considerably. I am also grateful to two anonymous readers for Harvard University Press for their excellent and helpful comments, as well as to my editors, Aida Donald, Elizabeth Suttell, and Anita Safran.

I owe a special debt to Daniel Tretiak, my first professor of Chinese politics, who has always told me I had the ability to be a scholar, and B. Michael Frolic, my second professor, who had nothing but doubts, which he has shared with me for a decade and a half. I dedicate this book to them, to my late father, and to my mother, who remains my staunchest supporter.

INTRODUCTION:
DILEMMAS OF THE
POST-REVOLUTIONARY
STRUGGLE

REVOLUTIONS DIE. Caught between the impetus of pursuing continuing socioeconomic and political transformations and the competing pull toward stasis, all successful revolutionary movements succumb to the Thermidor. Society, tiring of the constant revolutionary assaults and the high cost of incessant mobilization, demands a "convalescence from the fever of revolution,"[1] which allows forces favoring development to defeat those still trying to build utopia. Popular demands for economic prosperity increase, and beneficiaries of the inequalities generated during the early postrevolutionary stage develop a profound interest in preventing any challenges to the extant distribution of wealth, power, and prestige.[2]

The changes wrought by Deng Xiaoping since 1978, involving constant, themselves almost revolutionary assaults on post-Mao China, show that the goal of economic development has replaced the search for utopia. Slogans advocate raising the GNP and per capita living standards, while references to communism merely justify continued Party control of the political realm. The Party's historic mission—to help the proletariat overthrow the bourgeoisie, bring on socialist society, create selfless individuals without ties to private property, lead society close to communism and then wither away—has been set aside. In contemporary China, modernization and economic prosperity are the name of the game.

Other socialist regimes have tried to overturn the new socioeconomic and political hierarchies that develop during the postrevolutionary stage by reasserting the revolutionary process.[3] Stalin's "revolution from above" in the late 1920s and the early 1930s ended the liberal economic policies of the New Economic Policy (NEP) under which the private sector had made a comeback after the extreme controls of "war communism." Economic radicalization followed a renewed emphasis on proletarianizing culture, the arts, and educa-

1

tion policy begun in 1928.[4] Similarly, Cuba's "revolutionary offensive" of the late 1960s tried to destroy the private sector in commerce and agriculture and to replace material with moral incentives. Although nationalization had begun in the mid-1960s, this movement sought to crush the private trade sector that had been growing amidst wide-scale state control.[5] Both these situations reflect attempts by ruling communist leaders to attack the complacency which followed the establishment of political and economic control and to push society more rapidly and violently along the path of radicalism.

Of all modern revolutions, however, the Chinese case, both theoretically and practically, has seen the most significant attempts to keep the revolution alive in the postrevolutionary era. Guided by Mao Zedong's theories on change in postrevolutionary society, China first attempted its ill-fated Great Leap Forward of 1957–1959. During the Cultural Revolution decade (1966–1976) and continuing in part through the reign of Hua Guofeng (1976–1978), radical leaders in the Chinese Communist Party (CCP) tried not only to mobilize rural society for socioeconomic and political changes that would prevent private interests and inequalities from undermining the collectivization of the 1950s, but to move rural China to even higher stages of collectivism.

This book addresses the larger issue of ideology and politics by looking both at how China's leaders tried to introduce ideologically based policies into a peasant society, and at how local officials and peasants responded to that effort. It examines the values and goals that led Maoists to try and turn an impoverished countryside into a Marxist utopia to prevent the possible death of the revolution. It describes the political machinations that arose from their efforts and the innovative strategy they employed to introduce their policies into the local areas. Most important, it suggests that politicians' beliefs count, and some communists, motivated by a need to save the world, pursue those goals out of ideological commitment, not simply as instrumental choices in the pursuit of political power.

This book also addresses the theme of central-local and elite-mass relations and the dilemmas of policy implementation in hierarchical or bureaucratic systems. While national leaders have goals that inform their policy proposals, the need to delegate decision-making authority to the localities undermines their control over the entire process. Local leaders must survive under dual pressures for policy conformity and the need to adjust policies to mesh with local interests. The mixed incentives created by their position in the bureaucratic hierarchy force them to tamper with national policies. Fortunately, "information assymetry," created by local control over information flows to national leaders, and the difficulty of monitoring policy compliance create a "leakage of authority," which allows for false reportage and local policy evasion or adaptation.[6] Factors such as geography, topography, and level of economic development begin to affect the pattern of policy implementation, as do the policies themselves, which carry within them the seeds of evasion and adaptation.[7] As a result, final outcomes, while triggered by national leaders, often differ dramatically from their goals, reflecting instead the interests of the dominant sectors in the localities, whether they be local officials or local corporate groups who hold the reigns of power.

Finally, this book was also written to fill a gap which exists in the literature owing to limited interest in peasantry under postrevolutionary situations. The response of peasants and cadres to ideologically based policies that challenge the distribution of wealth and power shows that peasants, above all, respond rationally, and their behavior is determined by their position within the extant political economy.[8] Cadres and peasants, favored by the distribution of wealth, power, and opportunity prevailing in the current system, will resist those policies; and where resistance is impossible, they will adjust them to meet their own needs.

Similarly, since the ruling hegemony that legitimizes the distribution of resources and opportunities works to the disadvantage of some peasants,[9] losers under the extant regime can support alternative norms that offer them more protection or undermine the authority of those who benefit from the current rules. They may even appear to act against their own material interests, expressing instead concerns for moral and economic justice.[10] Driven by contradictory desires for prosperity and fears that others who employ the open economy more effectively will outstrip them politically and economically, disadvantaged peasants may support restricting everyone's opportunity to prosper. Although such policies may harm these peasants' absolute economic situation, they improve their relative status by narrowing the income or opportunity gap between themselves and the beneficiaries of the established political economy. While they appear to support equality, justice, and the strictures of a moral economy, their support is not based on an innate egalitarianism—except insofar as egalitarianism breeds redistribution of wealth. Instead, this anti-equity position of the Chinese peasant and his support for radical policies is based on a perceived threat to his own security and status. To this extent, morality and rationality are intertwined.

But before we can look at these efforts to reradicalize the countryside in 1968–1978 to prevent the Thermidor of the revolution, we need to look first at the initial postrevolutionary attempt to reinvigorate the revolutionary ethos. The failure of the Great Leap Forward (1957–1959) and the subsequent New Economic Policies (NEP) of 1960–1965 form a critical background to our study.

Prelude to Reradicalizing the Countryside, 1958–1966

Why did Mao and the radicals try to launch their rural crusade in 1968? In large part, their political experiences before, during, and after the Great Leap convinced them that it was necessary to push rural society beyond the degree of collectivization that existed in 1966. From their perspective, the 1950s Land Reform and incipient cooperation among peasants had not prevented the reintroduction of exploitation, usury, and traditional values. Yet without constant socioeconomic and political changes, China's peasant society would quickly revert to pre-1949 patterns. And while Mao's perceptions may have been wrong, or at least colored by his penchant for seeing class struggle and class enemies everywhere, many local cadres in the early- and mid-1950s had abandoned their role as social reformers and tried to become "new rich peasants."[11] National leaders, too, who felt that radical policies were pushing peasants too quickly into cooperatives, had dismantled collectives, dramatically slowing down social change and the transition to socialism. For Mao and the radicals, this was their first experience of a Chinese Thermidor, and it was intolerable. Their concerns about inequalities of power, wealth, and status generated by the Soviet model of development—as well as a desire to modernize China as rapidly as possible with a minimum of state investment—led Mao and other radical leaders to launch the Great Leap Forward in an attempt to catapult Chinese society into the communist utopia.[12]

They hoped that mass mobilization, organizational changes and revolutionary enthusiasm generated by the Great Leap would break down the regularized patterns of political and economic activity to which the Chinese peasants had succumbed and bring on the advent of the "heavenly temple" of the Chinese millennium. But slogans of "three years of hard work for 10,000 years of prosperity" could not alter the fact that China in 1959 was extremely poor, and the rural economy depended on good weather, careful planning and hard work. Beginning in 1959, terrible weather, poor harvests, excessive grain procurement brought on by exaggerated local crop reporting, and exhaustion among the population triggered the "three bad years" (1960–1962).[13] In the ensuing famine perhaps as many as 25 million people died. This catastrophic failure, which convinced many Chinese leaders and peasants that China needed economic development, not revolutionary rhetoric, had apparently ensured a return to more rational economic policies.

Following the Great Leap's collapse and Mao's subsequent withdrawal to what he called "the second line of command," the CCP came under the stewardship of Liu Shaoqi and Deng Xiaoping. They and more moderate Party leaders cut a deal with the peasants and introduced a Chinese version of NEP.[14] In the major policy statement on agriculture of the 1960s, called the *Sixty Articles on Agriculture*,[15] the CCP in 1962 promised to refrain from interfering in the peasants' private lives. This document legalized a major expansion of the private sector, the reintroduction of material incentives, the formation of smaller economic units—with the production team as the basic unit of ownership and account (see Table 1)—and a moratorium on mobilizing peasants for large-scale field and water conservation projects.[16] The document also restricted county, commune, and brigade control over the direction of social and economic change by criticizing their cadres for expropriating team labor, capital, or equipment for their own use without permission.

The concessions were short-lived, as Mao and his radical supporters had learned a very different lesson from the Great Leap's failure.[17] Having blamed its collapse on the obstructionism of central leaders, local vested interests opposed to socialism, and excessive haste in fullfilling the radical program, rather than the program itself, Mao had turned his attention in 1959 to explaining how "revisionism"—the Marxist version of Thermidor—had developed under socialism.[18] His polemics with the Soviet Union in the early 1960s and analysis of changes in that society eventually convinced Mao that a capitalist restoration could still occur even after the advent of socialism.[19] So in the early 1960s, at the very moment when Liu and Deng were striking their bargain with the peasants and introduc-

Table 1. Institutional structure in rural China, 1975.

Organizational level	Organizational realm	Party organizational unit	Number of units nation-wide	Average rural population per unit[a]
County	State	Committee	2,200	350,000
Commune	Collective	Committee	52,615	14,768
Brigade	Collective	Branch	677,000	1,148
Team	Collective	Cell[b]	4,820,000	161
Household	Private	Member	168,000,000	4.6

SOURCE: *Zhongguo nongye nianjian, 1980* (Chinese Agricultural Yearbook; Beijing: Nongye chubanshe, 1981), p. 5.
a. Total rural population in 1975 was 777,000,000.
b. Cell formed only if there were three party members in a team.

ing the *Sixty Articles*, Mao was interpreting rural prosperity, the reintroduction of rural social hierarchies, and cadre abuses of political power to increase their personal wealth as signals of the impending death of the revolution.

To strike back against Liu and Deng, whose moderate policies were facilitating the reemergence of the private sector, superstition, religious activities, and rural vested interests under socialism, Mao warned Party leaders in fall 1962 "never to forget the class struggle."[20] At that Tenth Plenum of the Eighth Party Committee he launched the Socialist Education Movement, where associations of the prerevolutionary poor and lower-middle peasants were to investigate and criticize local leaders.[21] Within this radicalized environment, petty corruption was translated into class enemy activity, and peasants who made money privately became "newborn capitalist elements." Cadres, too, were reminded of the high price of opposing national policies and national trends.

Mao's weakened political position limited the radical thrust of his Socialist Education Movement. Under Liu Shaoqi and Deng Xiaoping, the Party, not the masses, controlled the campaign. Bureaucrats and college students entered villages all over China, and they, not peasants, criticized local corruption, often replacing one group of local leaders with their opponents. In much of rural China, the movement had ground to a halt by 1965.

A policy the Party began in 1964, but about which foreigners knew almost nothing until 1987, facilitated the Maoist efforts to reradicalize the rural areas. Creating a Third Front—a strategic decision by China's top leaders including Mao—involved a massive redirection of state investment to construct immense heavy industrial projects deep within the Chinese interior: as much as two-thirds of all government funds went to build these projects between 1964 and 1972.[22] This strategy, driven mainly by the increasing American and Soviets threats, further illuminates why the Dazhai movement began in 1964; moreover, it resonates well with radical efforts to build communism in the Chinese countryside through local grain self-sufficiency, ideological transformation of the peasantry, and the reliance on moral incentives, high levels of forced capital formation, rural modernization through labor mobilization, shifts to larger accounting units, and restricting the private sector.

The Ideology and Strategy of Agrarian Radicalism

As Mao and the radicals saw the gap between the ultimate goal of a perfected society and the tactics employed to attain that utopia widen, they grew wary that supporters of capitalism had worked their way into the CCP. For them, policy differences reflected class struggle under socialism within the Party itself. So Mao and the radicals prepared for the day when they could redirect China back onto the revolutionary path and mobilize the masses for that "great leap into prosperity."

Once the Cultural Revolution routed the urban Party and managerial structures that had supported the NEP of the 1960s, the radical leaders turned their attention to reradicalizing the rural areas. Believing that a key obstacle to the revolutionary transition to communist society was the resilient, private petty-bourgeois economy and mentality of the Chinese peasant, while at the same time seeing the peasants' political and cultural backwardness as a clean slate upon which to draw "beautiful socialist pictures," these leaders advocated the wide-scale implementation of a panoply of policies within the countryside based on Mao's theory of "continuing the revolution under the dictatorship of the proletariat."[23]

Imbued by a "penchant for activism" common to most radical movements,[24] and motivated by the more voluntaristic side of Marxism,[25] the Maoists believed, as did the Calvinists before them, that great leaps of faith and continuous warfare against Satanic forces could bring about the ideal society.[26] They refused to compromise politically and continued to pursue their radical program, even though it endangered their political authority.

This program included class struggle by the poorer peasants against the vestiges of precollectivization rural leaders and the newly emerging local vested interests. As in other socialist systems, where increasing the size of collective units or turning those units into state farms demonstrated transitions to higher stages of socialism and communism,[27] the radicals advocated shifts in the level of ownership and income distribution of the rural production units from the team to the brigade, widespread amalgamation of production teams into larger ones, and the development of brigade and commune industries. As was the case with Cuba's "revolutionary offensive" of the late 1960s,[28] a "moral incentive economy" was to generate higher levels of political consciousness and a willingness to work for moral rather than material rewards, all the while weakening the peasants' ties to the private economy and private property by wide-scale restrictions on private plots, markets, and household sidelines. Finally, as in other resource-poor revolutionary regimes, where the primitive accumulation of capital was to create the material basis for communist society without state investment,[29] the radicals mobilized peasant labor and imposed high rates of forced savings on them. These structural, moral, and economic transformations were expected to prevent inequality and lay the basis for the shift to the communist utopia.

Elite Politics and Informal Policy Implementation

How was this program of renewal to be introduced? In almost all communist movements, disagreements between ideologues and modernizers, which remain muted during the revolutionary struggle for power, resurface as major intra-party disputes in the postrevolutionary stage.[30] Since all indigenous communist revolutions have occurred in the less developed societies, the issue of economic development versus continued socioeconomic and political change surfaces soon after order is established. For radicals, the revolution's purpose is the liberation of humanity, which can be attained only by the advent of communism. Policies undermining the movement towards utopia are labeled counter-revolutionary or revisionist. Modernizers, on the other hand, respond to demands for economic growth and improved living standards from a populace who see their impoverishment as the consequence of continued revolutionary struggles. Given this popular hunger for development and stability, the modernizers and their developmental policies are hard to defeat.

As a result of the popularity of the more moderate developmental program, victory for the ideologues and the defeat of the modernizers has depended on the active participation of the supreme leader. Without Stalin and Castro, postrevolutionary radicalization would not have occurred in their respective countries.[31] Yet between 1968 and 1976 Mao never openly supported the radicals' rural program and remained relatively inactive in this conflict, even though the radicals were applying his theory to the countryside. His wife's argument in 1975 that the Chairman favored certain revisions and additions to the *Sixty Articles* has not been substantiated.[32] In fact Mao reportedly opposed publishing the speech in which Jiang Qing made these remarks.[33] According to other sources, he tried to prevent his 1975–1976 political attack on Deng Xiaoping from spilling over into the countryside.[34] Mao's limited political role greatly weakened the Chinese radicals' ability to introduce their program.

Rather than being the leader of the radical forces and the consistent supporter of revolution over development, Mao thus played a far more ambiguous role in the struggle between radicals and moderates in the 1970s. Mao's ambivalence was rooted in power politics. From 1969 to 1971 he could ill afford to alienate conservative regional military leaders whose support he needed to defeat his erstwhile successor, Lin Biao. The absence of central directives supporting agrarian radicalism in 1969–1971 suggests that Mao refused to take a formal stand on this issue. Moreover, a late 1971 Central Party Document criticizing the radical policies may have been the quid pro quo for the military's help in purging Lin.[35] Second, Mao often played the great balancer, preferring to let the modernizers and ideologues fight, intervening only if one side's dominance threatened to lead the ship of state too much in any one direction.[36] In this way he undermined those who were fighting for the very values he espoused during the early 1960s and during the Cultural Revolution.

On the other hand, Mao maintained the legitimacy of the radical line by preventing the modernizers from controlling rural policy making. The draft constitution circulating in late 1970, which would have legitimized the private sector, was never adopted. According to the 1981 *Resolution on Party History*, Mao in 1972 was more concerned about an overemphasis on development than excessive attention to ideology.[37] Following the 1975 acceptance by the National People's Congress of the peasants' rights to private plots, household sidelines, and private marketing, Mao launched the Bourgeois Rights Campaign, which called for restricting, not expanding, these private freedoms. Finally, when Mao believed that Deng's moderate course was attacking the Cultural Revolution and becoming a revisionist line, he criticized Deng in late 1975 and removed him from his posts for the second time in spring 1976.

Without Mao's legitimation, advocates of agrarian radicalism were sorely pressed to mobilize and maintain support for their policies. Throughout most of this decade they never totally controlled central politics, confronting opposition from both moderate Party leaders in Beijing, who saw folly in their utopian goals, and from conservative regional military leaders, who in the wake of the Cultural Revolution feared that the continuing revolution would create political instability in the localities they controlled. Their more radical policies, which contravened the *Sixty Articles* and generated great hostility, never received the formal support of the Central Committee leadership.[38]

Facing this political opposition and Mao's ambivalence, the ideologues acted as a minority opposition to the dominant moderate forces in the leadership[39] and resorted to an alternative strategy for mobilizing support for their nonofficial policies. Relying on the weak degree of institutionalization at the center of the Chinese communist system, they went outside the formal policy implementation channels and introduced their policies into parts of the countryside between 1968 and 1978.

While analysts have presented various models or explanations of the policy making process in China and other socialist systems,[40] little attention has focused directly on the implementation of nonofficial policies.[41] Yet leaders in socialist systems who confront opposition at the center have at various times gone directly to the people and local officials to mobilize support for their own proposals. Stalin, Khrushchev, and now Gorbachev have all followed this pattern.

During the radical decade Chinese radicals used informal channels or "policy winds" to introduce their faction's policies onto local political agendas. Through speeches, newspaper articles, personal ties and networks of political allies, organized visits, and by inserting their policies into ongoing political or economic campaigns, like riders on congressional bills, they increased the degree of ideological fervor, fear, and coercion in the political system and generated a radical environment in many county and subcounty units of rural China. This way they often persuaded some elements of the local body politic to implement parts of the radical program, for within such a radical environment local cadres knew they risked being labeled class enemies if they opposed leftist policies. Fearful of rightist labels, or concerned with advancing some parochial political purpose, many local cadres chose to implement these unofficial policies.

Agrarian Radicalism at the Local Level

Although some analysts still employ a totalitarian framework for explaining politics in socialist systems, a model based on the centralized leadership of a single individual, a unified party, central planning and control of the means of production and communication cannot explain the extent of local diversity that existed in China at the end of the radical era. No doubt the Cultural Revolution in the cities often reached Kafkaesque proportions, as when the discovery of a headless Mao statuette sent a Nanjing city quarter into round-the-clock study meetings in search of the culprit.[42] Moreover, on rural policies about which national leaders were more united such as the widespread growing of grain, policy implementation was more uniform. But the tentative nature of the links between national and local leaders caused by the breakdown of the CCP, the great divergence between articulated, or formal, and informal national policies, the gap between nationally defined goals and local policy implementation, and the dynamic nature of local politics from the late 1960s through the mid-1970s necessitate a far more complex approach to local Chinese politics.[43]

This study attempts such an approach. It argues that the strength of supporters and opponents of each policy from the county to the village was critical. Moreover, the way the policy affected each region—how it filtered through a village's geographic location, its physical or topographical characteristics, its distance from urban centers and its level of economic development—as well as the policy's "content"—which affected the ease with which it could be altered or evaded—determined whether or not, and in what way, these radical policies were implemented.[44] National elites could put the radical policies onto local agendas, but without their direct intervention into local politics the critical factor in policy implementation were local interests, the local environment, and the way individual radical policies affected those interests.

These local interests were based on rational calculations made within a highly constrained environment. For peasants, collectivization had introduced a bureaucratic hierarchy penetrating into the villages that limited their political behavior and ensured the dominant position of the rural bureaucrat in most of rural China. The power of the CCP and the Party-State in postrevolutionary society was far greater than the power of any ancien regime, and although the Cultural Revolution greatly weakened the CCP, open opposition to Party or local policies during the radical decade invited confrontations with local militias of young peasants, controlled by brigade Party secretaries, who beat local "class enemies." Collectivization also stringently controlled the economic choices available to the peasant for the pursuit of prosperity. Rural cadres determined the type of work a peasant performed, the hours during which he labored, and the payment he received for it. They also totally limited the peasants' economic and social mobility. Thus cadre, more than peasant, activities determined the pattern of radical policy implementation.

The rural hierarchy also established the critical boundaries and determinants of cadre behavior. While the extent to which the collective institutional framework was entrenched varied from locality to locality, its hierarchy and the distribution of political, economic, and social resources among rural officials from the county down dictated the cadres' political influence over the peasants. More important, the politics of survival and advancement within that bureaucratic maze greatly affected the way cadres responded to radical policies. While "policy winds" and the radical environment often predetermined a local cadre's political agenda, how he responded to those policy initiatives was structurally determined. Only an analysis emphasizing the political culture of the rural bureaucracy and the radical environment's incentives for cadres and peasants within these structures can truly reflect the nature of local politics during this era and explain the micro-level response of various rural actors.[45]

From this perspective we find that Chinese peasants had no

ideological affinity for the continuing revolution and made rational choices within that constrained environment. They addressed each specific policy, rather than the overall program, on the basis of how it affected their personal, family, or collective interests. Beneficial policies received their support, regardless of their ideological content; but if policies hurt their interests, they sought to express their opposition.[46] Thus a small minority of peasants did support the radical program. Some peasants—such as the weak, the old, and those with smaller families or younger children—who were deeply concerned about others getting too rich supported constraints on the private sector. They feared that in a more laissez-faire economy the skilled, the strong, the larger families, or the well-connected peasants would prosper, while the more vulnerable ones would fall further behind. Poor villagers could fear that a more open system would expand the importance of comparative advantage, and they would suffer. Motivated less by jealousy or a belief in absolute equality, their support for the radicals' anti-equity program, which restricted inequalities of opportunities, was due to a rational calculation of the potential dangers of a more free-wheeling rural economy. They themselves could not prosper, and they feared that others who did so might use that power unfairly. Communist propaganda had incessantly reminded peasants of the extreme exploitation that had supposedly characterized pre-1949 rural China. Although these peasants might have used the language of a moral economy and expressed concerns about social justice, their low socioeconomic status within the prevailing political economy made it rational for them to do so. Nevertheless, this group formed a very weak base upon which to establish a radical, rural political economy.

The strongest group of peasant supporters lived in poorer villages and supported the redistributive ethos and policies of the radical era. Amalgamating teams or brigade accounting equalized incomes among the teams that joined together, instantly increasing the incomes of the peasants in the poorer villages. Similarly, poorer villages in the hills would find it to their advantage to accept policies that forced peasants from wealthier valley teams to come and improve their irrigation systems or level their land. These peasants, too, had a strong rational motivation for supporting many planks of the radical program.

Rural bureaucrats at various levels were the most supportive; yet their support also depended on how the policies affected the local distribution of political and economic resources, and whether they strengthened the rural bureaucracy in its ongoing struggle with the peasant over the rural social product. As a result, cadre support was not universal, and their actions were not unitary, since policies had different effects on each level of the bureaucracy. For example, a policy that benefited commune officials might weaken team leaders. Similarly, the incentives for cadres to implement different policies varied according to their units' location, topography, and economic and political chararacteristics. As one can see, the intersection of local interests and the impact of radical policies on those interests created a highly complex matrix.

However, adjusting or evading radical policies placed team and brigade cadres in a bind. The radical environment demanded judicious behavior, as overt resistance could earn a cadre political censure. Bureaucratic superiors, for their own self-protection, insisted on lower-level demonstrations of policy compliance. Yet local cadres also needed to survive in a world of face-to-face relations with peasant neighbors, who by and large rejected the radical policies and put pressure on these cadres to alter the policy's impact.

Under these dual pressures, cadres developed evasionary strategies that can be best analyzed through a framework emphasizing the difference between the form of a policy and its real content. This approach seems particularly useful for traditional societies confronted by demands for rapid social change, where pressures for demonstrating compliance surpass the peasants' ability or willingness to accept new values or policies.[47] Thus local cadres either delayed introducing a policy for as long as possible or tried to alter its content, removing its most contentious and radical parts. In either case they responded formalistically, creating the appearance of radical support. For example, they collectivized private plots in highly visible locations but allowed peasants to till barren land in hilly areas, so long as nobody reported this to outsiders. Elsewhere cadres planted grain only in areas near the road but grew cash crops in areas farther off the beaten path. Or they created local models for radical policies to which they took visitors, but allowed other places to continue with more pragmatic measures. The radicals' penchant for creating false models contributed to the seemingly pervasive radical veneer.

The strategy often worked. To the outside world—both foreign and Chinese—the radical Maoist program appeared to have struck deep roots. On brief visits, cadres and foreigners alike witnessed only widespread conformity, with happy peasants terracing fields and possessing no private plots. Nor could visitors discover if teams had really been amalgamated or if workpoints (the method through which collectives measured how much each peasant worked) were really distributed according to political criteria. And although foreigners complained of visits to Potemkin villages, assuming that they had been built to dupe them, the Chinese were far more interested in fooling each other and collectively maintaining the charade.

Nevertheless, one must not overstate the extent of formalism and underplay the substantive impact of the radical policies. These ten years witnessed an excessive emphasis on local self-reliance, particularly in grain production, that destroyed decades, if not centuries, of rural regional specialization. In parts of Guangdong Province, bamboo groves were razed; in Mongolia, pastureland was ploughed up; fish ponds in many parts of China were drained to make more paddy fields; and areas, such as eastern Shandong Province, which had grown wealthy producing cotton, or parts of Fujian Province, which had prospered growing sugar cane, all shifted to grain production.[48] Private plots were adjusted in various ways, but the overall trend was a decrease in total acreage nation-wide. Similarly, rural trade fairs dried up all over China. During these winters peasants were pressured, cajoled, and, at times, financially induced to work long hours terracing fields, leveling hilltops, and building reservoirs and canals; and while some of these projects helped create an economic base for future growth, others were useless monuments to local officials. At the same time county, commune, and brigade officials expropriated individual and collective labor, capital, and machinery to develop rural industries and erect new buildings to house an expanding rural bureaucracy with which they dominated and controlled the rural areas.

Thus the countryside that had limped out of the post-Great Leap famine had been dramatically transformed by 1978. The rural bureaucracy and many of its institutions had been stabilized, while many rural cadres had accommodated themselves to aspects of the radical program. County and commune officials, who had expropriated peasant resources and used peasant wealth to their own advantage, managed larger bureaucracies. Local leaders, too, had adapted the radical programs to match their local interests, so the collective economy in at least one-third of rural China was secure. In those areas peasants had acquired an economic interest in maintaining that stronger collective.[49] In this way, initially unpopular policies had developed retroactive support. The interests that had expanded during the radical decade stood as the first line of resistance to the new rural reforms introduced in the late 1970s.[50]

Regardless of these gains, the obstacles against introducing agrarian radicalism into the countryside were simply too great. The radical program was based on an ideology that saw the search for prosperity and its achievement as a threat to the revolution's future; yet it was introduced into a peasant society where economic rationality predominated and where subsistence remained a major issue. It confronted elite opposition that greatly limited the state's role as a driving force for ensuring policy implementation; all this in a bureaucratic hierarchical system where strong local interests had always refracted and twisted national programs and where monitoring local implementation had always been a major problem. Perhaps it was predestined to fail in China, for despite the intense propaganda of the late 1960s and mid-1970s, what the radicals called the peasant's petty-bourgeois mentality remained vibrant in 1978, leaving the peasant's entrepreneurial spirit and his desire to improve his family's economic interests intact. Once the reform leaders around Deng Xiaoping took control of rural policy and called for revamping the rural political economy by moving away from restrictive policies toward more liberal ones, peasants with comparative advantages, innate talents, or good political ties responded, as well as the several hundred million peasants who had remained hungry under collectivization. Together they squeezed local bureaucrats and forced them to accept significant reforms. And once the incipient stages of decollectivization removed the fetters on the pursuit of private interest, China's peasants once again expanded their new-found freedoms, ending the battle for utopia and replacing it with a long overdue emphasis on economic development.

1

AGRARIAN RADICALISM DEFINED: THEORETICAL PERSPECTIVES AND DEVELOPMENTAL STRATEGIES

CHINA'S RADICAL leaders, including Mao Zedong, Chen Boda, Kang Sheng, Lin Biao, Zhang Chunqiao, Jiang Qing and Hua Guofeng, believed that only continuous socioeconomic and political changes in the rural areas could prevent a capitalist restoration in the countryside and ensure the Chinese revolution's ultimate goal—the transition to a communist society. These elites took their ideology seriously. Although motivated by a desire for power, they fit Gouldner's category of "critical Marxists" who want desperately to change the world around them.[1] To do so, these radicals applied Mao's theory of "continuing the revolution under the dictatorship of the proletariat" to the rural areas.

But what was the theoretical and historical basis of this agrarian radicalism in China? Why did these radical leaders really believe that they could take a poor peasant society and lead it rapidly through socialism into the communist utopia? Marxists had expected the urban centers and the working class to lead the revolution. Why did these people focus on the rural areas for their radical experiment? Through what methods did they expect to motivate peasants to actively support and participate in these social changes? What kind of rural world did they hope to achieve?

The Theoretical Roots

The ideology behind agrarian radicalism had three key components: voluntarism, ruralism, and class struggle. Voluntarism implies that people make history and are not the prisoners of historical or economic forces. Chinese communists could not have succeeded without believing that it was within their power to bring about earthshaking changes in China.[2] After 1949, Mao and other Chinese radicals denied that China's economic backwardness could hold back a transition to higher stages of socialism and communism. If the

16

masses believed in and struggled for these changes, "great leaps" were possible.

Second, the Chinese revolution was a peasant revolution, which successfully mobilized the rural populace to overthrow urban-based elites. After the cities were conquered, the countryside remained a major, if not the major, setting for development and a major focus of conflict between radicals and moderates over the revolution's future. Ruralism also entailed the issue of whether rural backwardness was a brake or boon to the transition from socialism to communism.

Class struggle and the ongoing conflict with revisionist tendencies in rural society form the third key element. Class analysis helped the CCP organize support for their programs and isolate their opponents. Using attitudinal, as well as economic, criteria for demarcating class helped the radicals form their strategy for the communist transition. Most important, Mao's belief that class conflict and the possibility of a capitalist restoration persisted under socialism led to his theory of continuing the revolution, which formed the basis of agrarian radicalism in China.

These three components came together to make the radical program highly utopian. While the transition from capitalism to socialism involved fairly concrete changes in the pattern of property ownership and the distribution of power, the transition from socialism to communism was essentially a blind path. The fathers of socialism had left few guidelines on how to get there, while the Great Leap Forward had served more to illuminate the pitfalls on the way to communism. Still, the radicals persisted in the 1960s and 1970s in believing that they could build a prosperous and egalitarian world in China's impoverished countryside. The secret way to utopia lay in finding the proper strategy and introducing policies derived from it into the rural areas.

Voluntarism and Agrarian Radicalism

The history of the communist movement in China is a tapestry of epic events, with determined individuals successfully overcoming great odds and immense natural barriers. These successes intensified CCP leaders' confidence in the veracity of their beliefs and strategies. At the same time, many leaders, especially Mao, believed that the masses' subjective energy could overcome all political and economic bottlenecks to development. This belief in the primacy of politics over economics and the possibility for the subjective will of the masses to bring about objective change surpassed even Lenin's faith in the power of revolutionary momentum.[3]

Mao's voluntarism was not such an obvious divergence from his

Marxist forebears and their need for action. Marx attributed a great importance to human effort and the role of individuals in transforming ideas into objective reality.[4] And while he criticized anarchists for emphasizing human will, Marxism "as a politics . . . also premises that events depend crucially on people's efforts, struggle, capacity for sacrifice and self-discipline."[5] Moreover, both Marx and Engels saw the possibility of telescoping the revolution's stages.[6] For example, Engels raised the possibility that Russia, while moving from feudalism to socialism, might compress stages and pass rapidly through capitalism because the "mir," or Russian collective village, could form the basic building block of socialist society.[7] Lenin, too, had little patience to wait for the revolution and accepted the notion of telescoping stages when in April 1917 he called on the proletariat to take political power two months after the "bourgeois revolution."

Mao's voluntarism surpassed Marxist tradition in his belief that "social relations of production"—the relations among the leaders and the led, or those who owned or managed and those who worked with the tools of production—could change before the "forces of production"; his belief in the power and reliability of the masses was also stronger. Politics, not economics, became the leading factor in social and historical change. In the mid-1950s, in the face of strong opposition within the Party, Mao argued that the masses' subjective power could support collectivization, that collectivization could speed up mechanization, and rapid collectivization would stimulate the peasants' productive energies.[8] This approach marked "the revival of a voluntaristic approach to socio-historical change and a populist faith in the peasant masses to effect that change," similar to Maoism during the revolutionary years.[9]

This voluntarism lies at the heart of agrarian radicalism. It led Mao to believe, however contrary to classical Marxism, that consciousness could be transformed before the material conditions of society changed, and subjective factors, such as increased human consciousness and will, could transform the material world. This penchant for voluntarism also prompted Mao and the radicals to rely on mobilization techniques and campaigns to overcome political, psychological, and technological bottlenecks in China's development, to prevent the revolution's demise, and to bring about the next stage of history.

Ruralism, the Peasantry, and Backwardness

Radical leaders placed great emphasis on China's rural areas, believing that China's backwardness not only would not undermine revolutionary transitions, but in reality could facilitate those transitions. In fact, while Marxism-Leninism, as a Western ideology, suffered from an urban bias, in China it fostered an anti-urban one.

The emphasis on rural China in agrarian radical ideology bridges traditional and modern China. In traditional China the city and countryside were interdependent, and, as in Mao's China, the rural sector was seen as a repository of wisdom and virtue. In the words of Gu Yanwu, a seventeenth-century scholar-official, "Goodness develops only in the village, evil in the city. The city is the place of commerce and trade. People relate to one another only with the aim of making profits. They are superficial and pretentious. As a result, the city is a sink of iniquities. The village is different. There people are self-reliant and have deep emotional ties with each other."[10] Similarly, in 1949 Mao warned that urban life could foster ideological and moral impurities, while in 1969 he complained that occupying the cities was "a bad thing because it caused our Party to deteriorate."[11] In 1968, to revolutionize and purify China's urban youths, he ordered them to move to the countryside "to learn from poor and lower-middle peasants."

For Marx and Engels peasants were generally a regressive social force, numbed by the "idiocy of rural life," with each household existing in isolation; they could unite to form a nation only to the extent that "potatoes in a sack form a sackful of potatoes."[12] In his unpublished notes—which present a more positive view of the peasants than Marx had intended[13]—and in earlier works and letters, Marx (and Engels) stressed the revolutionary potential of rural laborers and small landholders during revolutionary periods. During such periods communists could go to the countryside to mobilize peasants, who were important allies for the proletariat when it was too small to carry off a successful revolution.[14] Of course, peasants needed proletarian leadership. Still, the despotism of the radical era proved Marx to be correct when he warned that socialism established in a peasant society could lead to "primitive" and "crude" forms of social leveling that would give rise to more extreme inequality and oppressive despotism.[15]

Lenin's position on the peasants' revolutionary role shifted according to historical events, as he responded to both the potential for revolution in each particular period and the peasants' level of revolutionary activity.[16] While he had anticipated no major peasant role in the bourgeois revolution before 1905, their spontaneous actions during the 1905 Revolution convinced him that peasants could help achieve a radical bourgeois revolution, and rural laborers and poor peasants could facilitate the shift to socialism by struggling with rich peasants. Yet for Lenin peasants were secondary and supportive to the proletariat in both revolutions.

Mao's position on the peasant's role constitutes therefore a clear break from the liturgy of Marxism-Leninism. For Schwartz, Mao's peasant strategy was "a heresy in act never made explicit in theory,"[17] while Schram emphasizes that Mao's original Hunan Report ignored proletarian leadership.[18] In fact, Schram asserts that after 1937, Mao believed the peasants could be the "sole force" in the revolutionary process.[19]

Mao's anti-urban bias, which differed greatly from Marxist-Leninist tradition, had historical roots. How could one find progressiveness in an urban environment that was the seat of foreign imperialism, foreign domination, and the exploitation of China's working class? Excluding Beijing and Guangzhou, China's largest cities developed as treaty ports under foreign management.[20] And although Mao was criticized for his pro-peasant bias—in 1929 Li Lisan accused him of "localism and conservatism characteristic of a peasant mentality," while in the early 1930s, the twenty-eight Bolsheviks (his major opponents at that time in the CCP) accused him of "right opportunism" for maintaining that the working class lagged behind the peasant movement—his belief in the peasants' revolutionary potential proved correct.[21]

After 1949 he fought with the Party over the importance of the peasants' role in building socialism.[22] His 31 July 1955 speech on agricultural cooperativization returned the focus of the struggle for socialism to the rural areas. In October 1955, Chen Boda emphasized the close tie between socializing industry and agriculture when he argued that "we cannot stand with one foot planted on socialist industry and the other on small-peasant economy. The victory of socialism is unthinkable unless we win over the five hundred million strong rural population to take part in socialist construction."[23] Chen's view was that the peasants, in contrast to the bourgeoisie, had already learned the benefits of following the proletariat and supported socialism[24]; this position helped mobilize the Great Leap Forward three years later.

By the 1958 Great Leap, the countryside again became the model for revolutionizing the cities. The 1958 Wuhan Declaration declared that "in the future Communist society, the people's communes will remain the basic unit of social structure"[25] and the major mechanism in Chinese society for completing the transition from socialism to communism.[26] And by 1961, in the throes of nation-wide famine, Mao foresaw class warfare between an exploiting and prosperous working class and an exploited and impoverished peasantry unless land ownership "by all the people" and rural prosperity were established.[27]

Even the Cultural Revolution was the indirect, if not direct, result of disputes over rural policy.[28] When peasants did not respond to the Socialist Education Movement, Mao blamed local power holders and "capitalist roaders" in the party elite and attacked them. Only after they were defeated could he reinvigorate socioeconomic transformations in the rural areas.[29]

Central to the leading role of the countryside in the socialist transition was the debate over whether the socioeconomic and ideological backwardness of China's rural areas was a benefit or barrier to revolutionary transformations. Although Marxism appeared to be a progressive theory whose forces for change were the advanced elements in society, Lenin's "dialectic of backwardness" had complicated the issue.[30] According to Lenin, a bourgeois revolution based on an active peasantry and followed by land nationalization created better conditions for a socialist transition than existed in societies with more developed bourgeois systems. The weakness of the Russian bourgeoisie, he argued, made the transition to socialism even more likely.[31]

For Mao and the agrarian radicals, the issue was unclear. Peasant "blankness" meant that they could easily be mobilized to support the socialist transition, and their purity made the countryside the potential model for revolutionizing the entire society. Objective backwardness increased the scope of subjective human will and political consciousness as a force for revolutionary action, thereby closely linking backwardness and voluntarism.[32] Backwardness implied fewer ideological constraints, while poverty gave peasants a weaker tie to property. According to Mao, "the more backward the economy, the easier, not the harder, a transition from capitalism to socialism. The poorer people are, the more they want a revolution."[33] Thus for Mao the poorer peasants were the most revolutionary social class.

In 1978 Chen Boda was accused of attributing positive value to backwardness and advocating a "transition through poverty" in the 1958 Great Leap.[34] Several articles in the post-1978 period also argue, albeit with no documentary support, that Zhang Chunqiao and Wang Hongwen advocated premature "transitions through poverty" in 1968–1969 and 1975–1976 as well.[35]

Yet radicals consistently depicted the countryside as a repository of the "small-scale, petty-bourgeois mentality" that, according to Lenin, could regenerate capitalism even after the proletariat had taken power and destroy the revolution.[36] They wanted to transform the countryside not because it could trigger the transition to communism, but because the peasants' petty-bourgeois mentality could undermine that transition. Collectivization and transitions to higher stages of socialism were critical for destroying the peasants' tie to private property, making them rural proletarians. Still, whether poverty and backwardness was a source of counter-revolution or a critical cog supporting revolutionary transitions, the battle for the future of the revolution was to occur among the rural inhabitants whose social, political, psychological, and economic world had to be transformed as quickly as possible.

Class, Class Struggle, and Anti-Revisionism

In the face of the cultural strain brought on by the collapse of the traditional Confucian and dynastic order, followed by the defeat of the republican alternative, some young Chinese intellectuals replaced Social Darwinism with Marxism as an explanation for China's weakness.[37] Marxism and its method of class analysis played this critical role; class warfare against imperialism and domestic exploiting classes, who were deemed responsible for China's dilemma, would overthrow external and internal class enemies and liberate China from her economic, political, and psychological oppression. Moreover, Marxism's deterministic laws ensured victory for China's downtrodden classes.

As with Mao's voluntarism, his class analysis and understanding of class consciousness also broke with accepted Marxist perspectives. While Marx saw class consciousness as the product of the social relations of production, Mao believed that consciousness could change before the relations of production. Moreover, since for Mao the relations of production could change before the forces of production, class consciousness and class allegiances faced no objective constraints. Just as Engels argued that Marx had stood Hegel's dialectic on its head, Mao stood Marx's ideas on class consciousness on their head. Thus class consciousness was determined in part by one's attitude. And as the major cleavages in society changed, one's attitude towards those contradictions could determine one's class status. Thus at times of acute struggle, Mao always searched for friends and enemies.

This dualism also provided Mao's class analysis with a progressive and regressive component and was an invaluable tool for organizing political struggle. If education and class struggle could change consciousness, then through propaganda and mobilizing progressive forces China's backward society, opposition classes, and limited proletariat need not slow down the advent of the revolution. Similarly, agrarian radicals could argue that advanced or progressive elements existed in postrevolutionary rural China that supported transitions to higher stages of socialism, even though in reality few peasants supported these policies.

On the other hand, the regressive side of this dualism led Mao to emphasize the perpetual potential for the rejuvenation of old opposition classes under already transformed relations of production. Landlords and peasants, long stripped of their land and authority and living under socialist relations of production, remained potent supporters of a capitalist restoration. Resistance to higher stages of socialism in the villages was always blamed on bad class elements who still harbored strong anti-socialist values.[38]

Thus whenever radical policies faced opposition, two groups were reportedly at work: one guilty of trying to hold back the tide; the other supportive of new pushes for socioeconomic change. Class struggle among these two forces would generate high tides and move China's rural areas to higher stages of socialism.

Mao's belief that class struggle and the potential for bourgeois revisionism persisted under socialism emerged slowly. Although Mao argued during the 1957 Anti-Rightist Campaign that class struggle between the proletariat and bourgeoisie could become "very acute,"[39] he saw Peng Dehuai's 1959 attack at Lushan on the Great Leap as a manifestation of class struggle by "old bourgeois elements," or what Chen Boda called "capitalist revolutionaries" who had never been transformed.[40] Even in 1960, Mao referred only to "vested interest groups" which had developed during collectivization.[41] Mao and the radicals were still not talking of the embourgeoisement of society and the generation of new bourgeois elements under socialism. At the Tenth Plenum of the Eighth Party Committee in September 1962, famous for Mao's slogan "never forget the class struggle," he began to unveil his ideas on the continued existence of class and class struggle under socialism. And the ensuing debate with the Soviet Union in the 1960s convinced him that a capitalist restoration, which he believed had occurred in the Soviet Union, was possible in China as well.[42]

To a large extent, Mao's theory of the continuing revolution under the dictatorship of the proletariat which was summarized and published in the *People's Daily* on 6 November 1967, implied a more linear, less dialectic transition from socialism to communism than his earlier "theory of uninterrupted revolution" (*buduan geming*) which had guided the Great Leap. Whereas the original theory emphasized "wave-like progressions" with troughs and crests, advances and retreats followed again by new advances, the new theory emphasized slower, more methodical shifts to higher stages of development.[43] But while great leaps were gone from the theory—though not from the practice—linearity in no way implied that revisionism was impossible. In fact, because the apocalyptic synthesis that might have brought on the rapid advent of communism did not occur, revisionism was even more likely.[44] However, since antagonistic class contradictions persisted under socialism, continued class struggle would combat that potential revisionism and ensure the communist transition.[45]

The target of that class struggle was to restrict bourgeois rights. In *Critique of the Gotha Programme*, Marx argued that people in socialist society would be paid on the basis of the amount of goods they produced. Since some people produced more than others, equal right of reward necessitated unequal payment, making equal right a bourgeois right of unequal remuneration.[46] The issue was first raised in China during the 1958 Great Leap, when Zhang Chunqiao advocated eradicating the wage system as a vestige of bourgeois rights.[47] Yet Mao's preface to the article cautioned against immediate changes. And although a year later he admitted that "we certainly want to destroy bourgeois rights thought—wages, preferential treatment, levels— these are all wrong," he also recognized that the establishment of a highly gradational wage scale in 1956 was correct and necessary.[48]

Mao resurrected the issue of bourgeois rights after the call for the Four Modernizations at the 1975 Fourth National People's Congress. Opposed to the congress's stress on economic development and its downplaying of class struggle, Mao suggested that unrestricted continuation of bourgeois rights afforded revisionists the opportunity to undermine the revolution.[49] The *People's Daily* of 9 February 1975 quoted him as saying the dictatorship of the proletariat was necessary to control and, step-by-step, limit bourgeois rights in China. Yao Wenyuan voiced similar fears, emphasizing that new bourgeois elements created during the socialist transformation could use the economic and political inequalities inherent in these bourgeois rights to protect and expand their vested interests and kill the revolution.[50]

The following year the authors of a book, entitled *The Socialist Collective Ownership System* argued that if the bourgeois rights in the private sector were not restricted, the old regressive classes would use these opportunities to undermine the rural collective economy. Citing a report from Yunnan, they suggested that continued existence of bourgeois rights in commodity exchange and the private sector— such as private plots, rural trade fairs, handicrafts and extra-collective labor—"always created among the peasants spontaneous capitalist tendencies."[51] And among those most affected by bourgeois tendencies, some individuals seriously threaten the socialist collective ownership system.[52] The publication of this book brought the theoretical basis and practical application of agrarian radicalism to maturity.

Building Communism in the Chinese Countryside

The Failure of Millennialism

The initial attempts to establish communism in the countryside relied on a blending of Marxism-Leninism and traditional millennialism. According to Meisner, the Great Leap's millennialism found roots in what he calls the "practical dilemma of building a Marxist-socialist world in a backward peasant society." While China's economic backwardness had made the communist victory easier, it complicated socialist construction. This poor, traditional society responded haltingly to the radicals' demands for rapid social change. Moreover, economic development generated inequalities and vested interests that favored a coming to terms with the social order and the end of guided socioeconomic transformation. But possessed of a "catastrophic imagery of abrupt and violent revolution,"[53] the radicals sought explosive solutions to historical and theoretical problems that in the short run remained insurmountable.

To narrow the gap between their vision of society and the world around them, the radicals relied on the uninterrupted revolution to mobilize society for great leaps of energy and faith that might overcome social reality and catapult society into the Marxist utopia. This penchant among Marxist-Leninists who take power in peasant societies to rely on human will to leap historical stages as a shortcut to utopia applies particularly to China's Great Leap Forward; it also fits Cuba's "revolutionary offensive" of the late 1960s and Cambodia under Pol Pot.[54]

The millennialism in agrarian radicalism also had social roots in the Chinese peasant aspirations for prosperity and equality. Mao, firmly rooted in peasant revolutionary traditions, saw himself building "a bond between his own utopian visions and popular aspirations for social change and economic abundance."[55] This desire for both equality (that is, social change) and prosperity is an important heritage of Chinese peasant rebellions (see Chapter 4 below). Thus the Great Leap, which in summer and fall of 1958 possessed a highly millennial component,[56] emphasized both extreme equality, in the form of the "communist wind," and attaining levels of Western prosperity in three years. The slogan was "three years of struggle for ten thousand years of happiness."

The Great Leap's failure, which brought economic chaos, famine, and death, eradicated the millennialism in the agrarian radical program. Mao became far more cautious in calling for rapid socioeconomic change in the 1960s and 1970s.[57] By 1962 he believed that the transition from "the realm of necessity" to the "realm of freedom"—

that is, into the communist utopia—would be a gradual process of indeterminate length; when pressed, he conjectured that it would take a hundred years to build a strong socialist society.[58] The radicals, particularly the Gang of Four, believed that the vitality of "capitalist relations of production" under socialism would make the transition long and arduous. In response they developed an amalgam of policies that may be seen as a radical rural developmental strategy for building their egalitarian, wealthy rural world—in essence, a form of "practical utopianism." Since radical leaders spoke infrequently on rural policy after the Great Leap, they may not have possessed a systematic perspective on rural development. Nevertheless, from the writings and policies advocated by radical elites during this era, one can draw the basic contours and outline the concrete policies of their program.

The Radical Development Strategy

The radical developmental strategy had four components: a political-organizational component, comprising concrete changes in rural political and economic structures; a psychological-moral component, which was to bring about changes in the peasants' attitudes toward those structures and work in general, as well as to create support for eliminating bourgeois values and narrowing class, income and status inequalities; an economic component, involving an improvement in the level of rural technology and standard of living; and a mobilizational component that defined the techniques by which the policies were to be implemented. This section addresses the first three aspects of the developmental strategy, leaving the fourth for the following chapter.[59]

Organizational Changes. The radicals expanded the scope of collective, party and state control in the countryside and transferred administrative authority from private to collective organizations, from lower to higher levels of the rural collective organization, or from collective to state control.[60] Key policies included brigade accounting, unifying production teams, placing Supply and Marketing Cooperatives under state control, and developing brigade and commune economy.

Shifting control over economic activity and the ownership of the means of production to higher levels in the structural hierarchy—a structural transition to higher stages of socialism—involved the vertical integration of the rural organizational framework. Establishing people's communes, with ownership and accounting at the commune level, signified to some Chinese that China was on the verge of entering the communist utopia.[61] And while vestiges of the Great Leap mentality persisted into the 1960s and 1970s—the size of the unit became an indicator of progress toward communism—slower steps to higher levels of socialism were advocated. Thus throughout this period radicals advocated shifting the level of ownership and account from the team to the brigade.

Another important organizational change was merging production teams. In the late 1960s Lin Biao merged teams in order to organize peasants for capital construction projects.[62] However, for advocates of brigade accounting, merging teams was also useful; it was easier to unite two teams with different income levels than a whole brigade, while decreasing the number of teams simplified the transition to brigade accounting.

Brigade and commune enterprises established the economic basis for transitions to higher stages of socialism. In his speech to the Second Dazhai Conference of 1976, Chen Yonggui called for the continued growth of the economy at the commune and brigade levels "so as to create conditions for the gradual transition."[63] Where inter-team inequality created opposition to brigade accounting, a developed brigade economy could narrow that inequality by employing a poor team's excess labor or loaning them funds.[64] Since organizational changes were to replace peasant self-interest with support for higher levels of the rural hierarchy, brigade factories could overcome the gap between social consciousness and the desired level of economic organization.[65]

Transferring control over supply and marketing cooperatives from peasants to the commune (that is, from true to forced collectives—peasants had bought shares in these co-ops in the 1950s) increased bureaucratic control. Management authority over restaurants, shops, and local hotels shifted from the peasants to the commune officials who were under the leadership of the county supply and marketing organization. Starting in the mid-1970s, another way of organizing the rural labor were the full-time capital construction teams, which controlled vast numbers of peasant laborers.

Creating a Moral Incentive Economy. China's impoverished countryside and weak national economy, the national security imperative for rapid industrial development after the 1968 Soviet invasion of Czechoslovakia, and the need to rely on the rural areas to finance all this left the radicals few incentives to generate rural support. They relied instead on mobilization and creating a "moral incentive economy."[66]

Given Mao's belief that attitudes could change before the economy developed, and that changed attitudes could precipitate economic and organizational changes, raising peasant political consciousness became a critical component of the radical developmental strategy.[67] Throughout much of this period, the radicals tried to break the hold traditional Confucian values and habits had on peasants and replace them with Marxism-Leninism Mao Zedong Thought. Political study and class struggle campaigns were to teach peasants the virtues of the collective and the socialist road and convince them of the evil of the private road to prosperity.

Focusing on Marx's concept of bourgeois rights as the way capitalist values could be resurrected and inequities expanded under socialism, the radicals favored restricting opportunities for any expansion of those inequalities. To do this they attacked all vestiges of the "small producer's economy."[68] Private plots, which created opportunities for additional income and maintained the peasants' attachment to private property, had to be restricted or collectivized.[69] Rural artisans, prohibited from practicing their trades, and peasants who traditionally had gone to the cities for work were all forced to return and work in the collective. Controls were placed on rural trade fairs, "the clearest manifestation of bourgeois rights,"[70] and some were replaced with "big socialist markets" (shehui zhuyi da ji), where peasants were forced to sell all private produce to supply and marketing co-ops.[71]

Since paying peasants for work performed permitted the stronger to get richer and households with more workers to prosper faster, the Dazhai payment system of "self-assessment and public discussion"— where peasants who demonstrated strong revolutionary commitment could receive financial rewards equivalent to the strongest workers, regardless of their concrete contribution—sought to alleviate this bourgeois right.[72] It also leveled incomes, the essence of a moral incentive economy.[73] Finally, restricting economic crops in collective and private plots sought to limit comparative advantage and prevent inter-regional inequalities.[74]

The transition from socialism to communism involved eradicating the "three great differences" (san da chabie)—between mental and manual labor, workers and peasants, and town and country— developed under capitalism and persisting under socialism. To prevent class differences between "mental laborers" (rural cadres) and "manual laborers" (peasants), rural officials were to participate in physical labor. To further prevent political authority in the teams from becoming class authority, peasants were to participate in political decision making and monitor cadre behavior. To resolve differences between rural factory workers and peasants, the former received workpoints, not salaries. Tying their incomes to their team's agricultural output gave them an incentive to help with farming during the busy season. Also, since enterprises supplemented the collective income of teams whose peasants worked in the factories, all peasants had incentives to support collective enterprises. Finally, the difference between town and country was to be redressed as rural industry brought modern, socialist values—proletarian consciousness —to the countryside. Cooperative health care at the brigade level, barefoot doctors at the team and brigade level, and medical clinics at the commune level also narrowed the urban-rural gap. Similarly, sending educated youth to the countryside was expected to help peasants learn to read and introduce technical knowhow into the countryside.[75]

Finally, moral exhortation and participation in inter-unit field and water conservation projects was to imbue peasants with a "communist spirit" of self-sacrifice and concern for neighboring units. When neighbors were in trouble, they were to help them for free. When neighbors confronted financial difficulties or shortages of some kind, peasants were not to take advantage of these opportunities to make quick profits.

Economic Development. Although Mao believed that national will could transform reality, changes in the material conditions of society could reinforce political consciousness and generate strong support for higher levels of socialism. Consequently, advocates of agrarian radicalism developed their own economic policy priorities.

The foremost goal was creating a "cellular" economy, with regional, if not local, self-sufficiency in food and resource development.[76] Units nation-wide were compelled to become self-reliant in cereal production.[77] Grazing land was ploughed up, as was land previously targeted for economic crops. Because quotas were passed down through the bureaucracy, the unit of cereal self-sufficiency often became the production team, not the county.[78] Restrictions on markets and trade fairs intensified this cellular economy as peasants and production teams had to grow all the foods they needed to consume. Horizontal exchanges of goods between units and across administrative boundaries died on the vine of self-sufficiency.[79]

Agrarian radicals also tried to limit peasant income and consumption levels, ensuring that all surplus went to strengthen the collective economy. Wealthy units able to distribute more than 1.50 *yuan* per day—the level set in the national model brigade, Dazhai—were forbidden to do so on the grounds that "units which distributed more than Dazhai could not learn from Dazhai."[80] Table 2 shows that although the levels of accumulation during this period did not compete with those during the Great Leap, they were quite high,

Agrarian Radicalism Defined

particularly in 1970 and 1974–1976. At the same time, income distributed to the peasants as a proportion of total income was quite low during the whole period, with a trough in 1976.[81]

The radicals tried to create a "guerilla" economy, with large groups of peasants transforming the face of rural China.[82] Particularly during the winter season, capital construction campaigns, during which peasants dug reservoirs, river beds and canals, and terraced and leveled fields, became a regular part of the rhythm of peasant life. Collective agriculture created slack time, so unless labor was mobilized for such projects, private endeavors could expand. Peasants who previously had gone to the cities were forced back to participate in these projects. Besides improving the rural economy, facilitating the use of modern technology, such as tractors or fertilizer, and

Table 2. Financial distribution of accounting units in People's Communes, 1958–1981 (total income = 100).

				Allocation of net income	
Year	Total costs	State taxes	Net income[a]	Retained by collective[b]	Distributed to commune members[c]
1958	26.64	9.51	63.85	11.56	52.29
1959	26.77	10.00	63.23	12.53	50.70
1960	28.96	9.90	61.14	4.41	56.73
1961	26.70	6.41	66.89	6.79	60.10
1962	28.25	6.50	65.25	6.52	58.73
1963	28.31	6.54	65.15	7.01	58.14
1964	28.88	6.78	64.34	9.33	55.01
1965	28.18	5.60	66.22	8.93	57.29
1970	30.82	4.53	64.65	9.78	54.87
1971	30.13	4.44	65.43	9.50	55.93
1972	32.07	4.42	63.51	8.56	54.95
1973	31.30	4.29	64.41	9.63	54.80
1974	32.22	4.42	63.36	10.10	53.60
1975	33.61	4.02	62.37	10.93	52.48
1976	35.39	3.89	60.72	10.07	50.73
1977	35.59	3.80	60.61	9.31	51.42
1978	34.88	3.35	62.07	9.30	52.59
1979	34.12	3.23	62.65	9.59	53.12
1980	34.63	3.07	62.30	8.40	53.98
1981	31.41	2.93	65.66	6.55	59.17

SOURCE: State Statistical Bureau, *Statistical Yearbook of China 1983* (Hong Kong: Economic Information Agency, 1983), p. 210.
a. Gross income less total costs and state taxes.
b. Accumulation fund plus welfare fund.
c. Most of the distributed income is used by peasants to buy their share of collective grain produced by the collective.

making hillside land into paddy fields, large- and medium-scale projects could create a psychological interdependence and spirit of mutual assistance and concern among neighboring villages. Socialist cooperation would replace capitalist relations of exchange as the major medium of inter-personal and inter-unit exchanges.[83]

Some agrarian radicals recognized the need for introducing new technologies, such as tractors and diesel pumps, to mold peasant consciousness and promote the productive forces, even though they did not put a high priority on technological developments. Land leveling facilitated the introduction of this technology, and high rates of capital formation were to supply funds for local units to buy the machinery. While Lin Biao emphasized labor mobilization, not mechanization, Hua Guofeng's functional responsibility for promoting agricultural mechanization, begun in 1971, influenced his perspective; his brand of radicalism stressed agricultural mechanization.

Yet for all their rational strategies, the drive for utopia remained a significant part of Mao's theory of the continuing revolution, and even during the late 1960s and 1970s, the radicals' impatience led to a resurgence of millennialism. As during the Great Leap, when the radicals lauded the "sprouts of communism," after the Cultural Revolution they fought to defend the "newly born socialist things" (xin sheng shiwu) wherever they found them. In late 1969, Lin Biao talked of "flying leaps," while in 1975 Hua Guofeng promised almost instant mechanization by 1980, all of which was to occur through the mobilization of the human will.

Guided by the "theory of the continuing revolution," the radicals tried to motivate peasants to set aside the goals of self and accept the selfless goal of building communism. Relying on class struggle against the revolution's so-called enemies to undermine the crystallization of bureaucratic power that otherwise would have doomed the revolution, the radicals tried to move rural China through organizational transformations that would bring collective ownership to higher and higher levels. But mobilizing peasants was not easy, and the radicals confronted national opposition and local resistance.

2

POLICY WINDS AND
AGRARIAN RADICALISM

HOW LEADERS INTERACT with each other influences the way they make decisions, the mobilizational techniques they use to implement those decisions, and the way people on the local levels respond to their policy initiatives.[1] Throughout this period, policy decisions were made in the midst of intense factional battles that permeated every aspect of politics in China. This factionalism confronted advocates of radical policies with serious obstacles as they tried to transform their rural development strategy into policy directives and implement them in the countryside.

Shifting coalitions and balances of power among various factions meant that at most times supporters of a less voluntaristic and more conservative path of development were part of the decision making elite. These elites, while supporting the people's communes and collectivization, also believed that the private sector, material incentives, and stable policies based on the *Sixty Articles on Agriculture* should play a role in rural development. Thus only during brief moments did elites who supported a radical solution to the rural problem in China have a major influence on the formal policy making process. As a result, advocates of agrarian radicalism were forced to seek informal channels—"policy winds"—to mobilize support for their policy program.

Shifting coalitions also affected the specific radical policies advocated in each period of the radical era. First of all, only when the radicals were dominant could they introduce their more extreme policies. Moreover, advocates of the radical strategy were not a unified faction and policy differences existed among them; thus as each radical group rose to power, it advocated its own variant of the radical strategy. And while all advocates of the radical strategy relied on policy winds and class struggle campaigns to generate a radical environment at the local level, they also relied on different organiza-

32

tions and social forces—such as the army, educated youths, or rural cadres—to bring their specific radical vision to fruition. Nevertheless, informal implementation strategies and generating fear in the villages allowed the radicals to introduce their policies into many parts of rural China. As we will see in the second half of the book, reliance on these informal strategies left the final form of implementation to the discretion of local elites, leading to wide variations in the pattern of implementation of the radical strategy.

ELITE STRUCTURE AND THE POLICY PROCESS

Factions and Decision Making

Policy making in China since 1949—and particularly during 1968–1978—has rarely approximated any ideal rational model.[2] And while analysts have drawn numerous portraits of China's policy process, policy making from 1968 to 1978 was the direct result of struggles between different factions, each seeking to control the policy-making process.[3] These factions formed the basic building blocks of elite structure during the radical era and were critical in the ensuing power struggle. Factions that were part of the ruling coalition could influence policy decisions, while their political networks, which often crossed organizational boundaries and reached the lowest levels of the state, military, or party bureaucracy, were a major component of the implementation process.[4]

Yet from 1968 to 1976, although Mao Zedong never openly advocated the radical developmental strategy, he did create a political context conducive to the radicals' policies. Although he purged people he considered ultra-left, he usually ensured that the ruling coalition would have some radical or leftist leaders. Even in 1971–1973, when radicals were not part of the ruling group and were attacked by this more conservative coalition, Mao protected the Gang of Four who supported his Cultural Revolution policies. According to Joseph, he may have stopped Zhou Enlai from persevering in his critique of leftism in 1972.[5] Finally, in 1975–1976, when Deng Xiaoping tried to overturn the policies of the Cultural Revolution, Mao took away Deng's power and ensured two more years of radical influence after his death by passing his mantle to Hua Guofeng in 1976.

Factions and Policy Choices

Different factional leaders subscribed to different political lines and policies, but only the leaders and factions included in the ruling coalition determined the policies emanating from Beijing. A broad sweep of policy directions since 1949 shows that three visions of rural development have dominated rural policy: a *radical* Maoist line, with its stress on structural transitions to higher stages of socialism, a guerilla economy, and a moral incentive economy, all generated by relying on class struggle; a *bureaucratic* line, emphasizing planned and stable growth under central control, with a secondary role for the market and private sector; and a *marketeer* strategy, which advocates a central role for the household, the private sector, and the market's role in economic development.[6] During the radical decade, when Mao placed the marketeer strategy beyond the pale of acceptable policies, the struggle was between advocates of the radical and bureaucratic tendency.

A careful and differentiated analysis of each tendency, however, may show that advocates of the same general tendency belonged to different factions, and these factions may have varied in their commitment to specific policies related to that general tendency.[7] Placing these factions in the same radical camp explains the persistence of radical policies; differentiating among the various strains within the radical tendency explains changes that occurred during the radical era.

Thus although it may seem unnecessary to determine how many factions can dance on the head of a radical pin, the differences between "hard" (Chen Boda, Gang of Four), "soft" (Hua Guofeng, Chen Yonggui, Ji Dengkui), and "military" (Lin Biao) radicalism had a significant impact on the entire 1968–1978 decade. Which radical leader had political influence or joined the ruling coalition affected what radical policies were pushed through the formal policy process, what policies were advocated through informal channels, how support for them was mobilized, and most important, what policies were implemented at the local level.

Military radicals, who had their greatest influence in 1969–1970 when for a brief period they confronted little opposition, were concerned about war with the Soviet Union, so they emphasized mass mobilization of peasant labor (to curb the need for investment), building economies of scale by amalgamating teams, and relying on army officers at the county level and below to mobilize local support. Unlike the other radical factions, they cared little about ideological issues.

Hard radicals were far more concerned with restricting bourgeois rights and controlling the private sector, raising peasant ideology, and shifting more rapidly to higher levels of socialism through brigade accounting. They were always the most impatient for the transition to communism and most concerned about revisionism.

They placed their faith in "mass representatives" as the best rallyers for their policies. One representative of this tendency, Chen Boda, had significant influence in 1968–1970 when he allied with Lin Biao. However, the Gang of Four, the most well-known advocates of the hard line, fought a running battle with Zhou Enlai and Deng Xiaoping from 1973 to 1976. Even in 1975–1976, the Gang of Four fought with advocates of a softer radical line.

Soft radicals were far more in touch with peasant needs; they were concerned about mechanization and the modernization of the rural economy and accepted more gradual transitions to higher stages of socialism by building brigade enterprises. Yet they did not deny the importance of restricting the private sector and shifting accounting levels. While they were simply part of the ongoing factional battles in 1974–1976, they had a virtual monopoly on agricultural policy from late 1976 through late 1977. Under their influence, almost 15 percent of rural labor was organized into "specialized labor groups" (*zhuanye zu*) or full-time agricultural construction teams between 1974 and 1977 to ensure the success of rural labor mobilization.[8]

Policy Winds and Implementation

While Mao could ensure that some radicals were always part of the ruling coalition, he also sought to keep some balance between the radical and bureaucratic lines. Through his personal relationship with Mao, Zhou Enlai was also able to ensure the presence of more moderate leaders in ruling coalitions after 1968. Thus during most of 1968–1978 the radicals never totally dominated the most important policy-making arenas. Chen Boda, Lin Biao, Kang Sheng, Zhang Chunqiao, Yao Wenyuan, or Jiang Qing, either jointly or as individuals, never had total decision-making authority within the State Council, the Politburo, or its Standing Committee. Even in the late 1960s, at the peak of Lin Biao's influence, Zhou Enlai, Li Xiannian, Xu Shiyou, Zhu De, Liu Bocheng, and Ye Jianying were all part of the ruling elite, and all reportedly opposed the radical program.[9] As long as Mao did not directly intervene in the policy process and push the radical program himself—and there is no basis to believe he ever did—it was easy for the radicals' opponents to prevent the radical line from becoming part of any formal Party program. Only after Mao and Zhou's death, Deng's purge, and the Gang's arrest did Hua Guofeng, with the help of Chen Yonggui and Ji Dengkui, briefly wield enough power over agricultural policy to advocate formally some of these policies—and even then his revisions of the *Sixty Articles* were minor at best.

Moreover, throughout much of this period, organizational problems or factional conflict kept the formal Party institutions for implementing policy in a state of chaos. Party committees throughout China had been demolished during the Cultural Revolution and were not completely reestablished at the provincial level and below until August 1971.[10] Intense factional fighting during the succession crisis of 1973–1976 debilitated the formal decision making process, preventing formal advocacy of almost any policy.[11]

Yet the radicals, particularly the Gang of Four, could not simply jettison their radical program. Although subscribers to factional or coalitional models, such as Pye or Fox, argue that power, not policy, motivates Chinese leaders, power and policy were intertwined for the ideologues who supported agrarian radicalism. Their drive for power arose from a desire to put their utopian vision of China into practice. According to Fenwick, "the Gang's ultimate defeat is inseparable from its principled uncompromising stand on issues and ideology."[12] Other radicals, such as Hua Guofeng, who were more amenable to policy compromises when confronted by opposition, nevertheless reverted to a more radical line when that opposition disappeared. Thus radicals followed a two-pronged strategy throughout much of this era. In formal statements they downplayed their more radical policies. But privately and informally, when the time was propitious, they pushed the radical program.

Informal messages had multiple purposes and were a safer strategy for mobilizing factional supporters for an unofficial policy. They measured the distribution of one's political support in the bureaucracy; if no one responded to the slogans, elites who sent them could pretend that nothing had happened.[13] Although vertical ties within factional networks were important for implementing policy, using them too openly and too often, except during critical power struggles, was politically unwise.[14]

Disrupted Party norms during the Cultural Revolution and sharp factionalism made concerns about "democratic centralism" superfluous for most elites.[15] Formal appeals for unity persisted. But the ideological gaps between radicals and moderates and the intensity of the issue for the radicals compelled them to go outside the formal channels, which in these times they did regularly with impunity.

Finally, informal policy channels were especially appropriate for policies which directly challenged the official guidelines of the *Sixty Articles*. As late as fall 1975, at the First National Conference on Learning From Dazhai in Agriculture, Jiang Qing tried again in vain to rewrite the *Sixty Articles*.[16] Unable to attain a formal revision of these guidelines, the radicals simply ignored them and made changes on their own.

Advocates of agrarian radicalism were not alone in relying on informal policy channels to mobilize support for their developmental program. In 1955, when Mao arbitrarily increased the pace of collectivization, he set a precedent for expanding the locus of decision making and going around the Party leadership to ensure implementation of a policy for which there was no consensus.[17] Similarly, in many Third World countries, when demands for social change outpace policy guidelines, leaders circumvent the formal, decision making arenas. For example, confronting opposition in his own party to rural cooperatives, President Kaunda of Zambia called on local officials directly to form cooperatives. In Chile's ruling coalition, disagreements with the Communist party over nationalizing industry prompted the Socialist party to mobilize workers to strike certain factories and bankrupt them, thereby making them legal targets for nationalization under extant laws.[18] As Pye argues, Third World politics is characterized by informal politics whereby top leaders regularly circumscribe formal policies and the wishes of their co-leaders.[19]

In many cases, this strategy reflects the lack of institutionalization in political systems and the intensity of the conflict. For example, in the early years Hitler used similar techniques to arrest socialists and communists.[20] However, communist parties have formal rules and procedures, and from 1949 to 1955 most CCP leaders abided by those rules. But after 1955, Mao constantly attempted to communicate directly with "ideologically primed local party leaders and the population itself."[21] The groundswell for his policies forced them onto the central agenda and sometimes presented his comrades with faits accomplis.

Similarly, most radical policies never achieved consensus among Beijing's leaders. Chinese informants argue that restricting private markets, closing rural trade fairs, and shifting from team to brigade accounting were not championed in central Party or State Council documents before 1977.[22] Documents in our possession criticized rather than advocated radical policies of this period.[23] Yet these policies had significant influence. By 1978 close to 10 percent of brigades had replaced production teams as the level of accounting in rural China; and most transitions occurred before 1977–1978. Restrictions on private plots, rural trade fairs and household sidelines occurred nation-wide. Even when not implemented, these policies still got onto many local agendas, forcing cadres and peasants to debate whether or not to implement them.

The radicals spread their policies by the use of "policy winds" (*zhengce feng*). Though policy winds in China blow both vertically and horizontally,[24] a "central wind" refers to the process by which some central leaders circumvent national-level officials and institutions and mobilize lower-level party and government bureaucrats to implement policies which had not attained consensus among all leadership groups and which were not advocated through official party or government channels. This metaphor imparts the somewhat amorphous nature of this process of mobilization in China. Yet it had some very concrete aspects. Through an assortment of techniques, such as speeches, newspaper articles, visits to local units, and other methods outlined below, radicals sent messages to activate the lower levels of their political networks and mobilize local cadres who supported aspects of the radical program.

By starting a wind the radicals hoped to create a radical environment.[25] Exhortations to demonstrate progressive actions and take progressive postures on policy debates threatened middle-level and local bureaucrats who were not part of the radicals' factional network. This insecurity was critical in persuading them to implement these radical policies. The radical nature of the entire era intensified the nation-wide radical environment. Implementation by local radical constituents increased this pressure on neighboring units. Rural cadres raised with concepts such as *ning zuo wu you*, or "better left than right," understood the dangers of rightist errors; they were political errors (*zhengzhi cuowu*), whereas leftist ones were only errors of leadership style (*zuofeng wenti*). Nonsupportive cadres, hearing that the policy was being implemented nearby, might reconsider their hostility to the new policy. As the wind blew stronger and the radical environment intensified, they might become more nervous and begin to believe that their support or opposition to the policy might become a yardstick of their "political stand" (*zhengzhi lichang*), making continued resistance a political error. This way opposition would crumble and implementation would occur nationwide. Peng Dehuai pinpointed this problem in his 1959 attack on the Great Leap Forward at Lushan when he stated that "in our Party it has always been difficult to correct leftist errors and comparatively easy to correct rightist mistakes. Whenever something leftist comes up, it always prevails over everything; many people dare not speak out."[26]

Techniques of Implementation

To generate winds, create a radical environment, and insure implementation of unofficial policies, the radicals had to maintain a great deal of pressure on the local areas. As their national influence increased they had to penetrate local communities and begin "perpetual campaigning"—mobilize cadres for this revolution from above, politicize policy choices, and intensify the radical environment, leaving cadres little choice but to implement the radical policies.[27] Class struggle campaigns, which gave policy choices a class content, totally politicized the decision making process. Thus mobilization entailed a sometimes subtle, and sometimes not so subtle, threat of coercion and terror. These techniques employed in 1968–1978 whipped up the winds of agrarian radicalism and created a radical environment conducive to its implementation.

Test Points and Model Units

Chinese communists have long relied on "test points" (*shi dian*) and "model units" (*mofan dui*) to implement their policies. Establishing such prototypes in the early stages of mobilization ensured that policies were tested and mass opinions were gauged before they were popularized. Although the radicals also employed these techniques, radical policies were rarely tested; since they were ideologically motivated, they were assumed to be a priori correct and could not be rejected on empirical grounds. In a major break with the CCP's "mass line" work style, test points became model units for spreading the policy, and information on them was disseminated through the press, unofficial speeches, organized visits by local bureaucrats, and by word of mouth. In spring 1968, Chen Boda set up an experimental site for restricting private plots and markets in Evergreen Commune (*Sijiqing*) outside Beijing. He told peasants there that in future they would not need private plots and markets.[28] The content of such a speech would travel quickly across the countryside by various local or national rumor mills. Lin Biao reportedly established a similar test point in Zhejiang, which journalists visited and supposedly discussed in the national press.[29] Restricting markets in 1975–1976 was based on the experiences of Heertao Commune in Liaoning Province, where Mao Yuanxin had established his test point.[30] Such test points and models were critical for brigade accounting as well. Shanxi Province had ten test points, and Anhui Province's Quanshu County established two test points in 1970.[31] In 1975–1976, Zhang Chunqiao created test points for brigade accounting in Shanghai's suburbs, as did officials in Nanjing in 1978.[32] Leaders in these model units, often the final nexus of a factional network, could be mobilized to publicly support these policies in return for political and economic rewards. However, when factional sponsors lost and the policy line changed, they could become targets in the next campaign.[33]

The need to create models for others to emulate often meant that the exemplary units were false. During the Grain as the Key Link Campaign of the early 1970s, one district Party secretary in Guangdong Province chose a Guangning County brigade as his model for how hilly units could replace economic crops with grain.[34] He sent in a group of cadres who terrified the peasants into leveling the bamboo on the hills. After tearfully obeying, the peasants then terraced the hills, but the soil was too poor, and there was too little water. So the peasants built a reservoir and a culvert to bring the water to the fields. When the rice still did not flourish, Japanese fertilizer was applied. When the fields were finally productive, the district Party secretary made a movie, which was shown county-wide, about how this locality, through self-reliance, mass mobilization, and hard work, was voluntarily growing more grain for the state. After other places emulated this model, the entire county became impoverished.

The Heertao model for closing markets, where peasants "volunteered" to sell their produce to the supply and marketing co-op, rather than on the free market, was also phony. A Nanjing cadre who visited it in 1976 recalled the performance that was arranged for him and other visitors.

> At first the square was empty, but then they set off fireworks and the procession began. Everyone was wearing new clothes. Brigade secretaries led the procession. Behind each secretary was a young girl with her hair in braids and wearing white top, black skirt and white shoes. Each carried a sign with the name of the brigade. Then came someone carrying a red flag. Behind them every brigade had a marching band with a leader, drums, and a trumpet player. Then came people on stilts, about ten for each brigade . . . Behind them all came the people, bringing goods in baskets that they carried with bamboo poles on their shoulders. The poles were exceptionally flexible so when people stood still the poles bobbed up and down and looked good. Then came carts and horses, with flowers on their heads and on their tails. The carts were brightly painted and contained pigs and vegetables for sale. The people in the Supply and Marketing Co-op called out as they bought the produce. The purpose was to show how peasants sold directly to the state and had overcome the habit of selling between people. But in reality, it was a performance.[35]

Every district in China probably had its own Dazhai model which received the lion's share of state investment, technology, and labor assistance from peasants all over the county.[36] In describing a model in Shandong Province, Diamond notes that

> what the model really demonstrates . . . is that a unit with a potentially high production value can achieve that potential if it is assisted with loans, technical advice, and purchase requisitions for the needed technology, not to mention the added input of high morale that comes with continuous encouragement and public praise for each economic advance that is made.[37]

Although most peasants knew these models were unattainable without similar assistance, they were compelled to try to implement the same kinds of policies.

The radicals also organized visits to these models so others could learn from their experience (*xuexi tamen de jingyan*). Leaders in these models tried to persuade visiting cadres to implement radical policies. The Nanjing official quoted earlier visited Heertao Commune at the behest of city officials who wanted to see if the model was applicable to Nanjing. In 1975 Jiangsu Province took all commune secretaries in Nanjing to visit Huaxi Brigade, Jiangsu's Dazhai model—one of the few brigades in the province with brigade accounting. All team leaders in Qingxiu Brigade outside Nanjing also visited Huaxi. At that time the state reportedly called on "all provinces to organize leading comrades at the front line of agriculture, at different times and in different groups to visit Dazhai and study."[38] These are merely a few examples of a nation-wide phenomenon.

Linking Campaigns

From 1968 to 1978, a plethora of local and central campaigns shook the Chinese countryside, and the most extreme aspects of the radical program were inserted into these campaigns at the center, middle, or local levels. During the 1968 Three Loyalties Campaign which advocated loyalty to Mao, his works, and his revolutionary line, peasants in a commune outside Nanjing demonstrated their loyalty to Mao by donating their private plots to the collective. Similar events occurred elsewhere.

Linking economic policies with political campaigns turned economic decisions into political ones, undermining economically rational policies. Linking campaigns was most effective when economic policies were connected to class-struggle campaigns, intensifying the danger of policy resistance. Today the Chinese admit the difficulties that arose in implementing economic aspects of the Dazhai movement because economic decisions became politicized when they were linked to dangerous political campaigns.[39] For example, in parts of Guangdong, where the Three Loyalties Campaign followed on the heels of the Cleaning Class Ranks Campaign, people with bad class labels were arrested or beaten. Under these circumstances, peasants submitted quiescently to pressures to demonstrate their loyalty.[40] Similarly, peasants and cadres were forced to support changes in the rural political economy during campaigns such as One Hit, Three Antis Campaign, and the 1976 Criticize Deng Xiaoping Campaign.[41]

The campaign to promote Grain as the Key Link, which followed the fall 1970 Northern Districts Agricultural Conference (*Beifang diqu nongye huiyi)*, devastated the private sector in many locations. The campaign dramatically increased the grain production quotas that were imposed on all villages throughout China. In response, local leaders adopted strict measures. Local cadres were compelled to cut trees, collectivize private plots, and restrict all aspects of the rural economy that allowed peasants to earn a private income. In Jurong County, Jiangsu Province, private plots were collectivized and peasants were forced to grow grain in them, while one Yunnan brigade leader, intent on increasing grain output, made peasants transfer topsoil from their private plots onto the collective fields.[42]

Most amenable to this linkage was the recrudescent Movement to Learn From Dazahai in Agriculture. Radical policies, such as restricting private plots, household sidelines, and markets; brigade ownership; free assistance among units; stopping peasants from working in the cities; and egalitarian work points (first introduced in Dazhai), were inserted into Dazhai campaigns unofficially. For example, in the 1969–1970 revival of the movement, a brigade Party secretary in Shanxi Province accused cadres who opposed brigade ownership of not wanting to learn from Dazhai, which showed their position on the "class struggle between the two roads."[43] In the 1970s, Dazhai's leaders criticized visitors whose units had not restricted private plots and markets.[44] Although official pronouncements called on units to learn from the general experience of Dazhai, local leaders felt more secure during a campaign if they carried out a concrete policy used by Dazhai. Some cadres believed that to learn from Dazhai really meant establishing brigade accounting; otherwise, one was "abstractly affirming and concretely denying" (*chouxiangde kending, jutide fouding*) Dazhai's experience, which during a political campaign could become a political error.[45] In one locality people did not oppose a 1969 shift to brigade accounting because "at that time there was a movement to learn from Dazhai and brigade accounting was considered a progressive thing; so people did not object."[46]

Much expropriation of team and peasant resources in 1968–1978 by commune and county officials, what the Chinese call "equalization and transfer" (*ping diao*), occurred during "high tides" in field and water conservation campaigns. In principle, each unit's quotas were determined through an iterative process; each level in the water conservation bureaucracy consulted with professional governmental officials above and below to delineate mutually acceptable projects. However, during national irrigation campaigns Party leaders from the county down were pressured to expand their commitment.[47] These Party officials took over the responsibility for determining the quota and mobilizing the masses from local governmental officials, forcing commune water conservation officials to obey the commune Party committee rather than county water conservation officials. This supremacy of horizontal Party ties (*kuai kuai lingdao*) over vertical professional authority (*tiao tiao lingdao*) in China's communist bureaucracy permitted Party officials during the radical years to dominate their governmental peers and withdraw team funds from commune banks or team grain from commune grain stations.[48]

One official from the Ministry of Water Conservation in Beijing described how Party organizations politicized rural irrigation work after Hua Guofeng's and Chen Yonggui's Second Dazhai Conference on Agriculture in December 1976.

> After the Second Dazhai Conference there was a National Conference on Capital Construction which included all provincial first secretaries. They studied, researched and decided to do a large amount of work. In this meeting they [national leaders] called for people to get the masses to do rural capital construction "in a big way" . . . Visits were also organized to the places that worked well, such as Shandong. We took them to see these places so they could return to their own areas and use them as models. But the Ministry of Water Conservation lacks the strength to mobilize the masses. We can only look after some of the projects. We need help to get the masses moving. At this time, the counties decided how much labor and land would be involved in the projects. They reported to the province, which rarely changed the figures.[49]

Politicizing the issue pressured county Party officials, who wanted to adopt revolutionary postures, to expand the work commitment, and if commune leaders resisted, the counties pressured them. One city agricultural official admitted that when communes resisted these inflated quotas the city and county did "some political thought work with them, helping them to see the larger picture so they eventually agreed."[50]

Politicizing irrigation campaigns also created the context in which brigade and team leaders could not resist the expropriation of resources by commune and county leaders. For example, in 1976, at the time of the Second Dazhai Conference, a commune Party committee emulated Hua and put out a "call" (*haozhao*) for all commune members to "do water conservation in a big way." Once participating in field work became political, few could resist. The reference to doing this work "in a big way" signaled that expropriating local resources was acceptable.

Local Elite Turnover

Introducing unpopular policy innovations was simpler when local cadres were insecure about their political and personal futures.[51] If they were not sufficiently intimidated to implement the radical policies, replacing them with more compliant officials became necessary. According to Joseph, the radicals attacked veteran cadres, promoting inexperienced new cadres who were "congenial with factionalists and merely their blind followers and yes men."[52] While such an evaluation may be overly harsh, Madsen shows that the shifting external political environment precipitated concomitant changes in the nature of local leaders. During rightist periods, villages promoted cadres adept at forming personal relationships and local networks, while during leftist periods they promoted more purist revolutionary cadres.[53]

Political campaigns offered the venue for changing local leadership. Local elite turnover in the countryside occurred frequently during the early days of the Cultural Revolution, particularly between 1969 and 1971, during the One Hit, Three Antis and the Cleansing Class Ranks campaigns.[54] The Line Education Campaign (1973–1977) changed many local leaders; in some locations its impact on elite turnover peaked in 1975–1977.[55] Local factional conflicts, usually unrelated to the ongoing campaign, were often resurrected during them, and cosmopolitans—whose eyes were turned upward and whose views were more amenable to the radical program—replaced more parochial cadres.[56]

When county leaders were purged from 1968 through 1972, military representatives in some locations took on responsibility for political work.[57] In Jiangpu County, Jiangsu Province, the officer who took control in 1969–1970 had a great deal of power, and in 1970 a similar shift occurred in a Guangdong county.[58] These military leaders were more willing than local cadres to employ coercive measures and institute irrational economic policies in response to Lin Biao's 1969–1970 radical wind.

"Kill the Chickens and Let the Monkey Watch"

Struggle meetings, where ex-landlords were castigated as class enemies, and other people with "bad class backgrounds" were the "chickens," fulfilled a critical function in creating the radical environment. A cadre who participated in these attacks on class enemies described the process in rather cynical terms.

In 1974, we also used the technique of criticizing landlords and dragging them out to frighten the peasants into following the policies. In all the reports we wrote, we always mentioned that we had struggled some landlords because *without grabbing some landlords there would be no class struggle, and there had to be class struggle in our reports.* We reported how many people we struggled, how many times, and the number of people that were involved in the struggle sessions (emphasis added).[59]

The strategy was often successful. Peasants in Taishan County, Guangdong Province privately opened barren land in 1972–1973. In 1974, after a "reactionary rich peasant" was "struggled," peasants turned over more than half a hectare of newly opened barren land to the collective.[60]

Another cadre who organized such meetings said that rather than force peasants to openly attack cadres who were targets of one campaign, they first attacked "bad elements." This sent the message to the cadres. These so-called bad elements "were rarely guilty of doing bad things, but this was the only way to get the peasants going."[61] However, subjecting landlords to public opprobrium was no mere formality. Peasants, witnessing the beating of a landlord by the local militia, would think twice before criticizing a policy. Also, by attributing opposition to radical policies to the "rumor mongering of bad elements," local cadres could ignore legitimate peasant complaints.

Local militias were important participants in these struggle sessions. When comprised of rusticated or "sent-down" urban youths, militias were more likely to support radical policies; local peasant youths, however, were more conservative.[62] According to Madsen's informant, "During big struggle meetings, you have to rely on the militia to push things forward. Old people, middle-aged people, don't like to struggle. They are afraid to hurt the feelings of people. But young people aren't afraid. They don't know anything at all about personal relationships, and during the struggle meetings will struggle and struggle with all their might."[63] According to Madsen, at least half the active participants in political struggle sessions during rectification campaigns were militia people.[64]

Work Teams

Campaign work teams (*gongzuo dui*), often composed of district and county officials, descended on the villages to educate peasants, rectify leadership, or help implement policies associated with particular campaigns.[65] District or county campaign offices were often in control and worked closely with government or Party committees at that level. If the campaign was run at the district, county officials suggested communes that could serve as test points for the campaign. District officials could accept or reject these localities. Work teams then visited these communes where, with commune officials, they chose brigades that would carry out the campaign.[66] Some work teams sought villages with pliable and obedient leaders to facilitate the initial implementation stage.

Campaign work teams had a great deal of power. They could abrogate leadership authority within a unit by forcing the local leaders to "step aside" (*kao bian*).[67] In the late 1960s and early 1970s they sometimes replaced older, more conservative cadres with younger leaders who carried out radical policies. They organized struggle meetings to criticize landlords and frighten peasants. In one locality they monitored incoming and outgoing mail to intensify the radical environment.

Work teams tried hard to implement the policies of each campaign. As outsiders, campaign work team members cared little about the peasants' economic interest. They simply had a job to perform, which would be judged by their bureaucratic superiors, so they often carried out these policies without question. Only in retrospect did one informant see the leftist nature of policies he had carried out while on a Line Education Campaign work team. At the time, he said, he had not thought about the policy itself, only that he had to carry it out.[68] Work teams also had deadlines and could not return home until they completed their task. According to one informant, "We had to fulfill the task in three months or else we would have to stay and continue to work for three more months."[69]

During the Line Education Campaign, work teams in Guangdong Province ranked production teams they visited according to the ratio of their peasants' private and collective income. According to their scale the power of capitalism was: (1) "especially serious" (*tebie yanzhong*), (2) "serious" (*yanzhong*), and (3) "rather serious" (*bijiao yanzhong*). Work teams also used terms such as "there are not a few problems" (*you bu shao wenti*) and "not very serious" (*bu hen yanzhong*). When peasants in one "serious" location planted vegetables, banana trees and cash crops everywhere, the work team expropriated the land beside the road that had been cultivated and cut down the banana trees around the fish ponds.[70]

Many work teams which were given a specific task to fulfill resorted to radical measures to ensure implementation. One Guangxi Province work team sent to resolve a food shortage in a brigade decided to build terraced fields on which peasants could plant grain. To ensure that all peasants took part in the field work, they collectivized all private fishing and confiscated all private boats.[71] In another case, a work team from a commune outside Nanjing that went to a poor unit to see why output had dropped, attributed the problem to excess private plots and restricted them. During the 1960s and 1970s many bureaucrats believed that the major impediment to rural change was the peasants' backward consciousness, so the private sector became the whipping boy of many work teams. Given the radical environment of this period, getting permission to attack the "tail of capitalism" was easy.

Media Manipulation

Manipulating the press at various levels of society helped create the winds and maintain a radical environment. Supporters of agrarian radicalism used the national press, such as the *People's Daily*, to mobilize support for their policies by floating policy ideas and seeing if local leaders picked up the cues.[72] In 1974 the writing groups of the Gang of Four took control of the *People's Daily*, while Yao Wenyuan took control of *Red Flag* (*Hongqi*).[73] At times they made movies to propel the campaigns.[74]

Local newspapers and propaganda sheets maintained grassroots psychological pressure. During campaigns, districts and counties disseminated information through campaign newspapers. An informant from Yunnan recalled that when her team collectivized private plots in 1970, this experience became reference material for the whole county. Another informant, who worked in a Line Education Campaign work team in 1974, wrote reports for the county propaganda committee as well as for *Southern Daily* (*Nanfang ribao*), Canton's major newspaper. His reports were published under the byline of "this paper's reporter" (*ben bao jizhe*).[75] District newspapers, such as *Foshan Report* (*Foshan bao*), also described the restrictions of excess private plots.[76]

Media coverage during campaigns was highly distorted.[77] Work teams went to units that were either advanced or backward in relation to the goals of the campaign.[78] Changes in backward units were often given the highest priority because if they could change, the campaign was likely to succeed. But by ignoring all the average units in the countryside, the press gave a false image of rural China to foreigners and Chinese alike. Two other factors increased the biased nature of the reporting. First, during campaigns there was great pressure to demonstrate success; unsuccessful attempts at change were never reported until the ideological line changed. One informant admitted that when he wrote reports for the district Party secretary, he told only of the successes. A few lines at the end of the report outlined several problems.[79] And second, when press reports lauded the changes in these backward units, they rarely mentioned that work teams, political pressure, and large financial investments had ensured the changes. These half-truths, which compounded the wind of this period, explain why so many new experiments failed in rural China.

Xia Fang (Sending Down)

During 1968–1978, a vast number of urban cadres and youths, who were sent to the countryside, introduced peasants to the radicals' policies and ideology and mobilized peasants to adopt these radical programs. Sent-down cadres were active in rural Hunan in "cutting the tail of capitalism,"[80] and they led political study classes that helped create the radical environment at the local level. They also supplied a cohort for campaign work teams. Given their anti-rural predilections and beliefs that the countryside suffered from the feudal vestiges of petty-bourgeois ideology, they responded to the pressures and restricted the private sector when ordered to do so.

Of greater importance to the generation of the radical environment were the millions of urban youths who were relocated in the rural areas after 1968.[81] Born and raised in post-Mao China, some of these youths were committed to Maoist values and the radical policies they generated. In Chen Village, educated youths led the radicalization of the village.[82] One informant sent to Jilin Province's countryside reported that only the educated youths supported the brigade Party secretary's call for brigade accounting.[83] As reporters for the collective's broadcast system, educated youths helped propagate radical policies.[84] They often formed the core of the village militias whose harshness radicalized the local environment. Admittedly, most peasants resented and looked down on these youths, whose limited competence in farming often left them dependent on others for food. Yet their constant espousal of Maoist slogans and agitation for radical policies intensified pressures on peasants to accede to the radical demands.

Conclusion

Factional struggles, opposition from more conservative leaders who rejected their policies, the need to participate in winning coalitions, and Mao's lack of open support for the radical program forced the radicals to use informal channels for mobilizing support for their rural development program. While sending messages to the local levels through policy winds demonstrated political ingenuity and flexibility, the radicals' political weakness and the unpopularity of their policies necessitated creating a radical environment at both the national and local levels to constrain local cadres' choices and pressure them to implement these policies. Doing so, however, involved harsh techniques.

No doubt the radicals hoped that ideological education would teach peasants voluntarily to accept restrictions on the private sector, expend all their energy on behalf of the collective and the state, and support shifts to higher stages of socialism. But the radicals failed to enervate any real, spontaneous peasant radicalism. Only by creating a local setting rife with political and personal insecurity; only by purging leaders with strong ties to the peasants and replacing them with leaders who had fewer direct links with them; only by beating landlords who in most instances had committed no offenses for twenty years; and only by press distortion, deceit, and the creation of false models could the radicals create the psychological environment necessary to compel cadres and peasants to respond to their goal of building a better society. But can one build utopia through compulsion?

The radical economic strategy called for creating self-reliant, autonomous rural units which had little market interaction with their neighbors and which needed little help from the state. At the same time the radicals also wanted to penetrate these villages and control the political and social change within them. But independent units rarely listen to outsiders who dictate to them, especially those with limited influence. Since the radicals had little to offer, the economic goal of generating greater autonomy and the political goal of a revolution from above were incompatible.

The radicals were forced to rely on a vast array of coercive techniques to compel localities to implement their policies. And while many local cadres did respond to their signals and implemented parts of the radical program, the limitations on the radicals' influence were great. For although many local cadres heard the messages and felt the pressures of the national winds and local radical environment, as locals they also had to respond to other demands—from peasants, local bureaucratic allies, and the needs of their own careers. Nevertheless, as we will see in the next chapter, supporters of agrarian radicalism kept the issue very much alive throughout much of 1968–1978 at both the national and local levels. These ten years were indeed quite radical, forcing local leaders to struggle with the external pressures which impinged on their policy choices.

3

PERIODIZATION OF
AGRARIAN RADICALISM

THE PRESSURE ON THE localities to implement the radical policies varied in relation to the political, economic and psychological trends of the 1968–1978 decade.[1] Primary among these factors was the changing balance of power between advocates and opponents of the radical developmental strategy. As radical power increased, radical winds blew more strongly, and the radical environment intensified. During peak periods of leftist power—1968–1970, 1973–1974, and 1976–1977—the influence of the radicals' policies on local agendas and decision making, albeit with a possible time lag, increased. Nonetheless, excluding 1971–1973 and summer 1975, when leftist influence was at its nadir, the trend throughout the entire period was radical, the only difference being the extent of leftist influence within each sub-period. As long as the radical line was not totally repudiated, leftism remained the dominant force in China,[2] affecting debates on agricultural policy, the policy proposals emanating from Beijing and the local response.

General Trends of the Radical Era

The political shifts of this era and the attempt to carry out the radical development strategy occurred within a specific historical, economic, and psychological environment.

The Mao cult, developed in the wake of the Red Guard era and the overall radicalism of the Cultural Revolution, created a mood of euphoria in the countryside which Chen Boda, Mao's personal secretary and the leader of the Cultural Revolution Small Group, used to push China towards communism. Figure 1, based on references to several radical policies in the *People's Daily*, reflects to a certain degree the pattern of radical pressures during the entire decade.[3] But Lin Biao's 1969 military mobilization, with its moral and coercive component, and Lin's political demise brought the Chinese people back to

50

Table 3. Major events in rural policy, 1966–1978.

LEFTISM IN ASCENDANCY, 1966–1969

1966: Spring–summer. Outbreak of Cultural Revolution.

1966–1967: Winter. Anhui report describes this as a period of anarchy.

1968: Spring. Chen Boda and Lin Biao establish test points in Beijing and Hangzhou to restrict private plots and markets and to introduce Dazhai workpoints.

1969: 17 January. *People's Daily* calls on poor and lower-middle peasant associations to take control of private markets throughout China.

Spring. Three Loyalties Campaign follows on heels of Cleaning Class Ranks Campaign.

April. Ninth Party Congress; Lin Biao chosen as Mao's successor.

November. Lin advocates "new and flying" leap; areas around China respond.

THE RIGHTIST MORATORIUM, 1970–1972

1970: February. *Red Flag* supports "three-level ownership system."

1 May. Ministry of Agriculture and Forestry reestablished.

June–September. Northern Districts Agricultural Conference meets.

15 August. Guangdong Province conference supports "payment according to labor."

23 August–6 September. Second Plenum, Ninth Central Committee, attacks Chen Boda.

23 September. *People's Daily* calls on all units to "learn from Dazhai."

October. Xu Shiyou attacks leftist agricultural policies.

December. Central Committee of Chinese Communist Party (CC-CCP) document on remuneration supports *Sixty Articles on Agriculture.*

Fall-winter. Provincial agricultural conferences reject radical policies.

1971: 18 February. *People's Daily* stresses "three-level ownership," "all-round development," and "payment according to labor."

21 March. *People's Daily* supports "rural economic policies."

1972: February. Zhou Enlai speech criticizes "learning from Dazhai."

Mao states that major task is to oppose "ultra-rightism."

THE ANTI-CONFUCIAN WIND, 1973–1974

1973: 7 August. Yang Rongguo article begins Movement to Criticize Confucius.

24–28 August. Tenth Party Congress; Wang Hongwen becomes third-ranking party leader.

August. Line Education Campaign begins; continues through summer 1977.

1973–1974. December–January. *People's Daily* supports leftist policies.

1974: April–September. Privately opened barren land collectivized in Foshan District, Guangdong Province.

Spring. Hebei work teams criticize "rural economic policies."

23 September. *People's Daily* calls for "handicraft service stations" to control private tradesmen.

THE GANG OF FOUR, HUA GUOFENG, AND DENG XIAOPING, 1975–1976

1975: January. Fourth National People's Congress (NPC) proclaims "four modernizations" and recognizes private sector as "necessary adjunct of the socialist economy."

January. Mao Yuanxin opens Heertao Commune experiment.

February. Bourgeois Rights Campaign begins.

2 July. Jiang Qing sends letter to Conference on Professional Work in Agriculture.

Table 3. Major events in rural policy, 1966–1978. (*continued*)

THE GANG OF FOUR, HUA GUOFENG, AND DENG XIAOPING, 1975–1976
(*continued*)

August. Mao Zedong criticizes rash restriction of bourgeois rights.

15 September. First National Conference on Learning from Dazhai in Agriculture; Jiang Qing, in Mao's name, calls for revision of *Sixty Articles*.

1976: January. Mao opposes attack on "industry, commerce, agriculture, or the army."

8 April. Deng Xiaoping removed from all party posts following Tian An Men Incident.

April–June. Gang of Four attacks Hua Guofeng, Chen Yonggui speeches and Dazhai.

9 September. Mao Zedong dies.

5 October. Hua Guofeng arrests Gang of Four and Mao Yuanxin.

THE ERA OF HUA GUOFENG, 1976–1978

1976: 10 December. Hua and Chen Yonggui convene Second Dazhai Conference.

1977: August. Rural Capital Construction Conference calls for "high tide" in rural capital construction.

11 December. *People's Daily* announces "new leap forward in agriculture."

19 December. CC-CCP's Report on Working Forum for Popularizing Dazhai Counties calls on 10 percent of brigades to shift to brigade accounting.

1978: February. First Session, Fifth NPC, echoes Hua's line for last time.

earth. That Mao's successor—whose praise had elevated Mao to god-like proportions—had tried to kill him planted the seeds of skepticism among China's rural inhabitants, and once rural Chinese began to appraise the world around them realistically, they saw entrenched poverty.

The 1971 emphasis on material incentives, increased scope for the private sector, and rural modernization thus struck a popular chord. Figure 2 shows the periods of rightist critique of leftism. Still, the Gang of Four resurrected the radical mantle after Lin's fall and weathered the rightist shift, preventing any major critique of leftism between 1971 and 1973. Only some policies were criticized. Moreover, in 1973–1974 they counter-attacked. Although Zhou Enlai and Deng Xiaoping called in 1975 for the Four Modernizations, increased living standards, and an enlivened economy, the Gang of Four and then Hua Guofeng undermined and postponed any major policy shift. "Continuing the revolution" and "taking class struggle as the key link," not economic development, remained the basic Party line until 1978.

The economic trends of this period, particularly the poor agricultural performance of the early 1970s, were not conducive to fulfilling the radical program. In 1965 China moved to direct planning in

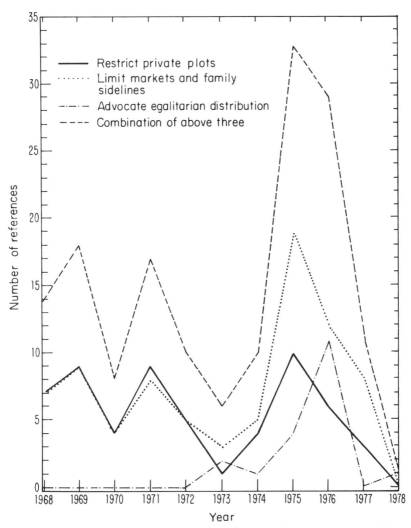

Figure 1. Articles in the *People's Daily* advocating specific radical policies, 1968–1978.

agriculture. Total output was determined in quantity terms, and each unit was given detailed plans outlining acreage, output, and the crops to be planted. Rigidity in the decision making process prevented units from seeking comparative advantage and decreased marginal productivity in agriculture throughout the 1970s.[4] Although we lack good systematic data, some indicators show the unfavorable overall economic trends of this period. From 1965 to 1976, total expenditure of the people's communes, as a ratio of total rural income, rose from 28.2

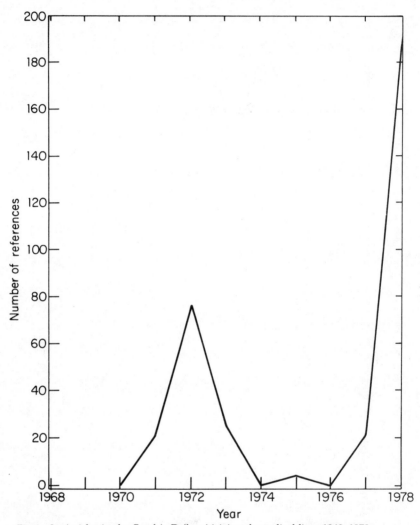

Figure 2. Articles in the *People's Daily* criticizing the radical line, 1968–1978.

percent to 35.4 percent; net income dropped from 71.8 percent to 64.6 percent; and the proportion distributed to commune members dropped from 57.3 percent to 50.7 percent (Table 2). Real rural incomes dropped in the mid-1970s, cotton rations did not increase between 1969 and 1979,[5] and per capita food consumption did not change from 1956 to the late 1970s.[6] Limited economic benefits did not create strong support for the radical line.

While economic conditions had often been preconditions for political and socioeconomic transformations, in this decade politics determined the economics. National policy and local leadership manipulations strengthened rural small-scale industries and the collective sector and constrained the private sector, including rural trade fairs, private plots, and household sidelines. The political priority placed on self-reliance led to an overemphasis on grain production to the detriment of economic crops. Figure 3 shows the dramatic increase in the area sown to rice during this decade.[7] Finally, leadership turnovers and incessant class struggle campaigns affected the peasants' work. By the end of the era all popular support for the radical policies had dissipated, leaving coercion as the main incentive for bringing about utopia.

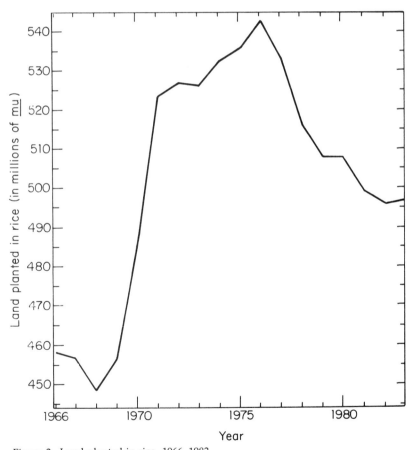

Figure 3. Land planted in rice, 1966–1983.

From the Outbreak of the Cultural Revolution to the
Ninth Party Congress, 1966–1969

During most of 1966, the center's prime concern was ensuring a successful fall harvest. Red Guards were forbidden from going to the countryside and peasants from flocking to the cities to participate in politics.[8] But by December 1966 and January 1967 the rural equivalent of the "January power seizures" occurred in many suburban localities, and local leadership began to disintegrate.[9] In some places old cadres had been moved out, and new, younger people had moved in.[10]

Unencumbered by state or collective bureaucratic controls, peasants pursued their own economic interests. According to a local leader in rural Jiangsu province, "during 1966–1968, which was a period of anarchism, some people expanded their private plots to 3–4 *mu*."[11] Black-marketeering and theft from collective granaries increased as well.[12] In January and March 1967 the Central Committee of the CCP (CC-CCP) called for a halt to encroachment on collective property and clearing of barren land.[13] Yet in 1967 demands for tighter control often went unheeded in light of the political anarchy that ensued.[14]

The first concerted central effort to introduce radical agricultural policies began in spring 1968,[15] when Cultural Revolution politics lurched leftward. The March 1968 purge of military Chief of Staff, Yang Chengwu, followed the "second February countercurrent," which included attacks on Chen Yi, Yu Qiuli, and—most important—on Tan Chenlin, who was responsible for agricultural policy. In an April editorial Mao shifted his support to the left,[16] and by June 1968 changes in the Politburo had left Lin Biao, Chen Boda, and the Gang of Four in a powerful position. The major opposition was from a weakened Zhou Enlai.

As radical power increased at the center, its proponents began a radical wind. Chen Boda and Lin Biao established test points in Beijing and Hangzhou, respectively, to restrict private plots and markets and introduce Dazhai workpoints. Chen Boda reportedly told peasants in Beijing's *Sijiqing* (Evergreen) Commune to unify their production teams (*bing dui*) and "grow your private plots collectively as they do in Dazhai."[17] In 1968 Zhang Chunqiao, at a Shanghai conference, reportedly outlined his views on poor units establishing brigade ownership.[18] In May and June 1968 *People's Daily* supported this radical wind by advocating restricting private plots, household sidelines and markets.[19] A May 1968 New China News Agency report criticized collective sidelines whose production forced the village to buy state grain for food.[20] This elite pressure affected local levels.

Brigade accounting was established in Jiangshan County, Zhejiang, in spring 1968,[21] while according to my interviews and letters from China collected by *Issues and Studies*, official private plots were collectivized in parts of Jurong, Jiangpu and Danyang counties in Jiangsu Province, in Yongxing County, Hunan Province, and Dong-huan County, Guangdong Province, while they were cut back in size in Guangdong, Heilongjiang, Beijing, Shanghai, Hunan, Fujian, and Jiangsu provinces. The first radical push of this era had begun.

Although the tempo of agricultural production caused events to quiet down in late summer-early fall 1968, radical pressures increased in September 1968 with the beginning of the nation-wide Learn from Dazhai Campaign.[22] Both Western and Chinese observers have characterized this period as one of intense radicalism.[23] Two campaigns—the Three Loyalties Campaign, which followed on the heels of the Cleaning Class Ranks Campaign—came together to radicalize this period. Particularly where the Cleaning Class Ranks Campaign had been violent, where many cadres had been criticized sharply, or where new cadres had replaced old ones, few peasants or cadres dared oppose the leftism in the Three Loyalties Campaign. Throughout China, private plots and private economic activities were restricted,[24] the role of the brigade increased dramatically,[25] the size of the units increased,[26] and following a September 1968 test point where county and commune cadres gave the Supply and Marketing Cooperatives control over the private commercial activities of the peasants,[27] *People's Daily* called on Poor and Lower-Middle Peasant Associations to take control of private markets throughout China.[28] Furthermore, the rustication of urban youth got a big push in December 1968 when Mao's directive was published in the *People's Daily* of 23 December. In 1968 over 1.7 million urban youth were sent to the rural areas, with the number increasing to 2.7 million in 1969.[29]

Lin Biao and the Year of Military Radicalism

Lin Biao had his greatest influence on rural China from the Ninth Party Congress of April 1969 until spring 1970.[30] External threats, particularly from the Soviet Union, gave Lin and other central and local military leaders a rallying point for mobilizing a new initiative. As financial investments shifted for a brief period from agriculture to heavy military spending,[31] the need for local and regional self-reliance increased. Collective accumulation expanded and peasant consumption suffered (Table 2).

Preparations for the Ninth Party Congress, the border conflict with the Soviet Union, and the needs of spring planting all led to a brief moderating trend in the rural areas;[32] however, the publication of Mao's slogan to prepare for war in the August 1969 issue of *Red Flag* gave momentum to Lin Biao's military and economic mobilization. In October Lin put forward Order Number One, which called for the evacuation of top leaders from several northern cities,[33] and in November 1969 he called for a "new flying leap."[34] The scope and intensity of this new leap was great.[35] As local grain self-sufficiency became a high priority, cash crops were dug up in some localities; hilly land was transformed into paddy fields; and local units were commanded to follow the state plan. A strict policy on cereal distribution was also advocated as peasants were pressured to eat less, save more, and increase sales to the state. Higher prices for above quota sales of grain and other agricultural by-products were also rescinded.[36] In 1969 savings deposits became subject to confiscation, which allowed the state and collectives to take money from citizens to finance the flying leap.[37]

When the One Hit, Three Antis Campaign went nation-wide in January 1970, it generated a radical environment conducive to the flying leap and the radical military mobilization.[38] While the campaign was not directly related to rural policy, the terror of the search for counter-revolutionaries probably strengthened the control of local military officials who in 1970 were most likely to replace the purged leftists.[39]

The amount of field work in rural China had already increased in winter 1968–1969, but military mobilization brought rural capital construction to new heights in winter 1969–1970. Data from Nanjing and Nickum's nation-wide data show a major increase in this period.[40] As pressure to fulfill rural capital construction projects intensified, local leaders expropriated more peasant land and labor.[41] Finally, to improve the economies of scale for labor mobilization, Lin and his military mobilizers pressured the rural areas to enlarge the production teams; their number had reached its post-Great Leap nadir in 1969–1970 (Figure 4).[42]

By February 1970 the campaign to eradicate capitalist tendencies, remake rural institutions, and alter China's physical environment had reached its zenith.

The Rightist Moratorium, 1970–1973

In late 1969 certain political events undermined the power base of Chen Boda and Kang Sheng, two of the leading radicals.[43] A November Central Committee directive "stipulated that implementation of the Tachai [Dazhai] distribution system could be postponed if the ideological level of the peasants in a people's commune or production brigade was not high enough."[44] Starting in early 1970 the

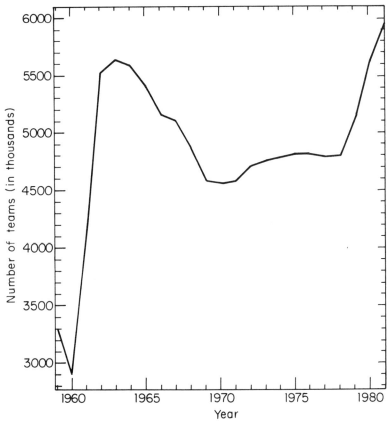

Figure 4. Number of teams in the Chinese countryside, 1959–1981. From *Zhongguo nongye nianjian, 1980* (Chinese Agricultural Yearbook; Beijing: Nongye chubanshe, 1981), p. 5, and *Zhongguo nongye nianjian, 1983* (Beijing: Nongye chubanshe, 1984), p. 19.

leftist program came in for sharper attacks. The February 1970 *Red Flag* supported the "three-level ownership system"—thereby criticizing brigade accounting—and questioned the voluntarism inherent in the ideology and strategy of agrarian radicalism: "Just as we could only lead the peasants step by step to move away from individual ownership to collective ownership in the past, so we can only lead the peasants step by step in their transition from a smaller system of collective ownership to a greater system of collective ownership, but we cannot and moreover should not attempt to complete this course at one stroke."[45] Establishing the Ministry of Agriculture and Forestry on 1 May 1970 signalled the beginning of a conservative trend.[46] Figure 5 shows the seasonal shifts in the critique of various radical policies.

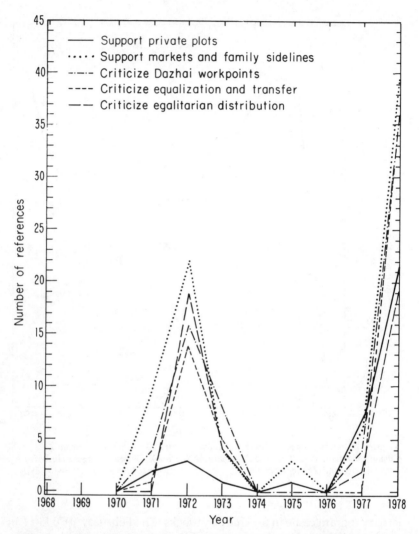

Figure 5. Articles in the *People's Daily* criticizing specific radical policies, 1968–1978.

June–October 1970 saw a major debate on agricultural policy, much of which surrounded the Northern Districts Agricultural Conference (*Beifang diqu nongye huiyi*),[47] which met to resolve the lack of grain self-sufficiency for 14 northern provinces and cities which relied on transporting grain from the south. The third session called for: (1) improving grain output in grain deficient northern provinces; (2) enlarging rural capital construction to increase the areas with stable and high yields—with a target of one *mu* of stable fields per peasant; (3) developing pig production and animal fertilizer—with a target of one pig per peasant; and (4) investing in agricultural mechanization so that 50 percent of the land would be farmed mechanically.[48] While the conference's overemphasis on both grain and rural capital construction work impoverished many parts of China and led to more equalization and transfer, the conference's stress on economic issues represented a moderation of the 1968–1970 radical trend. And although the conference's call for resurrecting the Sixty Articles went unheeded,[49] trends in the national press from mid-1970 show that the radical program was in a weakened state by the time the conference began.

In the weeks preceding the conference, numerous press articles criticized radical policies.[50] Three days after the Guangdong conference, People's Daily reminded local cadres of the importance of cash crops. Although some press reports still raised radical themes, such as restrictions on private plots and markets,[51] once the Second Plenum of the Ninth Party Committee, which met from 23 August to 6 September 1970, purged Chen Boda, criticism of leftist excesses intensified. A new Learn from Dazhai Campaign, begun in September 1970, had been deradicalized under the influence of the Northern Districts Agricultural Conference. Further criticisms ensued. In September 1970, the Shaanxi Provincial Revolutionary Committee announced that "revolutionary committees at all levels must act in accordance with Chairman Mao's policies on people's communes. . . . They should report and ask for instructions . . . and seriously carry out the system of ownership at the three levels, with the production team as the foundation."[52] In October, Xu Shiyou, head of the Nanjing Military Region and a conservative Politburo member, sharply attacked leftist agricultural policies. From another direction, China's draft Constitution circulating at this time reemphasized the team as the basic accounting unit and affirmed the peasants' right to private plots.[53]

Central politics facilitated further withdrawal from radical policies. A November 1970 meeting of the expanded Politburo criticized Chen Boda for his actions at the Second Plenum, and according to Oksenberg, Kang Sheng's political influence suffered egregious defeat in late 1970 as well. The December Politburo meeting attacked Lin Biao and began the critique of Chen Boda within the Party. With momentum in their favor, anti-radical forces organized provincial agricultural work conferences to repudiate radical policies and support the Sixty Articles.[54] For the next two-and-a-half to three years, Chinese agriculture followed a more moderate line.

Subnational political changes in 1971 moderated agricultural policy until mid-1973. Half a dozen provincial leaders who had

espoused the radical line were replaced.[55] Few Gang of Four supporters made it onto provincial revolutionary committees, and regional
military officials were paid off for supporting Mao in his showdown
with Lin Biao.[56] By 1971, 20 of 29 provincial first Party secretaries
were from the regional People's Liberation Army (PLA).[57] Within this
political environment Zhou Enlai took charge of most of the work of
the State Council and the Central Committee in 1971–1973 and
established a more liberal, rural political economy.[58]

On 21 August 1971 the CC-CCP raised the price for above quota
grain sales by 30 percent and allowed peasants to expand the private
sector. And on 26 December 1971 the Central Committee's directive
on "Distribution in the People's Communes" criticized "blindly
learning from Dazhai," Dazhai workpoints, and the excessive number
of officials who, without participating in productive labor, took a
supplement above that stipulated in the *Sixty Articles*.[59] This document, which supported expanding crop types, had an important
political impact at the local levels.[60] Peasants again cultivated land on
the side of the roads, on hills and around lakes, while in Guangdong
Province brigade cadres in Panyu County gave collective land to
peasants as private plots, instigating "a crooked capitalist wind of
privately opening barren land."[61] Many places replaced Dazhai
workpoints with piece or task rate systems,[62] while teams that had
been unified during 1968–1969 were again split. Some changes may
have been due to a February 1972 Zhou Enlai speech criticizing
learning from Dazhai.[63]

Nonetheless, most places simply stopped introducing the more
radical leftist policies without undoing their deleterious effects.
Private plots remained collectivized in many places until the late
1970s. Some places used Dazhai workpoints until the late 1970s as
well. Even the CC-CCP directive on distribution, long seen as an
important step in improving peasant livelihood during this era, had
no significant nation-wide impact.[64] Moreover this document sanc-
tioned equalization and transfer by allowing higher levels of the
collective to take funds from the teams.[65] Even *People's Daily*, which in
1972 criticized many radical policies, still argued that paying excessive
attention to diversification—that is, too little attention to grain—was
a bad thing.[66] In 1972 Mao still believed that the major task was
opposing ultra-rightism,[67] and with his support the Gang of Four
prevented a major leftist critique that was looming in 1971–1972.[68]

The Anti-Confucian Wind

The rehabilitation of senior cadres, the waning of the rightist trend, and
the knowledge that Zhou Enlai was dying of cancer increased radical

power in China in 1973. Mao, who preferred a balance between radicals amd moderates, undermined the 1971–1973 strengthening of the moderates by supporting the radicals at the Tenth Party Congress. Military representation on the Central Committee dropped from 40 percent at the Ninth Congress to 27 percent at the Tenth, while many leaders of the rebuilt provincial mass organizations, a major Gang-of-Four power base, moved to the center. And although the August 1973 congress was not a total victory for the radicals, it signified that their power was on the rebound. Wang Hongwen, the Shanghai factory rebel who became the third ranking Party leader and delivered one of the two major Congress speeches, took charge of much central Party work after this conference. Rumors circulated that Mao was seriously considering him as a potential successor. Radical power in the Politburo increased as well.[69] Still, much of the radicals' improved position within the Central Committee was window-dressing. Many cadres whom the radicals had purged in the Cultural Revolution returned to the Central Committee at this congress, and while mass representatives looked influential, all held posts below second Party secretary on their provincial Party committees. In fact, 28 of 48 did not even have positions on the standing committees of their provincial Party committees.[70]

Accordingly, after late 1972 the Gang of Four intensified factional conflict that would not subside for several years. In April 1973 they attacked Zhou Enlai's intellectual and educational policies and stopped the moderate trend that had been building since mid-1972 on this issue. Two weeks before the convening of the Tenth Party Congress on 24 August 1973, the Movement to Criticize Confucius began.[71] During this movement the radicals started their own journal, *Study and Criticism*, which became another forum for mobilizing radical support. Although most analysts argue that this campaign and the later Criticize Lin Biao and Confucius Campaign had little effect on rural policy[72]—during the entire campaign, from August 1973 to summer 1974, only five articles advocating agrarian radical policies appeared in *People's Daily*—informant interviews and later press reports suggest that the movement had an important local impact.[73]

Private plots were restricted and some teams were amal-gamated.[74] But the real radicalization occurred only in late 1973 and early 1974. Press reports assert that in Shanxi, Hebei, and Gansu provinces the 1971–1973 rightist trend, whereby some peasants had left collective labor, was criticized in 1974.[75] Many places using task rates returned to Dazhai workpoints in 1974.[76] A new wave of expropriation and transfer and the specialized construction groups, which facilitated much of the labor expropriation, began in 1973–1974 as well. Finally, private plots and household sidelines were attacked during 1973–1974.[77] While private craftsmen who had come under collective control during the Cultural Revolution had reverted to private employment in the early 1970s, *People's Daily* of 23 September 1974 called for "handicraft service stations" to reestablish controls over these tradesmen.

These restrictions were a response to a rather amorphous national campaign that local leaders may have used to their own advantage. The precise date of the Line Education Campaign is unclear, but various local campaigns to "strengthen education in the party's basic line" (*dangde jiben luxian jiaoyu*) ran from summer 1973 through summer 1977. A *People's Daily* article in late 1976 argues that a rural campaign to carry out education in the party's basic line began immediately after the Tenth Party Congress (August 1973), while work teams were sent to Yunnan Province in December 1973 to "help unfold education in the Party's basic line."[78] A work-team participant in this campaign in Guandong divides it into four phases: February–December 1974, January–October 1975, November 1975–August 1976, and August 1976–June 1977.[79]

The anarchic nature of rural policy during this era and cadre abilities to use national policies to bolster local interests are exemplified by the fact that the campaign's content and scope varied from place to place and year to year. A summer 1974 Line Education Campaign work team in Jiangpu County, Jiangsu Province labeled a commune bean curd factory "collective capitalism," cut back on expanded private plots, and criticized a commune official for embezzlement. But this campaign was never popularized in the rest of the province.[80] Privately cultivated barren land was collectivized in Foshan District, Guangdong Province from April through September 1974.[81] In 1975 under this campaign officials in Jinjiang County, Fujian Province, restricted rural trade fairs, while another work team restricted private plots and household sidelines in Guangxi Province.[82] According to Chen Yonggui, the Gang of Four tried to stop work teams from going to the countryside in 1976 because they attacked local cadres and stopped the masses from criticizing higher level officials.[83] Thus radical policies had greater impact on the countryside, specifically in spring-summer 1974 and from late 1973 until spring 1976 in general, than previously believed. Still, the CC-CCP directive of 1 July 1974, which ended the urban unrest associated with the Criticize Lin Biao and Confucius Campaign, probably strengthened conservative forces in the countryside as well.

The Gang of Four, Hua Guofeng, and Deng Xiaoping

From January 1975 until spring 1976 debates over rural development continued. The Fourth National People's Congress (NPC) of January 1975, which made the Four Modernizations (agriculture, industry, the military, and science and technology) the Party's basic task, used the language of the *Sixty Articles* to declare private plots a "necessary adjunct of the socialist economy." As in 1970–1971 economic development superseded class struggle and socioeconomic transformations.

However, as soon as the conference ended, the Gang of Four and their followers attacked the increasing surge for agrarian reform. In January 1975 Mao Yuanxin, Mao's nephew and a close ally of the Gang of Four, began an experiment in Heertao Commune to eradicate the private market and compel peasants to sell all sideline produce to the Supply and Marketing Cooperative.[84] In February several articles appeared in the *People's Daily* of which two alleged that class enemies had undermined the progressive politics of the late 1960s and early 1970s by advocating capitalist tendencies, private plots, household sidelines, and rural trade fairs.[85] Also in February Mao and the Gang of Four resurrected the contentious issue of bourgeois rights in a socialist society.[86] This campaign and Yao Wenyuan's article which suggested that "new-born bourgeois elements," the product of bourgeois rights, had formed the social base for Lin Biao's counter-revolutionary actions, made some rural cadres very nervous. What Zhang Chunqiao called a "fear of communization" swept rural China in February and March 1975.[87] Cadres no doubt were deeply concerned. In January the private sector had been formally legitimized; yet after two months Mao and the radicals told cadres that if they did not restrict the private sector it could generate a basis for counter-revolution. If they did not restrict private plots, markets, and sidelines could they be accused of building a social base for "anti-Party criminals" such as Lin? In response, some local officials restricted the private sector.[88]

Although the debate that followed seems to Westerners like splitting hairs, it was a critical policy struggle in the course of which the moderates tried to clarify the meaning of "restrict" (*xianzhi*). They could not ignore Mao's February directive, but restricting and abolishing bourgeois rights were not the same. The moderates, while recognizing the need to restrict bourgeois rights, argued that to ensure that these restrictions did not become leftist mistakes, the private-sector or material incentives that were acceptable under the *Sixty Articles* should be allowed to persist. Throughout April, May, and June *Red Flag* opposed brigade accounting, restricting private plots and household sidelines, Dazhai workpoints, and the closing of rural trade fairs.[89] As a clear message to local cadres *Heilongjiang Daily* stated that "we should not allow the restriction to exceed the limits set by the Party's present policy . . . We must draw a clear line . . . between what may and can be done today and what can only be done tomorrow."[90]

The attack on the Four Modernizations was intense. Bolstered by Mao's support in February, the Gang of Four launched a counter-offensive and created a "mini-wind." Any undeclared plans to expand the private sector were stopped cold as Zhou and Deng fought for the legitimacy of the *Sixty Articles* and the more liberal attitude towards the private sector established in January. But by August, after weathering the radical push, moderates received a boost from Mao when he reportedly called for "refraining from rashness" in the restriction of bourgeois rights.[91] With this assistance, Zhou and Deng staved off any reradicalization of the countryside throughout summer 1975.

Supporters of agrarian radicalism were now severely limited in their ability to mobilize the provinces or local leaders. Lin Bao was dead, Chen Boda was incarcerated, and Mao's health imprisoned him in the leadership compound of Zhongnanhai. Wang Hongwen, who only two years before had been a rising star, had lost Mao's support for his factional antics during the Criticize Lin Biao and Confucius Campaign.[92] This campaign also created great animosity against the Gang of Four among top leaders, making coalition building almost impossible. Peasants were unlikely to respond to another campaign based on peasant loyalty to Mao. Moreover, while in 1974 Deng Xiaoping was still rebuilding his power base, by spring-summer 1975 he was much stronger, as he purged more and more local leftists.[93]

Mao's unpopular wife, Jiang Qing, carried the major burden of fighting for agrarian radical policies. On 2 July 1975, in a letter to delegates at the All-China Conference of Professional Work in Agriculture, she criticized the concept that "the people regard food as the first requisite so when revolution and production are in conflict, the grasp of revolution should be somewhat slackened." She called on delegates to keep class struggle alive and avoid revisionist policies of Khrushchev- and Malenkov-type leaders. Wang Hongwen also attended the conference.[94] At the First Dazhai Conference, convened in September in Xiyang County and then in Beijing in October, she reemphasized the threat of a rural capitalist restoration, reminding delegates that "peasants still harbor to a serious degree the notion of a small peasant economy." She called for a "mass rectification campaign among all the people," and in Mao's name called for revising parts of the *Sixty Articles*.[95] However, her speech was not transmitted in some provinces in China.[96]

The First Dazhai Conference failed to generate a leftist policy wind or compel rural cadres to implement radical policies. Hua Guofeng's six-point program, a watered-down version of the radical strategy, was less radical than the program he initiated one year later at the Second Dazhai Conference after Deng and the Gang had been purged.[97] As Hua tried to build a winning coalition, Deng's presence prevented him from pushing a more radical program.

This absence of radicalism prompted the Gang of Four to attack Hua and Dazhai for selling out to revisionism. Yao Wenyuan reportedly refused to allow *Red Flag* to carry a summary of Hua's Dazhai speech,[98] and criticized this version of the movement because it "does not study how to attend to revolution in the superstructure in rural work," nor does it "study the question of restricting bourgeois rights as Chairman Mao many times directed."[99] And while the conference, as well as the ongoing Line Education Campaign, did trigger an enormous movement of cadres to the grass roots—figures quoted run as high as 1.6 million—Zhang Chunqiao refused to let these post-Dazhai work teams go to Shanghai's suburbs, saying that "who knows whether the education in the basic line is correct or not."[100] In fact, the Gang was so upset with the entire trend of the Dazhai campaign that from October 1975 until their political demise the Shanghai press never once mentioned Dazhai.[101] Although the conference did trigger a "high tide" in rural capital construction[102] and precipitate some minor leftist adjustments in a few localities,[103] only Zhou's death in January 1976 and Deng's purge following the 5 April 1976 Tien An Men Incident allowed the radicals to create a new radical wind.

Before that, the radicals had faced serious opposition. Hua Guofeng, who controlled Party work after January 1976, was not very supportive of the Gang's strategy. Civilian provincial leaders, who in 1973–1975 had replaced military officials, were rehabilitated pre-Cultural Revolution leaders who opposed the radical line.[104] Mao's early 1976 directive, which said "do not attack industry, commerce, agriculture or the army," did not help the radicals, nor did the February–March "warning" (*da zhaohu*) meeting.[105]

But throughout spring 1976 the Gang fought back on all fronts, bolstered in part by the weakness of the Politburo's Standing Committee and their own control over Mao, now under the watchful eye of his nephew, Mao Yuanxin. In February, Yao ordered those sections of the national media under his control to step up criticisms of the reformist program in agriculture and industry.[106] Zhang Tiesheng, a Liaoning youth whose blank exam had triggered a major attack on Zhou's 1973 educational reforms, made a provocative speech at Dazhai in February as well.[107] Although the warning meeting was partly aimed at weakening the Gang, they manipulated Mao's directives and turned the meeting to their advantage. Thus although the 5 April Tien An Men Incident had been a clear attack on them and a strong demonstration of support for Deng, Deng's purge as a result of the incident and the arrest of his supporters during the Double Pursuit and Investigation Campaign which followed it, allowed the Gang to become more feverish in their attacks.

From April on the radicals influenced rural policy making. In April a planned reaffirmation of Central Document No. 21 of 1975—Hua Guofeng's Dazhai speech—was snuffed out by the Gang of Four.[108] At one April 1976 conference in Wuxi, Jiangsu Province, Chen Yonggui reaffirmed the positive role of the Dazhai Conference, but in May and June his two addresses to agricultural conferences were attacked by officials in Suzhou and Shanghai for abandoning political struggle.[109] In April 1976 *Red Flag* accused Deng of ignoring Dazhai's experiences in class struggle, emphasized the positive aspects of the Dazhai movement in restricting bourgeois rights, and asserted the class character of agricultural mechanization, Hua's pet project.[110] And in May *People's Daily* reported how the "Heertao experience" controlled rural markets.[111]

By June the final debate on policy involving the Gang took place. The radicals argued that the post-April 1976 Criticize Deng Campaign and the search for class enemies in the Party should guide all work, including the Dazhai movement; their opponents, hoping to preserve the emphasis on production that came out of the October 1975 Dazhai meeting, tried to separate these two campaigns and called on Party committees to "grasp revolution and promote production"—a moderate buzz word—and implement the spirit of the Dazhai Conference.[112] The number of press reports on Dazhai in June suggests that Hua and Chen were trying to maximize attention on it.[113] But then, Yao Wenyuan called for a link between the search for capitalist roaders under the Criticize Deng Campaign and "reality throughout the country on all fronts," and at a meeting of representatives of provincial propaganda departments in June, officials were challenged to prove that they were not capitalist roaders themselves.[114] This they could do only by implementing radical policies.

These pressures led to the most radical policy wind in rural China since 1968–1969. Districts in Shandong Province introduced the

Heertao model to control trade fairs, as did a county in Yunnan.[115] Even a commune in conservative Nanjing sent two representatives to study the Heertao experience, although they refused to carry out the policy.[116] In many locations private plots and household sidelines were attacked.[117] The types of crops raised in private plots were restricted as well.[118] Finally, brigade accounting was introduced in several parts of China.[119] According to Chen Yonggui, Yunnan, Guizhou, Sichuan, Fujian, Zhejiang, and Jiangxi provinces were disrupted by the Gang of Four in this period.[120] Middle-level cadres, concerned that the radicals were about to take power, decided to demonstrate political "redness."[121]

The Era of Hua Guofeng

Although incarcerating the Gang of Four should have reversed the leftist trend in agricultural policy, the radical environment did not dissipate immediately. Throughout his reign Hua Guofeng supported a "soft" strain of agrarian radicalism, which placed more emphasis on economic growth, attacked the private sector with less fervor, and did not see an immediate communist transition. Nevertheless he promoted a 1977–1978 "sudden advance," which included continued overemphasis on heavy over light industry, grain over economic crops, accumulation, over consumption—which triggered a drop in living standards—and huge financial deficits.[122] Deficit spending, overemphasis on accumulation, and denigration of personal consumption and living standards mandated continued emphasis on moral incentives, mass mobilization, and some fear and coercion. Hua was an ardent Maoist, and while his policy positions were less radical than the Gang of Four's, his unrealistic targets and refusal to change the line in agricultural policy sent signals to local officials that the left line would be maintained.

The December 1976 Second Dazhai Conference, convened two months after the arrest of the Gang of Four, sent this message as well. Chen Yonggui, then in charge of agriculture, called for criticism of capitalist tendencies and the three freedoms—expanded private plots, rural trade fairs and household sidelines—for restricting bourgeois rights, continuing the youth to the countryside movement, and maintaining May 7th Cadre Schools. He also advocated consolidating and expanding the collective economy. Finally, he called for "an all out people's war for capital farmland construction."[123]

Local officials got the message. This conference showed one commune official in Nanjing that the leadership of Hua and Ye Jianying would in no way end mobilization or certain aspects of agrarian radicalism. A spate of transitions to brigade accounting followed the conference,[124] as did a series of restrictions on the private sector, including tightened controls on cash crops in private plots and privately owned trees in front of people's homes.[125] Finally, a great deal of equalization and transfer occurred in rural China.[126] In Nanjing the amount of earth moved in 1977 increased by 10 percent over 1976, which had already increased by 30 percent over 1975 as a result of the First Dazhai Conference; yet total state investment in 1977 dropped by 7 percent as compared to 1976 (see Table 4).

At the same time that Hua distanced himself politically from the Gang of Four, he maintained a radical line in rural development throughout 1977. A Rural Capital Construction Conference held in summer 1977 in Xiyang County (home of the Dazhai Brigade) and Beijing called for even greater efforts in rural capital construction work and competition among local units to create a new "high tide." Chen Yonggui's speech to that conference invoked many radical themes, as he linked enthusiasm for capital construction with a cadres' class stance. He also called for continued struggle against landlords and rich peasants, whom he called saboteurs, and continued criticism of capitalist tendencies. And although he recognized that field and water conservation projects should be undertaken for mutual benefit, he said that peasants "should not act like capitalists

Table 4. Nanjing rural capital construction data, 1968–1979.

Year[a]	Earth moved (thousands of cu. m.)	Land leveled[b] (thousands of cu. m.)	Labor used (days)	Investment (thousands of yuan)			Earth moved per yuan of state funds (cu. m.)
				State[c]	Local[d]	Total	
1968	18,020	—	116	2,650	35	2,685	6.7
1969	24,590	—	178	2,020	1	2,021	12.2
1970	28,820	—	206	3,836	239	4,075	7.1
1971	27,190	—	208	6,153	230	6,383	4.2
1972	29,160	—	209	3,372	—	3,372	8.6
1973	27,370	6,350	205	2,487	640	3,127	8.8
1974	41,300	11,580	299	2,033	980	3,013	13.7
1975	59,880	12,520	352	3,634	38	3,672	16.3
1976	89,230	34,450	357	7,980	310	8,363	10.7
1977	99,260	31,450	325	7,100	601	7,774	12.7
1978	89,110	35,250	377	21,520	2,930	21,894	4.0
1979	40,000	15,220	225	41,100	420	41,520	1.0

SOURCE: Nanjing City Agricultural Office, 1981.
a. From end of year listed to spring of following year.
b. City officials deny leveling land before 1973; it is more likely that they simply never organized such leveling, leaving local leaders to do it on their own.
c. Includes provincial and national funds.
d. Investment from the city level and below.

who give first consideration to narrow personal gains and losses in business transactions."[127] By October over 390,000 projects were under way, and by mid-November over 80 million rural laborers were involved.[128] An Pingshang's speech to a Yunnan Conference on Dazhai in October 1977 also suggested that rural class lines were sharpening and warned against allowing "middle" peasants to occupy more that one-third of the cadre posts in teams and brigades, because holding these posts would help poor and lower-middle peasants "struggle against capitalism," "resist and criticize spontaneous capitalist tendencies," and "solve the problems concerning unbridled growth of capitalism."[129]

Hua also tried to maintain support for the radical line in agriculture during winter 1977–1978, six months after Deng Xiaoping returned to power. On 19 December 1977 the Central Committee published the "Outline Report for the Politburo on the Working Forum for Popularizing Dazhai Counties," which shows that a previously unknown meeting on agriculture had occurred then.[130] A *People's Daily* editorial at that time announced that "our historical experience proves that each new leap forward in the national economy is invariably preceded by a new leap forward in agriculture . . . Now we are confronting a new high tide in economic and cultural development."[131] This conference also called for a "mini-Great Leap" in agricultural output, including a grain output of 350 million metric tons and a cotton output of 30 million metric tons by 1980. It called for basic agricultural mechanization by 1980 and for a "high tide" in rural capital construction. Later criticisms of Hua for instigating a "sudden advance" were not wrong.

Most interestingly, central leaders at this conference for the first time formally called for the transition to brigade accounting. While the conference's report recognized that team accounting was appropriate for most of rural China, it emphasized that shifting to brigade accounting was the major trend, and it called on Party committees at all levels to help create the necessary conditions for it. The meeting reportedly decided that from winter 1977 to spring 1978, approximately 10 percent of brigades in rural China should establish brigade accounting. This document resulted in a "wind of transitions" within the countryside[132] and continuing restrictions on the private sector. And while this document's formal nature means that it could not have generated a policy wind as defined here, it supports the contention that this was the only time when such a formal Party call for these restrictions or transitions occurred.

The meeting's impact was not as widespread as Hua and his allies had hoped. As Chapter 8 shows in detail, Deng's provincial supporters were attacking radical policies and initiating major agricultural reforms in the provinces during the same winter season. Nonetheless the public and formal Party line continued to be radical. At a Jilin Dazhai Conference called in response to the December national Dazhai conference, Wang Enmao, first Party secretary of Jilin, said that, "efforts should be made to energetically and steadily pass the basic accounting unit over to the brigade," thereby echoing Hua's line.

> The system of taking production teams as basic accounting units practiced by many production teams will not be able to meet the need of developing production. Such is an inevitable developmental tendency which leadership at all levels should clearly understand . . . According to an investigation, some of our brigades have favorable conditions for the transition of ownership from production teams to brigades. Party committees at various levels should conscientiously grasp this work and guide it along its course of development.[133]

Wang and Hua's position was echoed for the last time at the First Session of the Fifth National People's Congress in March 1978, when Marshal Ye Jianying, Hua's military backer, stated that "when conditions really are ripe, and one locality ripens, let us make the transition. If a group becomes ripe, let them shift." Yet he also injected a cautious note when he said that "when conditions are not ripe, we do not want to do it chaotically." And the Constitution this speech introduced supported transitions "when the brigades' conditions are ripe." Formal support for brigade accounting and the December document's stress on 10 percent helps explain why by 1978 the number of units with brigade accounting peaked at 66,712 or 9.5 percent of all brigades in China.[134]

    This formal support also explains why local leaders implemented radical policies in some rural areas during winter 1977–1978. Brigade accounting was once again introduced in both Shaanxi Province and Nanjing,[135] and one commune secretary admitted in the *People's Daily* that after the fall of the Gang of Four he maintained tight controls on private plots. Only in mid-1978 did he begin to change his policies. The Fifth National People's Congress and its Constitution helped some rural areas resist redividing collective private plots by allowing them to claim that these plots were "in accord with the general orientation."[136]

    Although these formal statements of support for the radical developmental strategy should have had an even greater impact on the localities than the reliance on informal policy winds of the preceding nine years, Deng's wind of reform had affected several provinces in late 1977 and early 1978. While local officials who preferred to follow the radical program could use Hua's radical line to maintain tight controls on the private sector, reform-minded officials could now find incentives in ongoing changes in Sichuan, Anhui, and Gansu provinces. These changes suggested to some local officials that a major battle was looming and that if Deng succeeded, agricultural reforms were forthcoming. Since 1978 became a year of uncertainty for local cadres, it was safest to avoid any changes; and if mistakes were to be made, it was still safer to err to the left.

Only the CC-CCP document of July 1978, heralding the Xiang-xiang Movement,[137] and particularly the Third Plenum documents of December 1978, convinced local officials that major changes were imminent and local radicalism had to stop.[138] Still, these reforms would take several years to wend their way through the political system and finally dismember the radical rural development strategy.

Conclusion

For more than ten years agricultural policy remained in flux, and political battles in Beijing over the control of the policy process led to shifting tides at the local level. Nevertheless, buoyed by support from different supporters of a radical solution to the process of rural development, the overall line remained radical. Even when moderate leaders, such as Zhou Enlai, established some control over agricultural policy, radical leaders sent out their messages through a variety of techniques. As we have seen, local leaders responded to these policy winds and the radical environment, kept tight control on the private sector, avoided obvious material incentives, pushed for rural capital construction work, and strengthened the collective economy.

As we will see in the following four chapters, this chapter only scratched the surface of the local response. Local responses to the same policy varied greatly from place to place, as each policy flowed down at different times into very different local environments. The countryside responded to many of these radical messages, but the radicals themselves had limited success in determining the final outcome.

4

THE LOCAL RESPONSE

The longings of the peasants were one truth, and the policies of the higher ups and the propaganda in the newspapers were quite another.

Liu Binyan, *People or Monsters*

THE RADICALS' motivations, techniques of implementation, and the agricultural policy conflicts that ensued at the national level from 1968 to 1978, need now to be translated to the local level. This chapter and the three that follow analyze and explain the impact of the radical program on rural China and show the ways in which local factors, including local value systems, the local political structure and its political culture, the way the policies affected the distribution of economic and political values, and how the characteristics of each location shaped the ultimate impact of the radical strategy on the location and its inhabitants. But although this chapter shows how the lay of the land, the structures that were built on it, and the interests of its inhabitants refracted radical policies as they meshed with local society, it presents few concrete illustrations of the conceptual points it raises. It is hoped that the three case studies following this discussion will amply fill that need.

Local Values and Agrarian Radicalism

The Elite-Mass Gap

The local world where policies were carried out differed greatly from the world in Beijing where policies were made. While the radicals thought in grand ideological terms, local leaders from the county down confronted mundane, yet practical, problems. Each group's values and concerns differed, as did the constraints under which they worked and the concreteness of the policies with which they dealt. These different pressures and variations in the bureaucratic framework surrounding them meant that national and local leaders lived in a different political culture, dominated by different formal ideologies, policies, and institutions, which in turn generated their own informal adaptive attitudes and behaviors.[1]

Moreover, the canvas on which national leaders practice their brushwork is all of China, and only highly perceptive and flexible leaders recognize the need to vary their brushstrokes for different parts of the painting. From the start, however, the radicals had only one brush and only one stroke for each sector of society. For the countryside until 1975 it was the Dazhai brigade; for industry, Daqing oilfield. But immense differences could exist even within one county. Some villages were in the hills, others in valleys; some were near water, others regularly suffered drought; some had high population densities, others lacked people; some were highly factionalized, others had coherent leadership groups. A local leader who ignored these differences was doomed to fail. Only by adapting central policies to local reality could one hope to mobilize support for the radical policies.

Finally, the radicals' overall developmental strategy was composed of a bundle of individual policies, each with its own local impact. Although in the radicals' minds these policies may have formed a somewhat coherent package, each affected the local struggle for political authority and control over resources in its own way. That effect, in turn, determined the way in which the policies were received at the local level and the extent to which they were or were not implemented.

As a result, perceptions of Marxism-Leninism, social change, and the value system they generated varied as well at the national and local levels.[2] As most national leaders learn belatedly, the messages they send to the peasantry, if accepted at all, are, according to Scott, "assimilated into an existing set of meanings, symbols and practices which frequently do great violence to the message as understood by its high priests in the capital city."[3] For the high priests of radical Maoism, the local world was a complex environment which twisted their policies in ways they may never have imagined.

Rational Motivations of Peasant Behavior

Chinese peasants and cadres evaluated the policies of agrarian radicalism and responded to them in the light of each policy's impact on their own self-interest. To this extent peasants and cadres responded as rational actors. After all, few peasants or local cadres could have understood the philosophical assumptions behind agrarian radicalism. Lacking what Converse calls "constrained belief systems," they were unable to view the policies within one overreaching ideological map.[4] Instead, they turned "remote, generic and abstract" issues into "simple and concrete ones."[5]

Several other reasons suggest the utility of the rational actor model. Rational choice models downplay elite preferences and central institutions, emphasizing instead, in Falkenheim's words, the "values, preferences and constraints that shape citizen behavior."[6] Since we are shifting gears to study the local response, the adoption of this model seems appropriate. Second, assumptions of rationality suit economic rather than political issues; while the radicals' goals were political, for peasants they were economic ones that became political only when peasants expressed opposition to them. Finally, by his own admission, Scott's critique of rational approaches to peasant rebellion does not apply to an analysis of small-scale, less mobilized forms of peasant political activity.[7] Yet as the case studies will show, that is precisely what we are studying.

However, while behavior reflects subjective evaluations of probabilities of personal gain and loss, whose goal is always maximizing personal utilities,[8] the utilities or values one wishes to maximize may vary. Under certain conditions Chinese peasants are risk avoiders, more concerned with maximizing household security than income.[9] When confronting unfavorable prices, they may choose to maximize their leisure rather than their income. Their concerns can extend beyond the narrow confines of their household to include social organizations, such as personal networks, lineages, or village communities. They may rebel over issues of social justice.[10] Yet they are hard working, shrewd planners who possess a spirit of enterprise and a strong desire to get ahead.[11] Underlying all these visions of the peasant is a recognition that at heart the peasant is a rational calculator; within the confines of his political, social, ecological, and economic environment he seeks to maximize his utilities, whether they be wealth, leisure, justice, security or equality.

Peasants and Prosperity

The peasants' desire for economic prosperity was a strong motivating force in the 1960s and 1970s. When political chaos and weakened leftist influence undermined local monitoring of economic activity, some peasants increased the amount of land they privately cultivated, expanded their household sideline activities, or sought work in towns. The hierarchical Confucian value system—which still influenced village life during the Maoist era—tolerated inequalities and respected those who got ahead fairly, particularly if they remembered to treat others in a "human way."[12] Prosperous collectives may have gained peasant respect, while cadres in those collectives were more likely to be promoted than those from poor ones. Ironically, the Maoist value system reinforced this trend. Wealthy collectives were upheld as models. Cadres wanting to prove that their village was learning from Dazhai strengthened the village's collective economy, since a stagnant collective economy proved that the wrong class was in power. This way both Maoist and traditional rural value systems legitimized economic prosperity, particularly collective prosperity.

Peasants and Equality

Yet Chinese peasants were also strongly motivated by a desire for greater equality of opportunity and outcome. Egalitarianism helped mobilize large-scale peasant rebellions in China and was also part of the bandits' moral code.[13] Traditional reflections of primitive communism in China, based on the "well-field system," linked egalitarianism with equal distribution and ownership of land. Egalitarianism also motivated peasant rebels. During the Taiping period there was "an honest desire on the part of the rank and file to do away with discriminatory distinctions."[14] According to Scott, peasants in Vietnam, Europe, and China during the revolution demonstrated a penchant for egalitarianism far more extreme than that of their revolutionary leaders.[15]

The peasant's desire for equality affected communist China as well. In April 1948, land reform in areas under CCP control was disrupted by what Mao called "absolute egalitarianism."[16] This problem reappeared in the Great Leap when local cadres demonstrated an egalitarian tendency towards "leveling of rich and poor and equal distribution." When Mao criticized this tendency toward egalitarianism, he meant "the tendency to deny that there should be differences in income among the various production brigades and various individuals."[17] Today, the Chinese castigate peasant "egalitarianism" (pingjunzhuyi) as a major source of the economic problems of the 1960s and 1970s, arguing that it infected elite (that is, Mao's) ideology and undermined efforts by strong peasants and collectives to get rich.

While some Chinese peasants and cadres favored egalitarian redistribution, others simply wanted equity. Since people's contributions to society differ, inequitable outcomes are unavoidable; so people should be paid according to their contributions. Such demands for equity by strong peasants undermined the use of Dazhai workpoints, while creating a "social basis for the policy changes of the late 1970s."[18]

Some local supporters of agrarian radicalism, however, may have favored a form of anti-equity or leveling, which restricted opportunities to generate inequitable outcomes. In this case redistribution was unnecessary; closing the opportunities, which advantaged peasants with preferred positions used for economic gain, ensured the same outcome. Even when inequalities were not expanding, some peasants may have feared that disparities in endowments could create inequalities; for them the fairest system would prohibit natural endowments from generating inequalities of outcome. If opportunities are not limited, but resources are finite, peasants who use their endowments to expand their share of the limited pie immiserate other peasants.[19]

Local cadres, who narrowed prerevolutionary inequalities through land reform and then saw inequalities reemerge in the mid-1950s before collectivization, could support restricting sectors where differential endowments could generate unequal outcomes—particularly private production and market exchange. Limited data suggests that between 1962 and 1965 most county and commune cadres were either old cadres—veterans of the anti-Japanese or civil wars—or land reform cadres, who had come to power by redistributing land.[20] These officials could have either an a priori sympathy for redistribution or an antipathy against renewed inequalities.[21] Several *People's Daily* articles reported that during the 1970s county or district officials prevented teams from using their comparative advantage to get wealthier than their neighbors.[22] Xiyang County's deputy secretary, reporting to the 1975 Dazhai conference, expressed concern that polarization could develop among teams if some of them tried to increase average per capita income by acting like "collective capitalist organizations."[23] The radicals displayed this anti-equity perspective most clearly in the 1975 debate over bourgeois rights. Even "soft" radicals, who in 1975 may not have supported narrowing bourgeois rights, opposed their expansion.

Equality and Prosperity

Clearly, we face a contradiction. While peasants and cadres sought to enrich their households and villages, other peasants and cadres supported limiting opportunities for personal and collective advancement. Yet Mao saw little contradiction between these two goals, believing that Chinese peasants suffered from "complementary tendencies towards selfishness and egalitarianism."[24] They wanted to get ahead, but feared that in a competitive system others may get too far ahead, and they would suffer privation. They preferred a system that delivered both wealth and equality. The unity of these two drives, prosperity and equality for all, created a wave of support for the Great Leap Forward in fall 1958. Mao saw the adoption of people's communes and the end of private property as proof that China was moving close to communism and predicted that within one or two years China could institute a "free supply system."[25] When this free supply system was in fact introduced in fall 1958, peasants believed that an era of abundance had arrived.[26] Elite promises of prosperity meshed with the ongoing equalization of income and property to convince peasants that the millennium had arrived.

A household's economic conditions may explain its attitude towards the search for wealth and equality. Poor, vulnerable, labor-weak households support policies that protect them and leaders who impart high value to inter-personal, inter-household, or inter-regional equality; labor-strong households support policies and leaders that allow them to utilize their preferred economic position. Thus a basis of support exists in rural China for both market-oriented and restrictive agricultural policies, allowing leaders who advocate each line to argue that they are responding to popular desires.

In the 1960s and 1970s, however, the radical developmental strategy, although promising prosperity and equality, served only to restrict economic opportunities. These nation-wide limitations on comparative advantage, collective capitalism, and market exchange undermined economic growth and collectively derived, individual incomes. Further restrictions on private activity constrained extra-collective household incomes. Although radical ideology stressed economic growth, peasants and cadres who supported growth by means at variance with the radical strategy were silenced, while supporters of restrictions syncretized the elite value system with local desires for equality or anti-equity and championed the leveling aspects of the egalitarian ideology. As we will see in the following chapters, egalitarian outcomes were at times due more to local values, local interests, and local interpretations of the radical message than to the elites' message. Still, the lack of prosperity severely undermined popular support for the radical strategy and instead drew support primarily from peasants and cadres who supported its egalitarian message.

The Local Political Structure

As winds blew down from the political center, they brushed the walls of local bureaucratic structures in various parts of rural China. Whether they penetrated those walls and became local political issues depended on two factors. First, each locality's autonomy and power affected its ability to resist external pressures. Second, leaders from the county level down evaluated each policy to see if it could strengthen their own political and economic power. Where radical power or support for radical policies was weak, the wind often blew by. But once the wind penetrated the local environment and became a political issue, the scope and form of its implementation depended on the interplay between local bureaucratic and collective interests, the local ecological and environmental setting, and the nature of each specific policy—in terms of the locus of authority for its implementation, its effect on cadre and peasant interests, and how easily it could be evaded.

Autonomy and Control in Center-Local Relations

All regimes in China, from the Qing Dynasty (1644–1911 A.D.) to the CCP radicals, sought an equilibrium between autonomy and control—or in the language of political development, between penetration and participation.[27] This equilibrium would ensure state control over resources, while generating popular support, political legitimacy, and voluntary compliance. However, autonomy and control constitute a double-edged sword. Without local actors to serve its interests, the state cannot penetrate very deeply; but powerful local actors promote local autonomy. Outsiders who push only the state's goals, but lack local support, can destroy the local spontaneity which leaders such as Kang Youwei, Chiang Kai-shek, and Mao Zedong tried to develop.[28] According to Mao, neglecting regional interests delayed China's economic development because since the Qin Dynasty, China "has been for the most part unified. One of its defects has been bureaucratism and excessively tight control. The localities could not develop independently . . . and economic development was slow."[29] But when the state relaxes its control and withdraws, "the cure"—replacing the central elite by a local one— "has often proven worse than the disease."[30] Similar problems plagued the radicals, as many of their policies were antithethical to local economic interests. Only a heavy state hand that stifled local initiative and popular support could ensure implementation in the villages.

In searching for control, different regimes have employed different institutional structures. Qing rulers favored "indigenous forms of coordination (that is, traditional elites) as the basis of control systems," while the Nationalists turned nineteenth-century tax farmers of commercial enterprises into twentieth-century tax collectors, forcing them to turn the funds over to the state.[31] To penetrate rural society deeply, the CCP built its modern bureaucratic structure on top of the extant, rural traditional structures, turning villages into production teams and standard marketing towns into commune headquarters. The CCP also fused informal networks of social power with formal organizations of local state power so that bureaucratic behavior was determined by both structural demands of formal posts and informal demands of traditional structures and networks.

The CCP's decision to fuse formal and informal structures

affected the balance between local autonomy and state control. Kuhn believes that the state's ability to expropriate the rural social product was never greater. Collectivization fused two previously dichotomous local frameworks: rural social units—such as market towns, dependent villages, and lineage structures—and territory and land usage. Official boundaries for taxation were established around the natural villages. Land sales, which historically had undermined the state's ability to collect taxes were prohibited. Local elites, incorporated into the state structure, could easily tax each village and control the productive output.[32] Others disagree with Kuhn's assessment. For Nee strong local government at the county or township (that is, commune) level could mobilize the peasantry on behalf of the state, but the "local elite gained access to and control over jobs and resources that stemmed from development and extension of local government."[33] Similarly, Parish argued that overlapping formal and informal power helped local leaders resist central control and penetration.[34]

Both viewpoints are correct. During the radical period local state cadres, particularly commune and county officials, extracted immense amounts of labor, capital, and materials from the villages. But these outsiders, as in traditional times, became powerful, rapacious local officials who invoked the state's authority in the pursuit of private gain. While the extraction of resources increased, that wealth was used to strengthen these lower-level state bureaucrats. The center's control over rural finances weakened,[35] while the real locals—brigade secretaries and team leaders—were left alone to defend the interests of peasants in the villages of rural China.

The Rural Bureaucratic Structure and Agrarian Radicalism

Although informal channels brought the radical message from the center and introduced it into the local areas, it was the formal rural bureaucracy that implemented radical policies. Here peasants, bureaucrats, and radical elites competed for political power, economic resources, and control over the policy process. And here, in this bounded social and political world, the local political drama of the radical era unfolded.

A cadre's position in the rural bureaucracy and the authority vested in his bureacratic post determined the scope and type of resources upon which he could draw. For example, commune officials, responsible for grain taxation and distribution, could extract grain from production teams to feed peasants who participated in commune-managed water conservation projects. Similarly, with the militia organized at the brigade level, brigade secretaries could wield this weapon to ensure support for their policy initiatives.

The information a cadre received varied with his bureaucratic post, as meetings at various levels channeled information to these cadres about the policies. Local cadres attended meetings two levels above their position in the bureaucracy; team leaders went to commune meetings, while brigade leaders joined meetings in the county seat. Since Central Party Documents were read at county meetings, brigade secretaries were better informed than team leaders.

Personal networks and factional ties developed within the bureaucracy. While competition for economic resources among the various bureaucratic levels was critical, inter-personal lineage or factional ties, which criss-crossed levels and economic systems from the brigade to the county, may have had more impact on policy outcomes.[36] Policy winds which permeated the local system became political issues affecting the ongoing struggle; similarly, how the wind affected extant cleavages and the distribution of power and wealth among those factions affected how the policy was implemented.

The bureaucratic structure also limited the effects of ideology on cadres' responses to agrarian radicalism. While experience may have determined a cadre's ideological predilections, where one sat in the bureaucracy was more likely to determine where one stood on any specific issue.[37] In fact, being a Party member during these years was dangerous, as Party members who failed to conform to the radical line received harsher punishments.[38]

The distribution of resources within the bureaucracy, the responsibilities of each post, the pressures for conformity, and the impact of factional conflict on policy implementation varied greatly during 1968–1978. After 1970 the expansion of small-scale rural industries gave some cadres more material rewards to distribute, including new jobs and increased resources, in the search for local compliance. Shifts in the Dazhai campaign affected cadre responsibilities. While brigade leaders were the major actors from 1964 to 1970, after 1970—and particularly after 1975—county leaders assumed authority for rural development.[39] As pressures for social tranformation shifted to demands for economic development, local cadres' tasks and leadership types changed.[40] Establishing revolutionary committees gave local radicals an entree into leadership positions, as did the 1968–1970 arrival of work teams which often sought alternative leaders. But by the mid-1970s demands to improve living standards and the Dazhai movement's emphasis on economic development gave rise to a more specialized, less ideological, leadership cohort.[41]

The County. During 1968–1978 the county (*xian*) was the lowest level of pure state power, maintaining close links with units as far down in the bureaucratic hierarchy as the brigade.[42] The county possessed a pervasive bureaucracy crossing many economic and political systems (*xitong*), which allocated funds, grain, fertilizer, and material for capital construction projects. The county also organized the marketing system, and all its bureaus had direct links with functionally equivalent structures at the district level (*zhuanqu*).

The county convened "three-level cadre meetings" (*san ji ganbu huiyi*) attended by county, commune, and brigade officials, where they introduced upper-level policies, read Central Documents, and also interpreted them. A county Party secretary who chose to respond to a wind could use these meetings to place the policy on each brigade Party branch's agenda. Since the county organizational bureau was the final authority for all brigade Party posts, it could replace brigade officials who resisted radical policies with more pliable ones. Campaign offices were often established in the county seat to monitor rural campaigns. These and more permanent county offices reported upward and remained ultimately responsible for the success or failure of any campaign. During the Dazhai campaigns of 1969–1971 and 1975–1977, Dazhai offices in some counties coordinated the different systems within the county government and Party structure.[43] The later Dazhai campaigns expanded the county's influence in almost all policy areas.[44]

As the case studies in the next three chapters suggest, this political authority and economic resource base made county cadres crucial in implementing radical policies.[45] Counties approved many policies before localities introduced them; at the same time they prevented their implementation. County-wide implementation of brigade accounting occurred in 1975–1977, while private plots were restricted across entire counties in the late 1960s. Also county officials were quite guilty of expropriating team resources throughout this period. Generally older and long-time Party members, these county secretaries supported egalitarianism, feared renewed polarization, and responded to pressures from above, making them the key level for introducing policy winds and mobilizing support for them within the local setting.

Yet county cadres were often too busy to monitor compliance. Before the Cultural Revolution they complained of the "five too manys"—too many meetings, too many organizations demanding attention, too many concurrent posts, too many documents and too many departments—which left them able only to transmit Party policy to the local levels but unable to investigate local implementation thoroughly.[46] The short duration of their visits and their preference for visiting only close and accessible model units caused peasants to describe busy officials as "dragonflies on water" or "birds which fly only to bright places." Thus, while they introduced policy winds into the rural setting, they were not as well equipped to ensure that the new policies were implemented. For that they needed to rely on commune and brigade leaders.

The Commune. Commune Party leaders were state cadres who often held urban residence permits and drew salaries and grain rations from the government. They were directly responsible to county officials. They were outsiders, brought in by the county and approved by the district to manage the commune for the state.[47] As outsiders they formed their own networks, whose boundaries were dictated by bureaucratic structures and whose content was dictated by bureaucratic interests, not personal ties to local peasants. While their responsibilities for meeting state grain quotas prevented them from totally ignoring agricultural production, their income was independent of collective output, so they often showed little concern for collective incomes. Recent criticisms in the Chinese press and by agricultural economists attributed rural economic problems to the commune's potential for "commandism." Controlling both politics and economics and more attuned to political, rather than agricultural, responsibilities as well as state, rather than collective, interests, the commune leaders served as the administrative link between the county and the brigade[48] and willingly imposed economically irrational policies on the brigades and the teams within them.

The resources commune leaders could mobilize to ensure compliance varied. Units with developed industrial bases controlled more resources, such as employment opportunities outside the agricultural sector, machinery for industrializing brigades, or funds and equipment for capital construction projects.[49] Allocating funds to poor brigades and teams also strengthened commune officials' political leverage. Leaders in poorer communes, however, had few material incentives with which to ensure compliance, so they preferred leftism over rightism, because during leftist periods cadres could more readily utilize their coercive powers.[50] Likewise, during leftist periods commune officials could expropriate team and brigade resources with impunity to strengthen commune enterprises, increasing their own political power and control.

The Brigade. As an organization that fit between the state and society, the brigade was situated at the critical nexus for resolving the conflict between autonomy and control. This unique location in the bureauc racy made it a major actor in dealing with radical agricultural policy. Its leader, the brigade Party secretary, was the highest local official maintaining direct loyalty to central authorities and personal ties with local residents. He could mobilize peasants on behalf of national interests; yet he could fend off the state if its demands became excessive. He alone could tap local spontaneity and outbursts of local energy. Unlike commune officials, brigade secretaries were not state cadres; nor were they mere peasants. Like a foreman in a factory, who is neither part of management nor truly a worker, the brigade official confronted dual pressures: from above he was pressed to maintain the state's interests and ensure policy compliance; from below he was pressured to maintain societal autonomy and protect peasant interests.

Three-level cadre meetings in the county seat kept brigade secretaries informed of events at the county and above. They knew if a policy was based on a local decision or a central document, whether it was official or merely a wind. They knew the extent to which county and commune officials supported a policy, clarifying the risks entailed in opposing it. They also knew the precise extent to which villages were following the policy. Too close to the real situation to be fooled, they could monitor implementation on foot and use their status as the lowest level in the formal, rural Party hierarchy to demand compliance. The increasing number of brigade officials during the radical era helped brigade secretaries keep track of local events.[51] They carried the policy from the county to the peasants indirectly through meetings with team leaders or directly through brigade-wide "transmission meetings" (chuanda huiyi). As purveyors of information, brigade secretaries influenced peasant perceptions of policy. If they supported it, they could paint it positively; if they opposed it, they could portray it in an unfavorable light.

As the lowest link in the Party hierarchy, the brigade secretary worked under serious constraints. He was expected to follow Party guidelines and faithfully implement Party policy. His appointment depended on authorization from the county organizational bureau, while his immediate superior, the commune Party secretary, could impose sanctions for improper conduct. His bureaucratic ties with upper levels were critical if he was to maintain his bureaucratic position. After all, he was probably promoted to brigade secretary because county and commune wanted someone who was fully convinced of the need to maintain state control.[52] Even when peasants were dissatisfied with a policy, the brigade secretary, more than anyone else, was responsible for persuading them to implement it.

From below, informal particularistic relationships complicated the brigade secretary's life. Unlike the commune secretary, a brigade secretary developed extensive local networks, making him ruler over a domain wherein his own personal ties and commitments abounded. The village looked to him to protect its autonomy vis à vis the state. Although he possessed formal bureaucratic authority, he was also subject to pressures from informal village leaders, especially where traditional structures were strong. In making decisions he had to consider their opinions, for long after the formal structures of power relationships had changed, the content of these traditional kinship ties persisted, reinforcing loyalties to the lineage rather than to the state or any larger corporate unit.[53]

With his family working in one of the brigade's production teams and his own personal income based on a ratio of all team incomes, the brigade's production directly affected a secretary's financial well-being. His political future was limited, with mobility into higher bureaucratic positions circumscribed.[54] While the possibility of employment at the commune level increased during the Cultural Revolution,[55] his gaining state cadre status and an urban residence permit remained highly unlikely. Another problem for the brigade secretary was that most brigades had few factories in the late 1960s and early 1970s. This limited resource base undermined his job as he tried to persuade peasants to implement unpopular policies.[56] On the whole, though, brigade Party secretaries were often both more attuned to local interests and reasonably well situated to parry the state's demands.

Team Leaders. Leaders of production teams were closely entwined in webs of interpersonal relationships within the team or village that tightly constrained their behavior. Of all local cadres, they confronted the strongest pressures to take the interests of the peasants and the production team as a whole into account. Because they were sometimes elected, they had to be responsive to other peasants; unpopular team leaders could not stay in office for long.[57] Even where brigade preselection of team leaders made elections a formality, unpopular leaders found it difficult to keep their jobs if they ignored peasant interests. In part their motivation for taking the job was "a general sense of duty or obligation to the community."[58] As with the brigade secretary, a team leader's income was almost totally determined by the collective's output.

While facing strong peasant pressures, team leaders could do little to resist brigade pressures. Since the brigade secretary's authority was derived from the CCP, resistance to radical agricultural policies during the Cultural Revolution decade was risky. Team leaders were rotated more often than other local officials, and since their position was not a Party post, their decisions were greatly influenced by brigade leaders. In large or mountainous brigades, where villages were widely dispersed, team leaders could be independent and influential characters. But where distances between villages were short or the brigade was a single large village, brigade leaders could easily monitor events in the teams. Unlike the commune secretary who, as an outsider living in the standard market town, had difficulty overseeing events in the brigades, the brigade secretary was a local community member with his own personal information network. Under these conditions team leaders had difficulty evading policies without brigade leaders knowing.

Once they had yielded to the pressure to comply, however, team leaders possessed important resources to ensure policy compliance. They controlled job allocations, access to loans, grain and relief distribution; many other services and opportunities under brigade jurisdiction were accessible only with the team leader's referral.[59] Also the leader of a rich team in a poor brigade probably could influence the brigade secretary. Model units were important resources for brigade leaders, and they could ill afford to alienate them. Moreover, if both team and brigade were poor, the brigade leader had few economic sanctions or inducements to wield over reluctant team leaders.[60]

Finally, the team leader's personal situation influenced his attitude towards the radical policies. If he had not enough time to make money from a private plot or household sideline, he would have little incentive to resist limitations on the private sector. In fact, team leaders may have supported measures, particularly those restricting the private sector, that prevented other peasants who were not busy with team responsibilities from earning extra income. The leaders had incentives to oppose capital construction projects from which their team did not benefit because team members who participated had to receive workpoints. And since the project did not improve the team's income, participation in the project simply decreased the value of each workpoint, which was the major indicator of a team's success. This lower workpoint value could lead peasants to question the team leader's abilities. Similarly, a peasant in one research site reported that a team leader's response to the state's demand for high levels of capital formation varied according to whether or not he planned to stay on. Retiring team leaders preferred to distribute more money at year's end so peasants would remember them fondly; those planning to stay on favored higher levels of accumulation to ensure that even if the following year's crop was not good, there would be sufficient funds to supplement the year-end distributed income. Protecting one's reputation within the community was an important motivation.

Peasants, Rural Structure, and Agrarian Radicalism

At the bottom of this bureaucratic hierarchy lies the Chinese peasant household. While both Townsend and Pye reject the concept of peasant political participation in postrevolutionary China, Burns and Falkenheim have shown that peasants pursue their economic and political interests in extensive ways.[61] However, while peasants found ways to advance their interests and influence decisions that directly affected their lives, severe limitations on political action existed throughout the radical decade. Given the negative value ascribed to bad class backgrounds and the tendency during this period to attribute opposition to class enemies, peasants of good class background were freer to express their views than those with less noble class roots.[62] Because peasants feared retribution for opposition, they hesitated to express opinions in formal settings, such as meetings, especially when Party officials were present. When decisions on how to implement a policy were in flux, peasants spoke more willingly. But once a decision was made, they adopted a passive public posture. Also pressure to display ritualistic support during these meetings was intense, because although most peasants were situated in the middle of an "activist-nonactivist continuum," one of their great fears was being labelled a "backward element."[63] During campaigns, previously inactive peasants attended meetings more regularly.[64]

Influence was advanced through personal approaches to team leaders, and when peasants did speak out they couched their complaints in economic, not political, terms.[65] In the face of intense pressure from political campaigns, policy winds, and the radical environment, peasants wisely avoided open dissent, choosing instead numerous informal, less confrontational ways of expressing their antipathy towards agrarian radicalism.

Finally, family size, dependency ratios, skills, relationships to team leaders, income levels of individuals and teams, and positions in networks and lineage structures all colored peasant views of radical policies during the 1960s and 1970s. Skilled craftsmen undoubtedly resented restrictions on household sidelines and the extension of collective controls over small-scale industry. Large households with many laborers had an economic incentive to support the expansion, rather than contraction, of private plots. Yet poorer families also supported some policies that restricted economic opportunities from which they could not benefit. Also, if capital construction projects helped poorer units, their members rarely complained when other peasants lost their right to winter leisure.

Systemic Variables and Agrarian Radicalism

Whether a policy wind affected a village depended in part on where the unit was, its geography and topography, the type of crops it produced, and its level of economic development. These systemic factors also affected the attitudes and decisions of actors in those units.

To understand the impact of radical agricultural policies on the countryside one should keep a map of China in mind. From this top-down perspective, villages surrounded by fields are connected to their respective brigade headquarters by small paths. In turn, brigades were usually connected at best by stony roads to commune centers. Roads also linked these small towns to larger towns and the seat of county government and Party authority. Consequently, teams whose fields were situated along a major thoroughfare used by county bureaucrats were pressured to level their land, plant grain, and restrict all private intrusions into the collective's fields. Otherwise brigade cadres would be criticized.

These spatial variations among units influenced the distribution of power and policy outcomes, so that distances from roads, fields, hills, state farms, bodies of water, or centers of political power all affected the impact of leftist policy winds. For example, proximity or accessibility to brigade or commune headquarters increased the likelihood of penetration, as units close to a seat of power or roads were more likely to be visited by local or outside officials. These units were more likely to become local models, so that outsiders, checking on policy implementation, would briefly monitor progress in that locality.[66] Where visits were unlikely, pressures for policy conformity decreased. The converse was also true. Local autonomy increased with the distance from the next level of bureaucratic authority.[67]

The limited spatial distribution of leftist influence during 1968–1978 made a unit's location important as well. Proximity to Hang-zhou, Shanghai, Beijing, or locations in Shanxi, Fujian, or several other provinces increased the likelihood that a radical environment would develop in a village (see Chapter 5, Table 5). As central supporters of radicalism changed throughout 1968–1978, the locus of radical environments varied as well.

Whether a unit happened to be situated in the hills or valleys, or close to a lake or river affected the impact of radical policies, particularly those related to capital construction or cropping patterns.

Hilly units which had to learn from Dazhai were under constant pressure to terrace their fields, while units near lakes and rivers drained them to expand crop acreage. Peasants in hilly areas could more easily enlarge their private plots by opening barren land; however, they often became targets during campaigns to restrict expanded private plots. Cropping patterns, often related to topography, also influenced a unit's response to radical policies. Many tea brigades established brigade accounting, while hilly locations which grew other cash crops, such as sugar cane or peanuts, were often exhorted to resist capitalist crops and grow more grain.

Were the wealthy or the poorer units more affected by radical policies? If local leaders responded to the egalitarian and redistributive nature of agrarian radicalism, wealthy units should have borne the brunt of this radical movement. In Parish and Whyte's study, wealthier teams were more likely to adopt Dazhai-type workpoints.[68] By attacking capitalist tendencies agrarian radicalism really restricted comparative advantage, and since wealthier units had more goods to market, market restrictions cost them more. Usually closer to towns, richer units were more likely than more distant units to be penetrated by radical policies. Moreover, since wealthy units became models, they were often the target of radical leaders. After all, if models did not support radical policies, how could ordinary units be motivated? Nevertheless, wealthy units had strong incentives to resist radical policies and may have been harder to penetrate.

Policy as a Variable

All radical policies had their own local impact, owing to their varying effects upon the distribution of economic and political goods. They affected some cadres and some families more than others. Some policies demanded greater changes in people's behaviors and values or were easier to resist than others because of difficulties in monitoring them.

Many radical policies transferred material resources from individual to individual, from individuals to the collective, or from one level of the collective to another. They shifted the locus of decision making across levels as well. As a result, each policy had its own constituency of supporters and opponents. For example, maintaining high levels of capital formation left more money with the production team and less with the peasants, while expropriation and transfer moved resources from peasants and their teams into the coffers of the brigade, commune, or county. Whereas the first policy pitted team leaders against team members, the second policy united these two groups in opposing higher levels of the collective.

Of critical importance was the extent to which the local officials could change the policy's "content" and still claim that they were really implementing it.[69] As with the leaders who advocated them, most radical policies had a "soft" and "hard" component. Although implementing a softer version of the policy diluted its radical content, less radical options often meshed with local bureaucratic interests and generated less hostility among the local populace, letting local elites build a wider and stronger coalition in support of the policy. For example, while brigade accounting transferred ownership and decision making authority from the team to the brigade, its main purpose was strengthening the brigade's economy so as to accelerate the transition to higher levels of socialism. But brigade cadres who built factories rather than establish brigade accounting still demonstrated a commitment to progressive policies and the goals of agrarian radicalism, all the while avoiding the complications and animosities generated by brigade accounting. Not surprisingly, many units chose the softer option.

A policy's locus of implementation varied, as did the actors and interests involved. While higher levels pronounced policy goals, the act of turning directives into reality depended on lower level officials. For example, Supply and Marketing Cooperatives were set up at the commune level, but if brigade cadres did not vigilantly prevent private marketing in their locale, the co-op would have little impact. Similarly, while a county secretary might decide to limit the size of private plots, their ultimate restriction depended on team and brigade cadres. Since the making and implementation of a policy often occurred at different levels for each policy, the political process varied as well.

Finally, the degree of concreteness of the indicators used to measure compliance varied across policies, making some policies easier to evade. For example, while reports of grain sold to the state or accounts of labor-hours used to dig canals could be, and were, falsified, the outcome was relatively finite. County officials could see the granaries and the amount of grain sold to the state, while water conservation projects were also quite visible. Without collusion by commune or county officials, these policies could not be evaded. However, if peasants and local cadres lied, how would a county cadre know from a short visit if a unit was really using Dazhai workpoints or had really established brigade accounting?

Form and Reality: A Framework for Analyzing Policy Evasion

The divergence of elite and mass goals and conflicts between radical policies and peasant interests resulted in a dilemma for rural cadres.

While bureaucratic superiors demanded demonstrations of policy compliance, local constituents preferred that the radicals' more irrational demands be deflected. Under these institutional and personal pressures, a local cadre had to be Janus-faced: the efficient bureaucrat and the compassionate local leader. Favoring any one side complicated the cadres' life by undermining relations with friends or bureaucratic superiors. Yet evading policies without detection was difficult and risky. Frequent transgressions, particularly by Party members, could lead to censure, the loss of a job or expulsion from the Party. The lessons of the Great Leap and the Anti-Rightist Campaign that followed it showed cadres the high cost of resisting leftist onslaughts.[70]

One strategy was to feign compliance by only appearing to carry out the policy or by carrying out only noncontentious parts of it without implementing the real content. For many reasons this duality of form and content is an appropriate conceptual framework for analyzing policy evasion in rural China, especially during the radical era. First, politics in the radical era, with its heavy emphasis on rapid sociopsychological changes, generated demands for outbursts of ritualistic behavior; second, Chinese traditional political culture reinforced the willingness of cadres to accept a formalistic response to many radical policies; third, these radical policies were divorced from the interests of the peasant masses who willingly participated in charades of implementation; fourth, the politicization of policy implementation and the reliance on mass mobilization, informal channels, and policy winds made the form/content dichotomy a useful evasionary strategy; finally, the countryside's enormous spatial and bureaucratic dimensions facilitated this evasionary strategy.

Both Mao Zedong and Zhou Enlai recognized the tendency towards pro-forma policy implementation in China and the dichotomy between form and content. As early as April 1943 Zhou pointed out that "we must pay attention to *content* rather than to *form* and examine whether a decision is really being correctly carried out or is being distorted" (emphasis added).[71] Mao explained some of the roots of policy formalism in a 1945 report on cultural work: "We should not make the change until through our work most of the masses have become conscious of the need for the change and are willing and determined to carry it out . . . Unless they are conscious and willing, any kind of work that requires their participation will turn out to be a mere formality and will fail."[72] Mao indirectly identifies an important explanation for formalism in rural policy implementation—pressures in societies undergoing extensive and rapid social change. In such societies the gap between established informal structures and inchoate formal structures is often great; and while the desire to protect the former is quite strong, attachments to the new structures remain weak.[73] Yet pressures to shift loyalties from prerevolutionary or prereform structures are intense. Formalism becomes a natural response to unpopular external pressures for change. Coterminous with demands for changing structures come pressures for inculcating and adopting new values and behavior patterns. For those who have not changed their consciousness, but feel the external need to demonstrate such change, formalistic responses—creating paper institutions, behaving ritualistically, or evoking new revolutionary images—are necessary.

The Chinese bureaucrat's penchant for ritualistic behavior is also related to a traditional need for consensus. After a major Party meeting, a purge, the publication of a new document, or a policy wind, elite and mass expectations of a new breakthrough triggers an "outburst of compulsive support" for this new consensus. This nation-wide expression of support in turn places a high priority on ritualistic behavior—that is, demonstrations of mass popular support—in every locality.[74]

Moreover, Chinese political culture had taught Chinese peasants to keep their real feelings inside and demonstrate only the proper external behavior. Deference to proper forms and speaking the correct words were more important for maintaining social order and avoiding chaos than having the correct inner feelings and attitudes.[75] Social integration, too, could be maintained if people stuck to the proper ritualized behavior.[76] Even if they knew that a deception was in process, Chinese peasants felt traditional pressures to maintain the facade.

Mao's stress on progressive behavior (*biaoxian*), rather than birth, as the indicator of a good class background fed into this tendency for ritualistic behavior. In Mao's "virtuocracy" acceptable social and political norms were predetermined and externally set; and yet, it was easy for local units or individuals to cheat and only look as if they were really progressive.[77] The penchant for labeling actions or policies "progressive" taught rural cadres that their road to social mobility and their unit's road to becoming a model lay through demonstrating such progressive behavior, while failure to adopt these postures led to political opprobrium. In 1981 *Shanxi Daily* recognized the problem inherent in establishing fixed guidelines for proper behavior when it argued that "if we mechanically affix 'progressive' to some forms, we are discouraging the proceeding of everything from reality and are encouraging the tendency to pursue formality."[78]

Given the bureaucratic nature of the rural hierarchy, politicizing the policy process through the use of progressive models contributed significantly to the rise of formalism. Models that were to be studied were often false, and local cadres who were taken to study them knew it.[79] But they too had to pretend they had adopted the model and attained the new levels, all the while knowing they were unattainable.

Yet officials at all levels had strong incentives to continue the charade and ignore the fact that responses were formalistic.[80] For actors in a bureaucracy, demonstrating conformity rather than implementing the policy itself may suffice to protect everyone. Bureaucratic superiors have their superiors to whom they must report. To avoid sanctions each level must simply verify that within its jurisdiction policies are being carried out. Creating the form of the policy— looking as if one is implementing the policy—protects everybody in the bureaucracy.

Politicizing rural policy led to formalism in other ways. It generated "commandism," where middle level officials, pressured by winds or legitimate Party policies, forced local cadres to implement unpopular policies. Squeezed from above and below, and with little time to generate genuine support among the peasantry for this social transformation, local cadres either imposed these policies on their constituents or feigned compliance. In these instances cadres could change the policy's content and resort to soft radical policies.

Third World countries whose national elites were trying to carry out rapid social change faced similar problems. Because pressures in these systems for demonstrating conformity are great, one must avoid alienating bureaucratic superiors while handling particularistic demands from inferiors in the villages. As a result, problems will be ignored and policies implemented when the "logic of political necessity" is stronger than the logic of policy analysis. Formalism grows from a "combination of ambitious substantive goals" (that is, extensive social change) "and intense pressure for results" (that is, politicization).[81] When Zambia's President Kaunda demanded the rapid establishment of rural cooperatives and the transformation of free-holding farms into collectives, he got many "paper" cooperatives. Similarly Nyerere's effort to collectivize Tanzania was described as "*ujamaa* through signpainting."[82] According to Hyden, pressures in Tanzania for "villagization" (*ujamaa*) triggered false reporting. Even if village collectivization was unsuccessful, the mere effort was reported as a success.[83] Although Africans lacked China's rural Party organization and history of mobilization, Chinese policy implementation fits this general trend almost perfectly.[84]

Demands for policy conformity based on mass mobilization through policy winds created the perfect context—short-term but intense pressures to demonstrate conformity—for evasionary strategies based on this dichotomy. Pressure was temporally limited; after a period of time it subsided. The cadre who could stretch out the period of implementation might never have to do it at all. In fact, some Chinese cadres, pressured to carry out unpopular policies, employed a four-step strategy of which form and reality were important components.[85] When first informed of the policy these cadres ignored it. When told a second time to implement it they began to study how to carry it out. A common expression for procrastination at this stage was "to do more research" (*jiayi yanjiu*). Creating a test point fit this stage of the strategy—a stage which in Western parlance is similar to commissioning a preliminary study. As pressure mounted, cadres established the form or external structure in which the policy could be carried out. Finally (and this occurred in only one of the two cases), when the pressure did not abate, implementation became mandatory.[86]

Politicization gave national elites incentives to perpetuate the charade of radicalism. According to Mao's "mass line theory," a policy is correct only if the original idea for it came from the masses and if they in turn accept the adjusted version as their own and implement it. While having little practical meaning, the mass line throughout the Cultural Revolution had significance for elite politics. In factional battles in Beijing over who was the apotheosis of the correct line, the only indicator of correctness was whether or not the masses followed policies derived from that line as their own and implemented them. Whether the policy was useful, enforced through coercion, or implemented only in form were secondary to the central leaders' need to demonstrate to their political rivals widespread implementation.[87] In many ways Pye is correct to refer to mass participation as "a new form of public pretense."[88]

Since local formalistic behavior was politically expedient to both national elites and middle level bureaucrats, they all had little reason to delve behind the facade of support and prove that evasion was occurring. At the same time, peasants who opposed the radical policies were placated by the form and joined in the deception. Thus, the Chinese erected an elaborate system of Potemkin villages to prove to each other that radical policies were in fact being implemented. And while cognitive dissonance generated by these frauds drove some Westerners to unmask the deception, Chinese cadres, attuned to the politics of "face," knew to play the game and were psychologically better equipped to do so. It was the rare cadre who announced that the Emperor had no clothes; they preferred the security of silently accepting the deception.

Structural problems in establishing bureaucratic feedback created a favorable environment for formalistic responses. According to Kaufman, lower administrative levels are unlikely to rebel when confronted by orders that sharply conflict with their values or interests; instead, "they quietly construe the orders in a way that makes them tolerable."[89] But feedback loops in rural China were particularly weak, as county and commune officials who investigated local policy implementation did so from a distance: what the Chinese call "looking at flowers from horseback" (qi ma kan hua). Middle level cadres could not simply cross to another office or take the elevator to another floor to check on implementation. Moreover, everyone in the locality knew that the county official would drive first to the commune headquarters for a briefing and then to the nearest brigade, and only then walk to the nearest team for a quick visit, rather than slog through the mud to really see if the policies were being implemented.[90] Thus local cadres could feel fairly safe that creating a facade of implementation would suffice.[91] In fact, most county and municipal officials relied on telephone conferences which simplified false reporting.[92]

The divergent goals of the center and the localities, the radicals' use of policy winds, the ambiguity of the guidelines for policy implementation, and the fact that authority to carry out any policy had to be delegated, created a "leakage of authority" which permitted extensive policy evasion.[93] As the level of implementation in the bureaucracy dropped, the degree of delegated authority increased.[94] The gap between elite and local goals also increased this leakage of authority; while ideology motivated central leaders, local leaders were driven by desires for political survival or increasing agricultural output. Moreover, the center's ideological goals were most alien to brigade and team cadres who were responsible for implementing radical policies. The peasants' hostility to these policies increased the cadres' willingness to establish only the form, because implementing these policies would have triggered much antipathy.

Because the radical line was not formally repudiated in 1972, cadres who had adopted radical policies in 1968–1971, but reintroduced policies of the bureaucratic line after the fall of Chen Boda and Lin Biao, did so as inconspicuously as possible.[95] Even before the 1978 Third Plenum, cadres were hesitant to reject Cultural Revolution slogans and policies totally.[96] According to Riskin, shifting tides between the Maoist and bureaucratic lines led to a form/content dichotomy which "robbed Maoist values of their substance, leaving only the rhetorical shell."[97] But just as Confucius stressed that rites must be continued even after the original meaning of the ritual had been lost if inner tranquility and social order were to be maintained,[98] many Cultural Revolution policies persisted long after the content had changed. The May 7 Cadre Schools remained long after cadre labor was replaced by sent-down youths and the schools became cadre retreats. Similarly, the Cultural Revolution only adjusted the forms of many Chinese societal traditions, but failed to change the real character of traditional behavior.[99] Through it all one had to maintain the facade; new radical forms had to be adopted even if content had not changed; and even as the radical content declined, the forms persisted.

Conclusion

Herein lies the framework for analyzing the impact of radical policies on the local setting. Although the radicals had their own views on how the policies were to be implemented and what the rural areas should look like after the policies were implemented, the complexity of rural China and its social, political, economic, and geophysical reality influenced how peasants and cadres responded to the radicals' messages. Although the radicals succeeded in putting their policies onto many local agendas, their policies remained prisoners of local political economies and rural value systems.

As the three case studies that follow suggest, most local actors reacted to radical policies from their own self-interest and tried vigorously to adjust each policy's impact to their own advantage. Those with more power—such as county, commune, and brigade cadres—gained more from each policy. And where those policies threatened their interests, they tried their best to fend them off. But even team leaders and peasants were able to have some impact on policy outcomes, especially when their interests meshed with those of some larger corporate or collective grouping or with the policy's specific goal.

5

BRIGADES AND
HIGHER STAGES OF
SOCIALISM

NO SINGLE POLICY better demonstrated the radicals' commitment to rapid shifts to higher stages of socialism than the emphasis on brigade accounting. During the Great Leap Forward it was the introduction of commune ownership that indicated to Mao and company that the millennium was at hand. The Great Leap's subsequent failure and the famine which followed forced the Chinese Communist Party to shift the level of ownership and accounting first to the brigade and then to the team. Tools, land, and property were all owned by the corporate body of team members; and each peasant's year-end financial distribution depended on the teams's collective income (see Table 5). Yet while team ownership and accounting still signified socialist, rather than private, ownership of the means of production, the reintroduction of family farming in the early 1960s and the radicals' intense fear of retrogression to capitalism made them demand constant advances in class relations and in the peasants' relation to the means of production. Thus, raising the ownership and accounting level to the brigade represented more than a simple administrative reform; it reflected the entire process of institutional transformation from small-scale to large-scale agricultural cooperatives, with the final goal of replacing collective ownership with a unitary system of "all people's ownership" under rural communism.

Yet of all radical policies none was more contentious than transferring ownership. As a reflection of the egalitarianism inherent in agrarian radicalism, raising the level of accounting to the brigade threatened to redistribute the resources and finances of wealthy teams to poorer ones, creating new or exacerbating old fissures along team lines. Where team divisions mirrored lineage or village divisions, this policy intensified previously suppressed traditional conflicts. Similarly, where factional conflicts among brigade leaders paralleled variations in team incomes, elite demands for brigade accounting further fueled those conflicts as leaders of poor teams advocated redistribution, while leaders of wealthy teams opposed it. These internecine disagreements over economic redistribution made these disputes analogous to conflict between social classes.

Unlike short-term brigade interventions into team or village life, to which peasants and cadres had grown accustomed, or even one-time expropriations of team land or funds which was common in this era, the shift to brigade accounting was a permanent power seizure by the CCP. In essence, this reflected one more step in the penetration of society by the Party-state. By removing decision-making authority regarding local capital formation, development of brigade enterprises, grain sales to the state, and the peasants' livelihood from the peasants and their team leaders, over whom peasants had much influence, and placing it directly in the hands of the lowest level of rural Party organization—the Party branch—brigade accounting redistributed power and control over scarce resources from the peasants to the Party.

Because this policy generated such intense hostility, partial solutions were utilized as well. Amalgamating or merging two production teams (*bing dui*) was one such solution. In 1968–1970 military radicals, such as Lin Biao, pushed it energetically because it helped mobilize labor for capital construction projects. Amalgamation also became a preliminary step toward brigade accounting by decreasing inequality between teams that were united—a single workpoint value was determined for all peasants in the new team—as well as enlarging the size of the team. However, with only two teams and not the entire brigade involved, this step was easier to implement.[1]

Similarly, strengthening the brigade economy was part of the tendency toward establishing higher levels of socialism in the Chinese countryside. Rather than precipitously equalizing incomes among all teams, brigade leaders could use factory profits to help poor teams catch up to their wealthier neighbors; after narrowing the gap, brigade accounting would be easier. For elite advocates of a softer radical line, and rural officials who opposed brigade accounting but who wanted to demonstrate their progressive politics without generating local conflicts, strengthening the brigade's economy offerred a most acceptable first step toward communism.

Explaining the Shift to Brigade Accounting

Conditions for Establishing Brigade Accounting

While the radicals strongly desired to shift accounting levels, they also recognized the complicated and contentious nature of this policy.

Table 5. Rural payment system of People's Communes, 1975.

$$\text{Step 1:} \quad \frac{\text{Gross team income} - \text{Costs and accumulation}}{\begin{array}{c}\text{Total number of workpoints}\\ \text{distributed to all team members}\\ \text{during one year}\end{array}} = \text{value of one workpoint}$$

Step 2: Value of one workpoint × Number of workpoints earned by a peasant in that year = The peasant's collectively derived income

Ever hopeful that peasants would overcome their petty bourgeois consciousness, the radicals were aware of the importance of material preconditions for successful ownership transfers. Thus they stipulated guidelines which, ironically, demonstrated that China's economy was too backward for this dramatic shift in the relations of production.

These preconditions involved five points: (1) a strong brigade economy; (2) average per capita income of over 150 *yuan* per person;[2] (3) relative income equality among production teams in the brigade; (4) strong brigade leadership;[3] and (5) the willingness of the masses. These criteria established a strong rationale for developing brigade industries, which by paying a very large portion of peasant incomes could increase the peasants' support for the brigade and overcome their more parochial support for the production team. Good leadership was also critical, because larger units with centralized decision making meant more people to be managed and more conflicts to be resolved.[4] Given China's limited supply of trained rural officials, this precondition was a serious constraint. Finally, in 1977, during Hua Guofeng's brief tenure, a debate ensued over whether the "willingness of the masses" should suffice.[5] This debate may have triggered some of the forced ownership transactions that occurred in 1977–1978, for unfortunately during the radical era the Chinese masses were often told what it was they were willing to do.

The radical guidelines reflected local difficulties with this policy. When the brigade's economy was weak or the income gap among teams was significant, richer teams opposed the policy. Without strong local leaders, peasant resistance to change and their ties to the team were not easily overcome. After the transition to brigade accounting, weak leaders were unable to run the brigade efficiently. And of course when the willingness of the masses was absent, the policy was forcibly implemented as a result of outside political pressures, and work enthusiasm suffered. While Chen Boda and Zhang Chunqiao may have believed that peasant enthusiasm could overcome material deficiencies, brigade accounting could not succeed if it totally ignored these local realities. Thus in 1972–1973 and after 1978, when the tide turned against this policy, many rural units quickly returned to team accounting.

The questions that immediately present themselves are: what kinds of localities established brigade accounting? Why were some areas more willing than others to do so? Did the areas meet the preconditions? What role did the local political economy and cadre interests play in implementing or resisting this policy? Finally, what kind of local politics did this policy generate, and what can it tell us about the relation between state and society and the radical ideology and peasant interests during the radical era?

Systemic Explanations

Several factors help explain why a unit implemented brigade accounting: (1) the province in which the brigade was located; (2) the level of inter-team equality; (3) the size of the brigade; (4) cropping patterns; (5) proximity to urban centres; (6) whether a brigade was a model unit; and (7) the nature of local and county leadership.

The province where a unit was located was very important. Thirty-five percent of all brigades in Shanxi Province and 38 percent in Beijing still had brigade accounting in 1979. The provinces with the largest percentage of brigade accounting and the largest percentage of such units nationally are listed in Table 6. Since these 12 provinces comprise 86.5 percent of all units with brigade accounting, the predominance of North China and the North China Plain is obvious.[6]

A relative degree of equality among the teams explains why some localities could implement the policy successfully. An informant from Shanxi Province observed that his locality established brigade accounting with little local opposition because inter-team differences were minor.[7] A brigade outside Nanjing was successful because for ten years before establishing brigade accounting it had helped poorer teams catch up with wealthier ones. Conversely, where inequalities were considerable but local leaders had been forced to establish brigade accounting, the experiment tended to collapse after a year or two. Still, in one Shanxi commune all brigades established brigade accounting in 1969, in spite of large income discrepancies among the teams. In this case commune-wide pressure to implement the policy was intense.[8]

Brigade size refers both to the population and the number of teams in the brigade. Brigades with many teams were more likely to have significant geophysical differences within the unit, exacerbating income differentials. A brigade south of Nanjing had some of its 26 teams in the hills, some in the valleys, and some on mixed terrain.

Table 6. Percentage of brigades utilizing brigade accounting, 1979.

Province	Brigades in province with brigade accounting	Brigades in province with brigade accounting as percentage of national total
Beijing	37.7	2.9
Shanxi	35.0	21.0
Tianjin	21.9	1.6
Shandong	21.0	13.0
Heilongjiang	17.0	4.0
Nei Mongol	14.0	3.0
Hebei	11.0	10.0
Xinjiang	11.0	2.0
Zhejiang	9.0	7.0
Fujian	7.0	2.0
Hubei	6.0	11.0
Shaanxi	5.0	9.0
Total		86.5

SOURCE: *Zhongguo nongye nianjian, 1980* (Chinese Agricultural Yearbook; Beijing: Nongye chubanshe, 1981), p. 6.

Although its economy was strong, workpoint values differed significantly among its teams. The brigade secretary did not respond when county and city officials in 1977 suggested a shift to brigade accounting because he considered so many teams with different workpoint values too difficult to manage. With the aid of published data on brigade accounting, this and other hypotheses are tested in Table 7.

Table 7. Systemic variables to explain brigade accounting.

Hypotheses	Correlation coefficient
1. Brigades with fewer teams more likely to adopt brigade accounting.	$-.483$ ($p < .01$)
2. Brigades with brigade accounting more likely to have amalgamated teams.	.617 ($p < .01$)
3. Provinces with greater density of CCP members more likely to adopt brigade accounting.[a]	.683 ($p < .01$)
4. Localities establishing lower-level Agricultural Producer Cooperatives in 1955 more likely to adopt brigade accounting.[a]	.657 ($p < .01$)

SOURCE: All data from *Zhongguo nongye nianjian,* 1980 (Chinese Agricultural Yearbook; Beijing: Nongye chubanshe, 1981) unless otherwise stated.
a. Fredrick C. Tiewes, "Provincial Politics in China," in John M. L. Lindbeck, ed., *China: Management of a Revolutionary Society* (Seattle: University of Washington Press, 1971), pp. 165, 168.

I used data from *The Chinese Agricultural Yearbook* to correlate the number of teams per brigade in each province with the percentage of brigades in that province adopting brigade accounting. A significant negative correlation means that provinces that had brigades with fewer teams per brigade were more likely to have more brigade accounting. The correlation between the percentage of brigades with brigade accounting per province and the number of teams per brigade per province was $-.483$ (p$<$ .01). Although some scholars would oppose using provincial-level data to make assumptions about local behavior, interview data support these findings.[9] In one commune, two of five brigades consisted of a single production team; in another locality the smallest brigade with only three or four teams had brigade ownership. It is highly probable that by 1979 many of the 67,000 brigades with brigade accounting were those with only a small number of teams.

This relationship between the number of teams per brigade and the percentage of brigades in a province that had brigade accounting may be due to the fact that more teams were amalgamated in these provinces than elsewhere; therefore, the number of teams per brigade was smaller. Although data on team amalgamation are unavailable at the provincial level, we can examine the average number of people per team for each province and assume that more people per team reflect a tendency to amalgamate teams. A positive correlation would suggest that brigades that amalgamated teams, not just brigades that already had fewer teams, were also likely to move to brigade accounting. The correlation between the number of people per team in each province and the percentage of brigades with brigade accounting in that province is .617 (p$<$ .01).

Size, in terms of the number of people in a brigade, could also explain brigade accounting, since brigades with fewer people were easier to manage than those with more people. Dazhai Brigade itself was small, with approximately 450 people in the early 1970s. In Xiyang County, where Dazhai is located, one brigade composed of a tiny village miles away in the hills had only nine laborers; Sungchuang Brigade in Chiliying Commune, Henan Province, which also had brigade accounting, had only 29 households and 1.4 hectares of land.[10] However, statistical analysis does not support this argument. Although it points in the right direction, the correlation of $-.270$ is not significant (p$>$ .05). Thus the number of people in a brigade may not have been an important factor in instituting brigade accounting.

Cropping patterns affected implementation. Units relying less on agriculture and more on sideline activities—such as fishing, forestry, raising tea, or industrial production—were more likely to make the transition. Of 54 units nation-wide with commune accounting in 1979, many were fishing villages.[11] Units emphasizing sideline activities were managed as large commercial enterprises rather than as agricultural ones, and because they could easily establish brigade enterprises, their brigades were wealthier. Furthermore, their investments generated inter-team equality more easily than investments in agriculture. In a famous tea commune near Hangzhou, 10 of 13 brigades had brigade accounting; the three still using team accounting grew grain. In these tea-growing brigades, workers lived in teams that were close together, with only slight income differences among teams or households. On the other hand, with habitation more dispersed in grain growing units, production teams played a greater economic role.[12]

Proximity to urban centres was important. Many units with brigade accounting were situated in the suburbs. Chen Boda's test point, Sijiqing Commune, was in the near suburbs of Beijing. Units with brigade accounting I visited in 1981 in both Nanjing and Xiamen (Amoy), Fujian Province, were in the periurban areas. And Zhang Chunqiao reportedly tried to establish brigade accounting throughout suburban Shanghai in 1975–1976. Two independent factors may explain this relationship. Since radical political power was primarily limited to certain urban centers and a few provinces—hence the high percentage of brigade accounting in Beijing, northern Zhejiang, and Shanxi—the radicals could more easily affect outcomes in the suburbs than in remote rural areas. Second, suburban units had higher population densities, and with more brigade industries they were wealthier. One unit in suburban Nanjing that established brigade accounting in 1978 fulfilled many of the criteria. Figure 6 shows that in this commune the brigade economies were quite strong.

Model units often had brigade accounting because they were closely tied into higher level politics.[13] When a new wind developed, they were called on to set an example. If they did not support new policies, other units would hesitate. On the other hand, cadres wanting to avoid wide-scale implementation of the policy could introduce the policy into a model unit as a form of political insurance. One informant reported that his unit, a model in learning from Dazhai, was his county's first to make the transition. Sinan County, where 80 percent of the brigades shifted to brigade accounting in 1977, was Guizhou Province's model in "learning from Dazhai and Xiyang County."[14] Dapu Brigade, a model in Gansu Province which had achieved national prominence in 1973, was pressured to make the transition in 1976.[15]

The nature of local and county leadership affected the implemen-

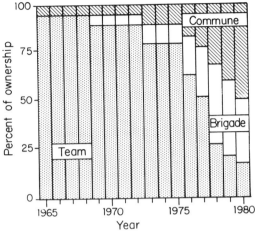

Figure 6. Three levels of economic ownership: changes in Zijingshan Commune, 1965–1980. Data supplied by commune officials in suburban Nanjing, 1981.

tation of brigade accounting. As Chinese scholars maintained, strong leaders could overcome local opposition and efficiently manage the larger production unit. One informant attributed the policy's success in his Shaanxi brigade to the abilities of the brigade secretary.[16] A Nanjing suburban brigade which introduced brigade accounting also had a very powerful brigade secretary. An example from Huiyang County, Guangdong Province, shows the obverse; there leadership was weak, and the policy failed.[17] Transitions also became more likely where county or brigade leaders were leftist or radical.

Equally important may have been the issue of Party membership. During the radical years Party members could ill afford rightist labels. They were also more easily affected by ideologically motivated policies. Areas with a high density of Party members, therefore, possessed a cadre of peasants who might respond to radical winds, even if the policies were unpopular. Using mid-1950s data on the percentage of the population in the CCP per province,[18] we can test the hypothesis that density of Party membership per province affected the adoption of brigade accounting. After reconstructing the data from the 1980 *Agricultural Yearbook*, we find a positive correlation of .683 ($p < .01$) between provinces with brigade accounting and Party density per province. The density of CCP members was greatest in North China, which also had the highest incidence of brigade accounting.

To a certain extent a unit's history of voluntarism, radicalism, or support for higher levels of socialism may have contributed to its willingness to adopt brigade accounting. In 1955 localities that established lower-level agricultural producer cooperatives (APCs) did so primarily on the initiative of collectivist-oriented local leaders. The correlation between the percentage of brigades with brigade accounting per province in 1979 and the percentage of households in lower-level APCs in 1955 per province was .657 (p< .01), showing that provinces, and perhaps localities, that quickly shifted to cooperatives also adopted brigade accounting.

To explain why brigade accounting was adopted in the North China Plain one must thus take into account the importance of its greater Party density and its history of voluntarism. Cropping patterns, suburban locations, inter-team income equality, and tendencies for team amalgamations were important factors in explaining brigade accounting in other locations as well.

Local Interests and Support for Brigade Accounting

Rural officials supported and implemented brigade accounting for personal, political, and economic reasons. In one prefecture officials who wanted to make their own locality famous took their local model team, combined it with two other wealthy teams to form a new brigade, and then pressured it to shift to brigade accounting. They felt that in order to create a nationally recognized model in their area, it had to be at least the size of a brigade.[19] On the other hand, county officials in Hubei Province decreased the embarrassingly high number of poor teams under their jurisdiction by uniting many poor teams into one poor brigade. "If we have seven or eight poor units and put them all together, we will only have one poor unit."[20] This action was probably in response to the 1974 national campaign to help poor teams become rich.

Some county officials admitted using this policy to overcome inequality. When asked how they overcame inter-team inequality, county officials in Hebei Province said that they advocated brigade accounting; it was a simple bureaucratic technique that involved little personal effort or capital expense.[21] Other officials used it to gain control over localities. In order to force peasants to double-crop their rice, county officials in Fujian Province first compelled them to shift to brigade accounting to increase the brigade's control over the type of crops peasants planted.[22] In another location, commune officials supported brigade accounting because it increased grain and pig sales to the state (for which they were responsible).[23]

By transfering authority over resources and their distribution and accumulation from teams to brigades, brigade accounting helped resolve economic and political difficulties. A brigade that controlled team granaries could sell more grain to the state or could pass sales quotas (*zhenggou renwu*) of the less productive teams onto more productive ones, ensuring fulfillment of state quotas. For example, Teams 2 and 3 in Dongliu Brigade, Laomiao Commune, Shaanxi Province, originally had similar state-imposed quotas. After it became the accounting unit, the brigade forced Team 3 to sell 10 tons to the state, while Team 2 sold only 4.5 tons.[24] In Jilin Province, two teams argued incessantly over a strip of land that divided them; brigade accounting solved the problem by transfering ownership of all land, including this strip, to the brigade.[25]

A number of local officials responded to ideological pressures of the radical environment. According to one informant, a thirty-year old brigade secretary who had been a school teacher and had studied Mao's writing more than most local leaders supported the policy because it indicated the depth to which his brigade was willing to learn from Dazhai.[26] Others, however, responded opportunistically, with little commitment to the policy's ideological goals. When commune leaders put forth the slogan to "take a great revolutionary step, don't be women with bound feet," they were concerned with demonstrating their revolutionary ardor.[27] Similarly, after April 1976, when the Gang of Four appeared to be on the edge of victory, political fears prompted some middle-level officials to implement the policy for self-protection.

Explaining Opposition to Brigade Accounting

Cadre Interests

Brigade accounting created numerous problems for rural officials. Precipitous transitions could alienate rich teams, causing drops in production that threatened the fulfillment of state tasks. Members of a wealthy production team were upset when their unit was forced to adopt brigade accounting because "if the distribution is not fair, peasant enthusiasm will not develop. Our team's peasants knew they would lose money. How the accounting would be done was publicized, so they had objections. They can count. They knew how much they would make."[28]

In addition, the bureaucratic procedures involved in shifting to brigade accounting were complicated. According to Central Committee rules set in the 1960s, "if a team wants to change, to be established or to split, it must get the permission of the county or the district under the city." But to establish brigade accounting, commune officials "had to write a report to the district and then the district wrote a report to the city."[29] Thus in 1969–1970 some units never tried to establish brigade accounting.

Managerial problems explain some local opposition. According to Fei Xiaotong, "when work is mainly done by hands and feet . . . extensive organization in such enterprises gives no appreciable profit but rather complicates human relations."[30] Brigade cadres would have to resolve these complicated human relations. Similarly, unifying teams or establishing brigade accounting forced peasants with long-standing feuds to work together. In one Nanjing locality, two teams which had been merged split over differing attitudes toward collective work. The argument ensued for several days and reached a crisis before the brigade secretary intervened. In another instance, an experiment in Huiyang County, Guangdong Province, where one poorly managed team was united with two well-run teams, collapsed after less than one month.[31]

Production team leaders also opposed brigade accounting because they lost control over local decisions. As a result, their team's unique conditions could be ignored, which could lead to economically irrational outcomes.[32] Mao had recognized this problem earlier on when he admitted that "original team cadres, at this time, will not be able to be 'masters of their own affairs' as before. Their managerial authority must be somewhat narrowed. Cannot they then oppose this type of change?"[33]

Resource Redistribution

The potential of brigade accounting for redistributing wealth among production teams was the most important reason for opposition to the policy at and below the brigade level. By compelling teams of unequal strength to combine their economic resources, the policy benefited the poorer teams. Table 6 showed how a workpoint was calculated. With brigade accounting the entire brigade's income was divided by all the workpoints distributed in the brigade. *Peking Review* of 1966 described the redistributive effects of brigade accounting:

> In one brigade a member of one team gets one *yuan* per workday, while in another team he gets only 0.7 *yuan* a workday. In such cases, if the brigade and not the team were taken as the basic accounting unit, distribution of income would have to be based on an average of the teams. This ignoring of the differences between teams would lead to a harmful egalitarianism, dampening the labor enthusiasm of members.[34]

In Nanjing redistribution precipitated conflicts. When the city established a test point in its nearby suburbs in 1978, the two wealthiest teams—as well as their peasant members—suffered serious financial losses, with both teams losing about 5,000 *yuan*. A team leader who learned at a meeting of the imminent shift to brigade accounting marched out of the meeting once he understood the costs to his team.

> The brigade called us to a meeting and handed out the outline of distribution (*fenpei an*). Before the meeting we didn't know what the policy was to be. We only learned of this method at the meeting. There was food and drink. I had only one drink and none of the four dishes, and then I got up and left. After the meeting the secretary and brigade leader came to my house and criticized me.[35]

As the peasants' representative and a man who was proud of his power, he had lost face in his constituents' eyes. The other team leader was more active in his opposition. "We didn't know much about it when it began. But we got 'ripped off.' In 1978 we complained a lot; everyone in our team complained. I didn't say anything in front of my team members, but I went to the brigade and the commune leaders to complain."[36] Per capita income in the larger of the two teams dropped by 40–50 *yuan*, while in the smaller team the per capita loss was greater; at 80 *yuan*, it amounted to approximately 15–20 percent of each peasant's income. Little wonder the team leader had stormed out of the brigade meeting when informed of the policy. However the decision to establish brigade accounting in this unit had been made at the municipal level, so local opposition was futile.

The Pattern of Opposition

Given the serious opposition to this policy, how did the 90 percent of locations who did not shift to brigade accounting respond to the wind? Localities responded in five ways. In some areas nothing happened; the wind had no effect at all. In conservative provinces such as Jiangsu, where pressures were minimal, local leaders demonstrated what Bachrach and Baratz have called "the other face of power."[37] Rather than use their power to enforce decisions, they used that power to prevent decisions from occurring. One Jiangsu informant recalled that when the wind of brigade accounting blew by, brigade officials told her that they would not let the peasants discuss it. As a third response, cadres in other areas merged teams or developed the brigade economy; implementing a related policy weakened upper-level pressures to adopt brigade accounting. Fourth, even places which established brigade accounting used the lack of specific criteria on policy implementation to cut back on the policy's redistributive content and alter the outcome preferred by the radicals. Finally, where the wind's strength forced the issue onto the local agenda, cadres still avoided implementing the policy because of the local power distribution and the policy's threat to the powerful groups in the countryside.

Changing Policy Content: Equality in Form or Reality?

Although brigade accounting redistributed wealth from richer to poorer teams, local cadres could establish the policy's form while altering its content. This way they could respond to pressures from above, but diffuse peasant hostility that would have resulted from a major redistribution of wealth among the teams. As a result, the degree of redistribution generated by brigade accounting reflected a continuum from major to minimal redistribution of team assets.

Under a "total equality" system, brigades used each team's gross income to pay their expenses, including salaries of brigade cadres. Brigade officials also recorded the number of workpoints peasants earned, because with brigade accounting team accountants became superfluous. Each peasant's income was based on the entire brigade's net profit rather than merely his own team's, allowing poor teams to derive part of their income from the rich teams' contributions.

This extreme form of redistribution took place occasionally,[38] but most units redistributed less. Xitang Brigade in Wuxi County, Jiangsu Province, only took half of each team's gross income, which was distributed among all the peasants after the brigade's expenses had been extracted. The remaining half of each team's gross income was kept and distributed within the team. This way the wealthier teams still had more funds to distribute, leaving their workpoint values higher than in the poorer teams.[39]

Two other units, one in Nanjing and another in Anhui Province, redistributed less than Xitang Brigade. Nanjing's suburban brigade rewarded each team 10 points for each 5 *yuan* worth of produce. For each 75 kg. of agricultural produce, regardless of the crop, they also paid 10 points. The profits from the sale of these goods covered team and brigade expenses, including brigade officials' salaries. Based on the total number of workpoints distributed, they determined a brigade-wide workpoint value. However, peasant income was not based on this workpoint value. Instead, each team determined its own workpoint value by dividing the number of points the brigade paid them by the number of workpoints their team's peasants had earned; the brigade-wide workpoint remained a mere formality, used to create the image of full-scale brigade accounting.

The policy was still redistributive, for several reasons. Wealthier teams received less than they contributed because they produced more valuable crops than the poorer teams; their total output was lower, but the value was higher. By paying every team 10 points for each 75 kg. of output, regardless of its market value, the brigade gave extra funds to poor teams which had a high output of cheap vegetables. Also, following Dazhai's example, this Nanjing brigade in 1978 restricted per capita income to 180 *yuan*, so wealthier teams accumulated more capital that year.[40] When the brigade became the unit of account that year, it took each team's year-end accumulation and never returned it. These two techniques, plus the fact that the brigade's and teams' expenses were paid from the original unequal contributions, caused the wealthiest two teams to suffer an economic loss.

A location in Anhui Province which established brigade account-ing in 1970 used the least redistributive variant of all:

> All teams gave the same percentage of their total income (*zong shouru*) to the brigade. The brigade then put aside money for the accumulation fund, the welfare fund, and for expenses. The brigade also paid the taxes. It then figured out a basic workpoint value (*di fen*) for the whole brigade, which determined how much each unit would give out. Then it took each team's contribution to the brigade as a percentage of the total contribution of all the teams and determined what percentage of the remaining funds would go to which unit . . . This method cut down on the inequality, but it was also fair in that each team got back an amount based upon how much they contributed. If your unit contributed more, you got more.[41]

Wealthy teams paid a larger share of the brigade's expenses, but the final per capita distribution was still based on each team's collective output. Therefore there was no redistribution of funds from one team to another.

Although the last two units described above formally established brigade accounting, there was less redistribution than the concept implied. Local leaders avoided accusations from wealthy units of excessive egalitarianism and protected themselves politically from upper-level officials who supported the policy. Because it was a policy wind, no formal guidelines had been established for brigade account-ing, leaving local leaders leeway to implement the policy in a form dictated by local interests. And because the policy's redistributive content triggered opposition, some local leaders changed the content and implemented less redistributive methods.

Policy Alternatives: Merging Production Teams

Two policies—amalgamating production teams and expanding the brigade's economy—reflect the tendency of moving to higher stages of socialism. Yet they also offerred local officials an opportunity to avoid problems inherent in brigade accounting. Since 1958 the appropriate size of the production team had been a contentious issue.[42] In 1965–1966 the number of teams decreased by 4.6 percent, and from 1967 to 1969 the number again dropped by over 10 percent (see Figure 4). Once radical power diminished after 1978, the number of teams increased dramatically.

In order to establish larger units of labor organization, Lin Biao and military radicals who mobilized peasants for large-scale capital construction projects demanded the amalgamation of small production teams. One commune official in Nanjing who felt that pressure in 1970 recalled that

> At the end of the Cultural Revolution, the province, the city and the district were under military control. The city was run by Fang Ming; the province by Xu Shiyou. They didn't know much about the countryside. They felt that the teams were too small, especially for construction work. So we united eight teams in 1970 . . . We had no orders from the "center," the province or the city. We didn't know whose idea it was, but it was the military who decided it at the city or district level. They had a meeting and they told us that with the units so small we couldn't do a good job running agriculture.[43]

Economist Xu Dixin also believes that the rash of team amalgamations in 1970 was related to capital construction work.[44]

However, for hard radicals who were principally concerned with revolutionary transformations to higher stages of socialism, merging teams was expedient for brigade accounting: it gradually reduced inter-team inequality; uniting two teams with different income levels was easier than transforming a whole brigade; and decreasing the number of teams simplified the eventual transition to brigade accounting.[45] Still, hard radicals who favored brigade accounting were less supportive of team amalgamations than were military radicals.

Local officials who evaded brigade accounting could find some protection in amalgamating production teams, since doing so demonstrated commitment to progressive policies. However, amalgamating teams was no easy process. If two teams had split before, due to financial or lineage conflicts, deep rooted conflicts could resurface.[46] Furthermore, amalgamating teams was redistributive. A team leader in suburban Nanjing admitted that initially his team's members opposed amalgamation because the other team was poorer and had many "overdrawn households" (chaozhi hu) who owed the collective money. These debts became the new unified team's responsibility. Thus amalgamating teams was not as useful a policy alternative to brigade accounting as strengthening the brigade economy.

Expanding the Brigade Economy

Expanding the brigade economy had practical implications for the transition to communism. It increased the percentage of the local economy under brigade control and could narrow inter-team and intra-brigade inequality. Poor teams with too many peasants and not enough land could send laborers to brigade factories, while brigade enterprise profits could help needy teams fund field levelling work.[47]

On the other hand, developing the brigade economy could undermine the transition to brigade accounting. If brigade leaders supported brigade ownership because this increased the resources under their control, developing the brigade economy fulfilled that goal with fewer complications. While strengthening the brigade economy helped lay the groundwork for a successful ownership transition in the long run, in the short run it removed the urgency of immediate ownership transitions by allowing officials to appear to follow the main trend.

In the early radical period, when pressures for amalgamating teams and brigade accounting were intense, some units chose to develop the brigade economy instead. After a brigade in Shaoxing County, Zhejiang Province, rejected brigade accounting in 1969, it compelled all teams to give money to establish a brigade tea farm; this demonstrated a commitment to strengthening the brigade's economy.[48] In the mid-1970s, the Dazhai movement's idea of shifting to brigade accounting led to the expansion of the brigade's economic role. An informant from Taishan County, Guangdong, reported that "1975 was the big year of Dazhai." Moreover,

> The collective was stressed and distribution was affected. We did more things at the brigade level . . . In 1975 the brigade built new buildings and a new factory. We built a pig farm for them. Before, the teams and the brigade had almost none of these things. They also began to do propaganda work that soon, step by step, they would make the brigade the accounting unit. They told us they wanted to shift the collective to ownership by the whole people.[49]

But by advocating developing the brigade economy in 1975–1976, both Zhang Chunqiao and Hua Guofeng may have supplied local officials the opportunity to choose this less radical option. While Chinese officials claim that in 1976 Zhang tried to engineer a Shanghai-wide shift to brigade accounting, in March 1975 he publicly opted for a more gradual transition to higher stages of socialism by stressing the importance of increasing the brigade's and commune's share of fixed assets within the collective economy.[50] At the fall 1975 Dazhai Conference, which presented a softer version of the radical program, Hua Guofeng referred to brigade and commune factories as rural China's "great hope."[51] That year Hua reportedly insisted on developing "exactly these two levels," in order to change the situation where "there are three levels of ownership but two levels possess nothing" (san ji suoyou, liang ji meiyou).[52]

This economy-strengthening policy received much support because it was acceptable to a wide selection of national leaders. Zhou Enlai reportedly supported developing commune and brigade industries at the August 1970 Northern Districts Agricultural Conference,[53] and in fact may have pushed this policy to slow down the shift to brigade accounting occurring in the preceding radical period. By the mid-1970s, radicals and moderates alike were advocating this policy, which increased the likelihood of its implementation.

Moreover, the policy was rather popular with most rural inhabitants. Although commune and county officials may have competed with brigade leaders over the resources necessary to start and expand brigade enterprises, they, unlike the partisans of brigade accounting, rarely undermined team production. Expanding the brigade's role offered peasants opportunities to escape collective field work and get a fixed salary. However, it also harmed peasant incomes, for as the brigade's tasks increased, the number of brigade officials who no longer labored in the fields increased dramatically, and their salaries were drawn from team accumulation funds.[54] Four brigades for which I received data in China corroborate this trend (Figure 7). Moreover, the major increases for most teams occurred between 1965–1970 and after 1975. Although the number of brigade cadres was to be decided by people's congresses and submitted to the county people's committees to be "kept on record,"[55] so many people were placed on the brigade payroll that the 1978 Third Plenum stipulated that only three to five brigade cadres were excused from physical labor.

Peasants also supported expanding the brigade's economy, particularly when relatives, friends, and fellow team members who were employed in the factories were paid in workpoints and their salaries were remitted to their respective team for distribution among all peasants. In Qingxiu Brigade, outside Nanjing, where the brigade followed this remuneration policy, agricultural income had dropped but per capita income had risen, buoyed by these financial inputs from the brigade.[56] Knowing this, the radicals advocated that all brigade and commune factories use workpoints rather than salary systems to create support for collective enterprises and strengthening socialism. Thus most rural bureaucrats and peasants supported strengthening the brigade economy, making this policy a popular and effective alternative to brigade accounting.

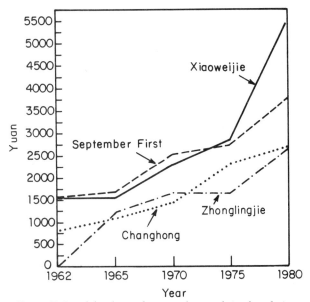

Figure 7. Local funds used to supplement brigade salaries in four brigades, 1962–1980. Data supplied by commune officials in suburban Nanjing, 1981.

Vested Interests and Rural Class Conflict

In any political system institutional stability creates entrenched political and economic interests. Post-1949 China was no different. After 1962, production teams developed collective interests which reflected institutional class interests in rural China. As a result, brigade accounting's redistributive nature triggered a form of class conflict between wealthy and poor units in parts of rural China.

In 1960, Mao recognized that attempts to move to higher levels of socialism would confront "cliques of vested interests":

> Although socialist society destroys classes, during the developmental process there will possibly be a problem of "cliques of vested interests." They will not be willing to change the established system . . . The establishment of any new system always destroys some of the old. There can be no construction without destruction. But destruction causes some people to oppose it. Man is a strange animal; when he has superior conditions (*youyue de tiaojian*), he puts on airs (*you jiazi*). If we don't pay attention to this, it will be very dangerous.[57]

These forces would have to be defeated and the institutions destroyed if China were to continue toward a communist society. Thus for Mao political development meant "deinstitutionalization" rather than "institutionalization."[58]

Evidence suggests, however, that the vested interests—in this case the rich teams—undermined this Maoist effort at institutional restructuring and the movement to higher stages of socialism. Since a team's wealth determined a large part of each family's income, production team members developed collective economic interests, especially during 1968–1978 when private household economic activity was tightly restricted. Although conflicts among households may have existed, peasants depended on each other for approximately three-quarters of their income. These economic interests reinforced collective consciousness so that peasants grew accustomed to working as a team and "a mild hostility to other teams" arose.[59] Barriers separating teams and villages rigidified.[60] Informants suggest that even after the Cultural Revolution spontaneous inter-team cooperation was almost nonexistent.[61] In fact, where brigade economies were weak, peasants probably felt little loyalty to any organization beyond the team.

Given these entrenched team-level interests and the inter-team redistribution of resources involved in shifting to brigade accounting, how can we characterize the conflicts that developed over brigade accounting? According to Lowi, redistributive policies lead to patterns of conflict which reflect a "power elite" rather than a "pluralist" model of political interaction.[62] Under the former, a sharp demarcation of interests develops along bureaucratic and institutional lines, and a ruling elite uses its preferred political position to keep issues inimical to its interests off the political agenda. Of all policy types, argues Lowi, redistributive issues most closely reflect class conflict in terms of intensity; structurally they also cut closest to class lines.

Because brigade accounting was redistributive, brigade officials from rich teams had material incentives to oppose the policy, while those who relied on the rich teams to run the brigade had political incentives to protect the interests of the wealthy. Therefore, when neither the winds nor the penetration from above were overpowering, brigade leaders often acted on behalf of the rich teams and kept the issue of brigade ownership off the local agenda. And if it got on the agenda, they prevented its implementation.

The analogy of class conflict can be extended further. In the absence of private ownership in a bureaucratic system, class and class power depend on the distribution of authority within "imperatively coordinated associations."[63] In the 1960s and 1970s rural power relations among brigade officials, team leaders, and peasants reflected Dahrendorf's model of industrial society. Little private property existed; structures were bureaucratic; and decisions—particularly on distributing or redistributing resources—were controlled by "administrative commands" (*xinzheng mingling*) in the brigade. Furthermore, wealthier teams often influenced brigade decisions by controlling the post of brigade Party secretary. In fact, four of five brigade secretaries I interviewed in Nanjing came from relatively rich teams, while in another case cited above two leading brigade officials from richer teams had kept the issue of brigade ownership off the local agenda.[64]

A major indicator of class dominance in a socialist society is inequitable access to resources, such as education, which permits those from the preferred economic groups to claim more than their fair share of political power.[65] This situation, which had existed in pre-1949 China, persisted under the communist regime in parts of rural China. For example, rich villages in rural Shanxi Province had been sending their children to school since the 1920s. Poorer villages, however, had developed no such tradition. After 1949 these wealthy teams continued to stress education; consequently, brigade officials— who should know how to read and write—consistently came from the wealthier teams. The inequitable access to education created institutionally based political inequality which directly affected the local response to brigade accounting. As one informant from that locality recalled,

> The people in my team liked the idea of brigade accounting because it would help them financially. But the people in Team No. 5 did not like it because they would lose a lot if they had such an accounting system. The cadres in the brigade came mostly out of Team No. 5, partly because their population was bigger but also because they were richer and so could afford to send their children to school to learn to read. So they came back and became the brigade leaders and had all the power.[66]

Since this was a radical province and the wind of brigade accounting was strong, local leaders were unable to keep the topic off the agenda. However, cadres consistently used their political leverage to avoid implementing the policy. "They had a brigade meeting every year to discuss the question of brigade accounting and once they even had a study meeting (*xuexi ban*) for twenty days at the county level for cadres from four levels, but they never carried out the policy . . . The main reason was the big differences in the teams' incomes."[67] Here rich people used their wealth to gain more education which, when translated into political power, was employed to protect their economic interests. And even as the state tried to introduce redistributive policies to overcome those inequalities, powerful rural interests resisted the state's intrusion.

A final example shows in some detail how wealthy teams used their control over the brigade's political structures to defeat poor teams and prevent brigade accounting and the redistribution of resources. In 1968 or 1969, in Zhejiang Province's Shaoxing County, Lin Biao's test point for brigade accounting outside Hangzhou intensified the radical environment during these two years.[68] However, in this particular brigade cadres never introduced brigade accounting.

> It was a policy decided from below. No one at the higher levels made you do it, but there was this "wind." It occurred twice, once after the Ninth Central Committee meeting (1969), which was called the "Ninth Congress's East Wind," while another occurred later. We thought about it but didn't do anything about it because the cadres who had real power were all from the rich teams. Had they been from the poor teams, they would have supported it. The decision not to get together was not one team's decision; it was made by brigade cadres.[69]

Table 8 shows that the brigade power structure favored Teams 3 and 4, which controlled the major positions. The 1969 workpoint value differed only slightly among the teams, but the long-term economic prospects were more favorable for Teams 3 and 4. They managed their forests well and were accumulating money yearly. Since they were expecting large payoffs in the future, amalgamation would cost them dearly. Representatives from Team 2 had little or no power, and only the Party branch member from Team 1 had authority to challenge the monopoly of Teams 3 and 4.

Table 8. Brigade power structure in Shaoxing County, Zhejiang Province.

Organization	Production team no.
Party branch (three members)	
Brigade secretary	3
Brigade accountant	4
Branch member	1
Brigade revolutionary committee (R.C.) (in decreasing order of political power)	
Brigade party secretary	3
Head, brigade R.C.	4
Brigade accountant	4
Member, party branch	1
Vice-head, brigade R.C.	2
Member, brigade R.C.	3
Member, brigade R.C.	4
Member, brigade R.C.	1
Women's representative	2

SOURCE: Hong Kong interview, 1980.

The three most powerful people were the brigade secretary, the brigade accountant, and the head of the revolutionary committee. All were from Teams 3 and 4. They deliberately avoided the question of amalgamating teams. They could avoid raising it altogether or raise it but not stress it. What they did was just let it flow by. There was no "order" (*mingling*) and no central document (*wenjian*). The *Sixty Articles* were still the key ruling articles.

But because many units in this county were adopting brigade accounting, they could not avoid the issue.

So we had an expanded brigade meeting with the members of the Party branch, the revolutionary committee, production team cadres, and representatives of the commune members. There were 40 to 50 people at the meeting to discuss the problem. It was a special meeting to discuss amalgamation. I was there. The meeting was extremely intense (*jilie*). There was real arguing (*zhenglun*). People stood up to put forward their positions, and then someone else would get up and oppose their position.

The divisions were very much along the lines of rich-versus-poor teams as the richer peasants tried to stop the state from forcing them to redistribute their wealth. The poorer peasants, however, strongly supported this policy. "People in Teams 1 and 2 all supported amalgamation. They argued that since everyone did it, why shouldn't we? If we don't amalgamate how can we say we are learning from Dazhai? Centralizing leadership is good for production and developing socialist enterprises." The poor teams believed the brigade economy could increase their individual or collective wealth.

Representatives of the wealthier teams also used the slogan "Learning from Dazhai" but would not accept brigade accounting. My informant recalled that "the opposition argued that one could study Dazhai without amalgamating. To develop production it is not necessary to unite teams, and leadership can be centralized without amalgamating. One side raised a point and the other side opposed it." But without any formal document demanding policy implementation, the final outcome was determined by the power distribution in the brigade. "So in the end we did not act upon this issue. We simply dismissed the meeting without resolving the issue (*bu huan er san*), which of course left everyone angry." Soon after, this unit expanded its brigade-owned enterprises.

Conclusion

The shift from team to brigade accounting occurred infrequently in China in the period under study, and by 1978 not quite 10 percent of rural brigades had established brigade accounting. Most transitions took place when middle-level officials at the county or above decided to enforce compliance upon a few model units or en masse in an entire district or county. Location, cropping patterns, and other systemic variables affected the propensity for establishing brigade accounting. Yet even when the transition was imposed from above, local leaders often manipulated the policy's content to limit the extent of redistribution.

This rapid shift to higher stages of socialism generated too many conflicts and too much opposition. Although theoretically and structurally this policy was central to the radical strategy and radical leaders, its redistributive content brought it into direct conflict with powerful local interests who sharply limited its nation-wide impact. Poor teams could expect some support, but the wealthy preferred to maintain the extant distribution of wealth. Without upper-level bureaucratic fiat, the rich teams controlled the final outcome. Through their political or class authority, based on their control over economic and political resources, brigade secretaries acted in their own teams' interests and prevented the outcome favored by China's radical leaders. The elite ideological goal of preventing Thermidor by restructuring rural institutions and re-revolutionizing society was undercut by the vested interests who were the target of the campaign and whom the radicals had wanted to defeat. On this issue, entrenched rural interests won.

The most commom strategy by which local cadres avoided brigade accounting was strengthening the brigade economy, making strong brigades a legacy of the radical period in wealthy areas. In some wealthy areas, where peasants benefited greatly from rural enterprises, their support for them intensified. To this extent the radical strategy generated mass support for slowly strengthening higher levels of the collective economy. After the radicals' collapse and the introduction of the "responsibility system," these peasants resisted decollectivization, fearing it would undermine the inchoate benefits they were receiving from the brigade.

Using policy winds and the radical environment, the radicals put the issue of moving to higher stages of socialism on local decision making agendas. In response to these pressures, most rural cadres, who had the final say on the form in which they built stronger collectives, chose to implement the less contentious parts of the policy. They eschewed the policy preferred by the more radical national leaders, choosing instead policy alternatives that garnered wider support, were easier to carry out, and strengthened their own political and economic power without redistributing resources from the wealthy to the poor. Ironically, the local decision to develop brigade industries is having a major impact on rural economics and politics. Rural industries today are growing at unprecedented rates, increasing the resources under the control of the vested interests who still dominate the brigade's political economy.

The radicals may have failed to introduce brigade accounting and move China closer to communism; they also failed to undermine the power of the rich teams and redistribute wealth from them to their poorer neighbors. But by creating a political environment in which cadres expanded the brigade's role in the rural economy, the radicals left their mark behind. In the long run, strengthening the brigade's industrial base may be their most important legacy.

6

RESTRICTING PRIVATE PLOTS

Property is theft.

Proudhon

THROUGH ALL THE policy perturbations on land policy since 1949, the Chinese peasant in 1968 still maintained control over a small piece of land. Land Reform had redistributed over 30 percent of the land from landlords to peasants, ensuring that all peasants had some land. Under the agricultural producer cooperatives, peasants retained access to private plots. After the Great Leap Forward—which collectivized all rural private property—had collapsed, private plots were returned to the peasants and declared a "necessary adjunct to the socialist economy."[1] The *Sixty Articles* of 1962 officially sanctified the private sector's reemergence.

But for the radicals, private plots were a remnant of the peasant small ownership system and a drag on the transition to higher stages of socialism. They were a bourgeois right left over from the previous society and the soil for a capitalist restoration. And they helped some peasants get rich, increased inter-personal inequality, and sustained the individual's desire for property which directly conflicted with strengthening the collective sector. As a result, during the Great Leap Forward the radicals tried swiftly to eradicate private property and private ownership, while in the 1968–1978 decade they tried to break the peasants' tie to private ownership of land through the constant restriction of private plots.

The way a village restricted its private plots varied according to several factors, including: (1) the type of private plots the unit and its peasants possessed—between 1968 and 1978, seven types of private plots existed; (2) the unit's structural characteristics—topography, cropping patterns, particulars of location, such as proximity to cities, forests, rivers, and so on, and its level of economic development; (3) the period when the restriction occurred—in 1968–1970, 1973, or 1975–1977;[2] and (4) the attitudes and interests of middle level and local cadres and peasants towards these restrictions.

As with brigade accounting, local views varied according to bureaucratic and personal interests, the nature of the political environment in a particular location, and the policy's impact on peasant and collective resources. While in some locations elite penetration predetermined local decisions, the importance of private plots to the peasants and the mixed pressures on local cadres necessitated negotiations between local leaders and peasants. In most instances local leaders compromised by limiting the restrictions or by evading the wind entirely. As a result, this "vestige of capitalism" was never totally eradicated and launched a comeback after the demise of the Maoist era.

Types of Private Plots and Modes of Restrictions

A local leader's decision to restrict the private plots was limited at the outset by the type of private plots his unit possessed. While the 1962 *Sixty Articles* referred to four types of private plots, informants and press reports speak of seven types: principal private plots (*zi liu di*), yard household plots (*zhu zai di*), marginal land (*wu bian di* and *shi bian di*), opened barren land (*kai huang di*), feed plots (*siliao di*), vegetable plots (*cai di*), and collective private plots (*jiti ziliu di*).[3] This variety gave local leaders many options if they decided to restrict their "capitalist sprouts." An appropriate choice often resolved pressures from above and allayed the fears of the villagers with whom they had to coexist daily.

As with brigade accounting, the modes of restriction of private plots lie on a continuum running from total expropriation to merely deciding what crops to plant, without reducing the area peasants controlled. Local leaders altered this policy's content as well and diminished its harmful effects on local politics, while still implementing its form for self-protection. Nevertheless some local cadres did find it in their interest to implement the policy, even if it angered their peasant constituents.

1. Total Expropriation. Total expropriation of principal private plots, where peasants lost all benefits from the land, rarely if ever occurred after 1958. Of 63 examples of restrictions gleaned from the press and interviews in Hong Kong and China, none ever totally expropriated the principal private plots (see Table 9),[4] suggesting that the most radical option was unacceptable to local cadres; what was acceptable were the more moderate options of collectivizing or restricting the size of principal private plots.

2. Collectivization. Collectivization was the most radical yet widespread technique for controlling principal private plots. This policy

Table 9. Pattern of private plot restrictions.

Type of restrictions	Number of cases	Percentage of total cases
Collectivized plots	17	26.9
Official plots	9	14.2
Marginal land	11	17.5
Yard land	7	11.1
Opened waste land	8	12.7
Crop types	8	12.7
Moving plots	3	4.8
Total	63	99.9

SOURCE: Interviews in Hong Kong and the PRC, and references in *People's Daily* and *Foshan Report.*

occurred in Shanxi, Shandong, Jiangsu, Tibet, Hebei, Guizhou, and Liaoning provinces.[5] Of the examples listed above, 26.9 percent opted for collectivizing private plots. The land could then be worked fulltime by older peasants, allowing other peasants to spend their energies on collective cultivation. After the harvest the collective divided some or all of the output among the peasants on a per capita basis. In some places peasants paid workpoints for the food, while in other places it was free. Collectives often grew grain in these new collective private plots, thus helping to resolve the higher quotas instituted after 1969–1970. In locations in Shandong, Shanxi, and southern Jiangsu provinces, peasants each year received 30 kg. of grain per person, irrespective of the output of the collectivized private plot or the type of crops grown.

3. *Restricting the Size of Principal Private Plots.* In other locations, collectives took only part of the land allocated for private plots, so each peasant's plot was decreased. This procedure often was the result of compromise, given peasant opposition to total collectivization. Still, by restricting the size of the private plots, cadres followed the trend of the times.

4. *Limiting Marginal Land.* Chinese peasants, grasping any opportunity for minor extensions of tilled land, often increased the size of their private plots by cultivating soil beside roads, rivers and lakes. This type of private plot revealed periods of lax rural leadership, because only in such periods could peasants risk visibly demonstrating an attachment to land, property and self-interest. However, marginal land's visibility meant it had to be restricted whenever a new campaign arose. During 1968–1978, therefore, this restriction occurred frequently and was a major target of the early years of the

Line Education Campaign of 1973–1977. At the same time, because the soil often was not fertile and the plots were small and highly vulnerable to expropriation, peasants rarely invested much time or effort into cultivating them; for the cadres, therefore, they became a highly visible, noncontentious method for demonstrating their willingness to struggle "the tail of capitalism."

5. *Restricting Barren Land.* Cultivating barren land occurred during periods of lax leadership as well, because it was simpler then for peasants to sneak into the hills and open new land. However, these plots were larger than marginal land, so when restricted they often became part of the collective fields. In fact, following the restriction of principal private plots, the collective sometimes allowed peasants to open new plots on collectively owned barren land. But once the land became fertile, the collective might appropriate it.

A work team participant described how outside work teams often had to become detectives to discover these plots.

> People had planted their excess private plots in the middle of the forests, so it was very hard to find them. They would go out to graze animals and then sneak into the forest and work on their private plots. So we always tried to find either people who did not have private plots or people who had a particular disagreement with another person to lead us to the private plots. Then we would get other people to lead us to the private plots of the person who had reported to us . . . We would then call a meeting and ask the people to admit that they had extra private plots. If they refused, we would take them to the land and ask them if, in fact, this was their land.[6]

6. *Restricting Household Yard Land.* After principal, marginal, and opened barren plots were widely restricted in 1968–1971, peasants sought new ways to expand and protect their private plots. Some built big yards around their homes and grew crops in them. When one team threatened to collectivize the trees in front of peasants' homes, peasants extended their yards, building walls around the trees.[7] In Dinghuan County, Shanxi Province, "The only place peasants could grow anything was in the yards within the walls of their homes. But in the 1970s they began to restrict the size of the yard that the peasants could have in order to limit their ability to grow crops on the side . . . They never forced people to limit the size of their gardens but only set limits on the people who were building new homes."[8] But in rural China making additions to old homes or building new ones could not occur without Party certification, so brigades could control yard size.[9]

"Residential planning" (*jumin guihua*), which occurred in much of rural China, led to restrictions on household yard land. Part and parcel of the Dazhai movement, this policy's primary goal was to move peasant homes from cultivable land and resettle them in neat rows in the hills, as in Dazhai. Although the *Sixty Articles* stated that peasants could not be forced to move, some leaders pressured peasants to move from the fields into the hills. In one location cadres reportedly tore down people's homes; in another, those who refused to move could not cultivate the land in front of their homes.[10] But once they moved, not only could the team or brigade control the size of their new yard, but with Dazhai-type semi-detached houses there were no front or back yards at all.

7. Crop Types. Another restriction—controling the crops grown in the private plots—was rather widespread in 1976. In Jiangpu County, Jiangsu Province, the collective restricted the growing of cash crops such as bamboo, sugar cane, and tree seedlings, as well as vegetables such as tomatoes, cabbages, and onions. A brigade secretary recited one of the slogans used at that time.

> If you grow ginger, onions, and cabbage,
> Hundreds of *yuan* you can make.
> But the spirit and interest to learn from Dazhai,
> That you will surely forsake.[11]

One leader in that area complained that if not for the commune's pressure he would have made an additional 600 *yuan* raising tree seedlings. This policy was a major part of the 1975–1976 campaign to restrict bourgeois rights.

8. Moving Private Plots. Local leaders, particularly in hilly areas, would force peasants to move their private plots, which were often reclaimed barren land. Once the soil was enriched, team and brigade leaders wanted it for collective land. In one brigade where teams turned dry land into paddy fields, they made the original private plots into paddy fields and farmed them collectively. One team leader said that they did this almost every year. The land was particularly valuable to collectives because it was rarely registered, so no taxes were paid on its output and production quotas were much easier to fulfill. After the land was taken the peasants moved their plots further into the hills.[12] In other cases, when peasants increased the fertility of marginal land near the collective or barren fields, the collective expanded its own fields to include this land. In return, peasants were allowed to open even larger pieces of land on their own.[13]

9. Rectification and Redistribution. The last restriction was rectifying the size of plots and redistributing them on the basis of population changes. This mode often involved no restriction at all, but merely triggered other forms of restrictions; cadres used the rectification process to restrict marginal or barren land or move principal plots onto infertile barren land, taking the good land for the collective.[14] According to the 1962 *Sixty Articles*, private plots were to be readjusted every few years; but these redistributions occurred infrequently. Some localities never adjusted their private plots after 1962. One Jiangsu informant recalled that "the private plots were divided according to population in the 1960s and were not changed even if people died or were born."[15] In 1979, to remedy the inequalities that had developed over the years, Jiangsu Province ordered all local units to reorganize the size of private plots.

Explaining the Restriction of Private Plots

Structural Factors

A few structural factors that affected the restriction of private plots include the level of economic development, location, and a unit's cropping patterns.

1. *Level of Economic Development.* Poorer areas confronted less pressure to restrict private plots than did wealthy units. Where collectives offered little financial security, private plots were often the only thing keeping peasants in impoverished areas above the subsistence level. An informant from Huaiyang County, one of the poorest parts of northern Jiangsu Province, reported that in his area, "the private plots were never taken away. We always had .10 or .12 *mu*. They didn't do it in the surrounding communes either . . . They couldn't take them away because without them there was no food."[16] In fact, in Hunan Province some areas expanded private plots in 1973. According to one informant, everyone in his unit got .2 *mu* more of land in spring 1973 because "there was no food to eat." There the collective did not work well, and "production was poor."[17] This expansion may have been a response to the nation-wide poor harvest of 1972.

Even when they tried to restrict private plots in very poor areas, intense peasant opposition prevented cadres from carrying it out. Yan'an District is extremely poor; private plots were very important for people's survival. Only once in five years did peasants in one locality receive money at the year-end distribution—a paltry 8 *yuan*.[18] When the county leaders tried to force this place to collectivize its private plots, strong peasant resistance compelled the county to reduce the size of the plots rather than take them away entirely.[19]

Wealthy units suffered the most restrictions. Guangdong Province work teams, sent to "cut the tail of capitalism" during the 1974 Line Education Campaign, went most often to rich units. According to a participant in this campaign, "there were two types of areas that we went to, rich and poor. The middle were left alone . . . At that time most of the work teams went to rich teams; the ratio was at least two to one for the rich teams." Why did they chose rich teams? "In reality, the units that were moving towards capitalism were the rich units. The emphasis was then placed on the rich teams."[20] Also, since peasants in wealthy units could find markets for their cash crops and make a lot of money,[21] cadres in wealthy areas restricted the type of crops grown in private plots. With the collective supplying most of their daily needs, peasants in wealthy areas responded more passively to the restrictions than did peasants in very poor areas, facilitating the restriction of private plots for the cadres.

2. *Location.* A unit's location affected the amount of land available for private plots. Hunan peasants in the hills got more land than those in the valleys.[22] Peasants living near hills or forests could cultivate more private land. Judging from all interviews, peasants in these locations had both opened barren land and been subjected to stiff restrictions during 1968–1971 and 1973–1974. Of 33 articles in *People's Daily* (1968–1977) which specified the location of the restricted private plots, 19 referred to hilly units, 10 to level land, and four referred to suburban units. Moreover, combining interview data and 1978 *People's Daily* articles criticizing these restrictions, we find that of 41 references to locations where restrictions occurred, 19 again referred to hilly land, 12 to level land, and seven to suburban units, with three falling into various other categories.[23]

Suburban units confronting urban sprawl were under severe pressure for land, so urban officials used political campaigns to cut back on the size of private plots in suburban units, while those closer to the city suffered even greater restrictions.[24] Among seven brigades in greater Nanjing for which I have data, the suburban brigades had the smallest private plots. Of 15 articles on restricting private plots from late 1974 to August 1976, 47 percent (7 of 15) referred to restrictions in suburban units.

3. *Cropping Patterns.* Some units responded to the pressure to produce more grain by relocating or collectivizing their private plots. Once the peasants made barren land fertile, cadres took that land and forced peasants to open new plots in the hills. Units which harvested a second summer rice crop—triple cropping—faced serious labor constraints for most of the summer, making it expedient to collectivize

private plots. According to one local leader whose unit raised two crops of rice, "the people were off working on their private plots and would not come back to work on the collective, so we took in the land."[25]

Support for Restrictions

To restrict private plots and destroy the peasants' attachment to private property and land, advocates of agrarian radicalism promoted policy winds to bring pressure on middle- and local-level cadres. Yet for rural cadres this issue, which limited the peasants' economic freedom and household welfare, was contentious. Pressured from above and below, cadres had to weigh several competing interests: furthering their own political future, advancing state interests, strengthening the collective economy, increasing peasant prosperity, and maintaining personal relations with peasant constituents.

Cadres and peasants supported the restriction of private plots for economic and political reasons. Cadres at different levels were concerned with fulfilling state quotas and strengthening the collective economy and collective control over peasant economic activity. At the brigade and team level, some cadres and peasants also supported restrictions for personal economic reasons. This policy wind could be both a threat—evasion could bring political disaster—and an opportunity for political advancement.

For county and commune cadres fulfilling state quotas was an important responsibility. When Jiangsu's provincial government imposed high grain quotas in the late 1960s, Jurong County officials collectivized private plots county-wide and forced peasants to grow grain in them.[26] A more important motivating force was the imputed contradiction between private plots and strong collective agriculture. County and commune officials often believed that restricting private plots increased peasant support for collective labor and prevented peasants from dissipating their energies on private endeavors. While investigating a nearby brigade in 1976, one commune Party secretary restricted their expanded private plots. Not only did he believe that larger private plots undermined collective work, but peasants, who now needed their fertilizer, had stopped delivering it to their teams.[27] He also supported collectivized private plots. When one team expanded the size of its collectivized private plots to ensure a marketable surplus, he had thought it a good idea because all the money went to the collective.

Some team leaders restricted private plots to improve collective output and increase collective fertilizer supplies. One team leader reported that in 1970, private plots were cut from .4 *mu* to .1 *mu*, and the collective area was expanded. "After, people worked harder, had better work habits, and gave more fertilizer to the state." In fact, he reportedly believed that "if private plots were too large, collective work would suffer, and that was not good for anyone."[28] In Chen Village, some cadres supported the 1969 Three Loyalties Campaign's attack on private plots because they too believed that the collective suffered when peasants worked too hard on their private plots.[29] Not only did many local cadres see a close relationship between restricting private plots and fertilizer supplies,[30] but in a team where they had recently expanded the private plots, peasants who planted sweet potatoes in those plots avoided collective rice planting which took place at the same time.[31]

Finally, even in the radical period, material incentives and personal economic interest generated some support for the policy. Unlike the state salaries of commune officials, brigade leaders' salaries were based on the average workpoint value of all teams or the average of the richest and poorest teams in the brigade. Expanding collective land and wealth increased the brigade secretary's income. Team leaders with many young children also had a financial incentive to collectivize private plots. While some peasants profited from working their land in the evenings and mornings, cadres had little time for their own plots. But collectivizing private plots and distributing the output on a per capita basis not only prevented other peasants from getting rich, but ensured that team leaders with large families benefited most. One team leader with eight children distributed produce from the private plots based on household population; this way he "could benefit from others' work."[32] Thus some team leaders preferred collectivizing rather than eradicating private plots.

Peasants who wanted to stop others from getting ahead criticized those with strong interests in prospering from their private plots.[33] According to an older peasant woman,

> We have .1 *mu* of private plot per person. Some families have opened more, but I won't do it. If I did that much work I would be dead tired. I take care of the private plot. I grow vegetables, rapeseed, and sweet potatoes. Our life is pleasant. We have enough grain to eat . . . Some families opened up .2 to .3 *mu* of land. These people have different thoughts. They don't think about resting or playing. They sell on the private market.[34]

According to some informants, weak and lazy people resented the expansion of private plots.[35] One peasant who had opened up a lot of land remarked that "the strong people don't say anything. It is the lazy ones who talk. Some people like to sleep late and go to bed early."[36] Indolent peasants also supported restricting marginal plots or cleared land because while such restrictions did not limit their private plots, they did limit opportunities for stronger households. As will be shown below, principal private plots were important for small households who, with few collective workers, made little money from the collective. Thus it was the opportunity for creating inequality that these weaker or lazy peasants wanted to foreclose, not the plots themselves.

This support for restrictions on the actions of energetic peasants was, however, usually passive. By speaking at meetings, lazy peasants might convince others that they wanted to become activists at the expense of the richer, more powerful families. According to one team leader, "some people are unwilling to work so they don't want others to work. Some spoke on behalf of limiting private plots. Not at the team meetings, but you could tell from their behavior and what they said that they liked the policy."[37]

But peasants who wanted to see their neighbors' plots cut back could also advocate the redistribution of plots within the whole team. Because the *Sixty Articles* authorized redistribution to accommodate demographic changes, these peasants could assert that their goals followed state policy. In a team in Zhejiang Province, some peasants received large principal private plots because the land's quality was poor. In 1975, however, once they improved the soil, other peasants who resented their larger plots called for a re-measurement and redistribution of these plots.[38]

Political interests also mobilized support for restricting private plots. Rural bureaucrats knew the importance of demonstrating their "redness" and avoiding rightist labels. An official in Jiangpu County, Jiangsu Province, returned from a 1976 visit to Dazhai, and to prove his redness tried to eradicate cash crops from private plots throughout the county. In Yunnan Province, county officials supported similar restrictions to demonstrate their county's progressive nature.[39] Commune officials had to be even more cautious. They had just made it to the first rung of the state bureaucracy; one slip could put them back in the brigade, with the status and income loss such a demotion entailed. Thus one commune secretary in Guangxi Province restricted private plots to make his unit a model; this would increase his own prestige and, quite ironically, make his unit eligible for outside aid.[40] A self-confessed, leftist commune secretary had impoverished his peasants; when they grew rich from private plots he had called it "capitalism coming up and socialism being put aside" and pulled the "capitalist roots" out of the private plots.[41]

Some team leaders restricted marginal land to prevent intra-team inequalities and the conflict they could entail. Unable to continually ignore the weak and indolent peasants who complained when others got rich, and responsible for limiting inter-household conflict, the team leader's easiest option was to cut back on expanded land or prohibit further expansions.[42]

Peasants, too, used this policy to advance their own political careers. Looking for what one team leader called "political capital" (*zhengzhi ziben*), such peasants hoped that a radical image would make them activists (*jiji fenzi*). And if they could make the transition from activist to model (*mofan*), they "could attend meetings . . . and still get paid for a day's work."[43]

Finally, economic interest created support for collectivized private plots where they had been run well. In Jiangning County, Jiangsu Province, peasants in three teams reportedly refused to redistribute the collective private plots after 1979; not only did they receive an ample supply of free vegetables, but the collective always had a surplus to sell, which increased everyone's income. Ironically, only pressure from commune officials forced them to redistribute the private plots.[44] Similar situations existed throughout China, especially where the amount of food distributed by the collective in lieu of private plots exceeded what peasants could produce from the land.[45] According to Blecher, once peasants in one brigade were forced to grow grain in their private plots, they supported collectivization because it facilitated the use of machinery, which reduced the drudgery of tending the fields.[46] However, opportunities for marketing produce from private plots were also tightly controlled during this period. Once rural trade fairs expanded and peasants could do more with the land and the produce, support for collective plots dried up.

Opposition to Restricting Private Plots

The Importance of Private Plots to the Peasants

Private plots were important to the peasants' livelihood. They could make peasants in some localities self-sufficient in food production, while in other areas they provided peasants with vegetables for maintaining a balanced diet.[47] In poor areas such as western Sichuan, northern Guangdong, and Gansu, Guizhou, and Guangxi provinces, private plots may have been the only thing keeping peasants from going hungry.

Where average incomes prevailed, peasants relied on the collective for food grains and on their private plots for cash.[48] These plots also supplied fodder for pigs and fowl, whose sale was the peasants' major source of cash. In three teams in Four Families (*Sijia*) Brigade, in Jiangning Commune, Jiangning County, Jiangsu Province, the private plots directly supplied less than 10 percent of household income; for over 83 percent of the people, direct income from the plots comprised less than 5 percent of total household income. But private animal husbandry as well as the crops raised in these private plots comprised 20 to 25 percent of the average total household income.[49]

In other places cash crops from private plots directly expanded household incomes. From 1973 through 1977, in a brigade in the hills of Nanjing, peasants grew tree seedlings in their private plots. The number of households raising them and the income each household earned from them doubled from 1973 to 1977. For these households raising trees comprised 15 percent of their total household income by 1980, and including income from raising pigs and fowl, more than 36 percent of their income came from the private sector.[50] Here, too, each household earned 21 percent of its income from raising animals for which private plots supplied fodder.

Distributing private plots to peasants served political, economic, and psychological goals as well. Walker argued that distributing private plots to the peasants in 1955 helped smooth collectivization by providing incentives to stay in the collective.[51] Collective income was distributed at most twice a year, so peasants staggered the crops they sold from their private plots to make cash available year-round. Otherwise, at points during the year they would be strapped for cash. Also, without private plots peasants could not grow the vegetables they preferred.

Peasant support for private plots varied according to the household age structure, a peasant's willingness to forgo leisure time to make more money, and the type of plots that were being restricted. Peasants who worked harder than others and always sought ways to expand family income wanted more private plots. In 1981, one peasant in a brigade south of Nanjing worked five hours a day on his plot, before and after collective work. In the course of 1980 he had extended his plot from .2 to 2 *mu*, equaling the size of his former private farm, and he had made over 500 *yuan* from the private sector to support his son in college.

Generational variations made some households better able to use their private plots. Households with older family members who retired from collective labor supported private plots. The members of one of the wealthiest families in a Jilin team relied almost entirely on their private plots for their income and strongly opposed their restriction, even speaking out in the formal setting of a team meeting.

One commune member was thirty-five years old. He had two parents, a wife, and two kids in school but only one could work. So his parents looked after the private plot. His courtyard garden is the biggest, and he is the best potato grower. Each year he grew 1,500–2,000 kg. He also grew sorghum which he swapped for other crops . . . His parents worked really carefully on the private plots. And even after the area [in the courtyard] was cut from .05 to .03 *mu*, they got almost as much.[52]

Large households with strong laborers could take advantage of the larger strips they received for having a larger household.

The most vehement opposition arose over restricting yard land. Traditionally some peasants built high walls to keep the state out, and while peasants in socialist China may have grown accustomed to state interference in their work, they resented intrusions into their private domain. Jiangpu County peasants reacted violently to attempts to uproot crops in household yard plots. One team leader refused to implement the policy after peasants beat the brigade Party secretary and tore his clothes when he tried to smash the tomatoes and rip out the tree seedlings in the household yard plots.[53]

Dazhai and Peasant Opposition

When the radicals employed normative incentives to mobilize support for restricting private plots, they constantly called on peasants to emulate peasants in the Dazhai Brigade, who had given up their private plots. Yet most peasants knew that Dazhai was a model; so they argued that their own conditions, rather than those of a wealthy model, should determine local policy. One informant from Yunnan Province reported that "to carry out all the policies they told us how Dazhai did it . . . They told people that attitudes in Dazhai were so good because they had no private plots. At every meeting they told us how good Dazhai was." But according to this informant, "Most people thought there was little relationship between their situation and Dazhai's. Some people did believe it while others did not. For most peasants this was too abstract. They didn't know where Dazhai was . . . But young people believed in Dazhai and wanted to be like them."[54] According to an informant from Jilin Province, peasants in his unit did not care that Dazhai had no private plots and argued that "Dazhai is Dazhai and here is here. They are not the same."[55] In another locality, "peasants didn't know what Dazhai was. They heard local cadres talk about it and knew it was in the papers, but they still really didn't know what it was."[56] Finally, peasants in one village felt that since they were not as rich as Dazhai, their financial conditions made it impossible to learn from Dazhai at that time. Only after they reached Dazhai's standard of living could they restrict private plots.[57]

Bureaucratic Interest and Support for Private Plots

Middle-level rural bureaucrats resisted restricting private plots because the unintended policy consequences could complicate county or commune leaders' jobs. County leaders in Guangxi Province rejected a commune official's request to collectivize all private plots; this would have necessitated banning peasants from going to the hills. But since firewood in the hills was the sole source for fueling their stoves, this ban would have generated a county-wide fuel shortage.[58] A commune leader in suburban Nanjing resisted this policy in 1969–1970 because he recalled the lessons of the Great Leap. "In 1958 we took away the private plots and peasants had to eat whatever was served in the dining hall. But people like different things so they really got angry. So in 1969–1970 we learned from the lessons of 1958 and didn't take away their private plots entirely." Clearly the radical pressures were not as great as during the Great Leap.

However, brigade and team leaders opposed this policy for other reasons. Brigade leaders were more vulnerable to pressure from peasants and team leaders whose income deteriorated when private plots were cut back. Personal ties with their neighbors informed brigade leaders of peasant opposition to this policy, increasing the pressure on them to resist it. While one brigade Party secretary, concerned about maintaining his reputation as a good fellow (lao hao ren), ignored outside directives, another rejected a work team's demand that he take away all the principal private plots. Why had he not listened to the work team? "We are basically peasants as well," he explained. "We understand peasants, the bitterness they have had to eat. But city people don't know peasants. They simply follow rules."[59]

With access to county-level information, brigade secretaries knew whether a policy was authorized by higher levels and if there was elite opposition to it. One fellow resisted the restrictions on private plots because he had insider information.

> In May 1976 we saw that other brigades had not done it, so we objected because we didn't want to do it. The city at that time sent out a work team to [a certain] commune to investigate this policy. They [the city] thought that it was incorrect. Our brigade has one person who works in the county, and he took part in the work team. He told us that the city thought that it was wrong, so we held off.[60]

Opposition from above decreased the risk of delaying implementation, because the policy would probably blow by.

If it was the county that initiated the policy, brigade secretaries had a measure of distance from it originators. Brigade secretaries met county leaders face to face infrequently, so they avoided the pressures confronting commune leaders. And without county or commune work teams to monitor implementation, brigade officials were cushioned by one level from the watchful eye of the county officials. Because of local pressure, access to information, and its unique position in the rural bureaucracy, the brigade became the strategic level for evading or altering this policy.

Team leaders, who also had dual attitudes towards the policy, experienced stronger pressures from below. Team leaders had private plots; restricting everyone else's meant restricting their own. Thus they often preferred to avoid total restrictions. In the late 1960s, team leaders in a village in Yan'an District resisted collectivizing private plots because their family income depended greatly on them. While "at first the team leaders agreed with the upper levels," their support for the policy was not strong.

> Their families . . . could get more money from their private plots so they didn't want to lose them either . . . The team leader . . . opposed this policy because he had the biggest family which was the largest lineage in the village, so they had the most plots. In the team meeting he presented the brigade's case and then told people that he opposed the policy.[61]

Following his report on local opposition, the county limited only the size of the private plots but did not collectivize them. Similarly, an assistant team leader in Guangdong Province, whose family was larger than average and made a lot of money from the private plot, opposed the team and brigade leaders' decision to move the peasants' private plots from more to less fertile soil.[62]

Team leaders were also dreadfully aware of the importance of private plots to team members' incomes. Given that only an immense investment of collective labor could even begin to improve per capita income, team leaders favored increasing the peasant's freedom to pursue wealth privately. One team leader outlined the relationship between overdrawn households and the need for private plots.[63] Without private plots, he argued, these households' demands on the team would have been immense; with them, peasants could grow grain in their private plots and therefore not borrow from the team. Only resolving the problem of overdrawn households in 1969 permitted the team to restrict private plots the following year.

A brigade secretary explained why one team leader had opposed restricting private plots in 1968:

The leader of Team 1 opposed the policy, saying that the *Sixty Articles* had stipulated that private plots would be safe for thirty years. His peasants were really angry but in the end he had to follow the policy . . . Team 1 was in the hills. Their collective was poor. They relied on private plots to supplement their livelihood. They grew grain in their private plots to supplement their food supply. After this their livelihood suffered. They also often had gone to the forests to cut firewood to sell.[64]

When peasant income dropped in a team which had collectivized private plots, a leader in a neighboring team did not introduce the policy in his own team the following year.

We saw that peasants in the next team did not have enough ration grain, that they sold too much to the state and that they had to use their own money to buy grain. But in our team where private plots had not changed, we got 10 kg. less per person than them but were not short of grain. We discovered that this was because we had the private plots as a supplement. Peasants in our unit grew grain and vegetables in the private plots. So team members and leaders were unwilling to change.[65]

Team leaders also feared violent confrontations if they uprooted crops already in the ground. In Zhejiang Province a team leader told his brigade secretary he would restrict the marginal plots, but he never did it because "It would have been very hard to pull out the plants that were already in the ground. We live with these people; it would have been hard to continue our face to face relations with them if we simply ignored all the hard work they put into this."[66] In another location the brigade Party secretary, knowing that team leaders could not do this in their own villages, forced them to pull up crops in neighboring villages. A team leader in that brigade was convinced the peasants would have cursed him.

I was afraid, so I didn't do it. I told the secretary that if he wanted it done, he could do it. I wouldn't. He came to see if we had done it, but he didn't dare do it either . . . I told the upper levels that if they wanted to criticize me that was okay. I wouldn't object . . . They couldn't beat me for not pulling up the crops, but if I pulled up the private plots the peasants could. At that time I saw that the peasants wanted to beat other cadres, so I wouldn't do it.[67]

Negotiations and Evasion at the Village Level

While radical winds and local interests pressured middle- and local-level cadres to demonstrate support for limiting peasants' capitalist tendencies, resistance was also significant, placing local actors in a bind. Private plots were important for the livelihood of many peasants and team leaders. Brigade officials, entwined in personal relationships with their neighbors, hesitated to implement certain restrictions when confronted by significant peasant opposition. And in numerous cases, because the issue affected their economic interests, peasants articulated their positions on it.[68] So how did each resolve his own needs and still protect himself from the political dangers of resisting a radical policy?

Local bureaucrats had five options: (1) ignore peasant protests and carry out the policy; (2) change the policy's content; (3) enforce the policy but minimize conflict with the peasants; (4) negotiate with the peasants; and (5) evade the policy. Although the outcomes of several of these strategies were the same—the private plots were in part restricted—the dynamic of the process varied, showing that most local cadres felt it necessary to respond to peasant interests in some meaningful way. In the first instance, decisions were made unilaterally; peasant complaints were ignored once the decision was made. However, in most instances, once the cadres decided to respond to this policy wind, the way they restricted the private plots resulted in part from the expressed or anticipated concerns of the peasants, thereby undermining the radicals' goal of totally eradicating peasant ties to private land.

The Authoritarian Response

When external political pressures were great or when local cadres were totally self-interested—either because of strong leftist predilections or desires to prove their "redness"—peasants' objections were ignored, and they were forced to accede to the restriction of their private plots.

In the radical days of fall 1969, at the height of the Three Loyalties Campaign and the One Hit, Three Antis Campaign, a production team leader decided to make his unit the brigade model in Learning from Dazhai.[69] For one year the entire brigade had been a test point for raising grain output, so the brigade Party secretary wanted to increase this unit's grain output as well. In response, the team leader decided to relocate his team's lakeside principal private plots into the hills and use the fertile land for cultivating collective grain. The village's political climate had been intense, with meetings occurring as often as four times a week. The brigade secretary, who was quite radical and very concerned about the collective, was feared by the peasants. Under his heavy-handed rule peasants had toiled in the hills, building Dazhai-type terraced fields. The number of political activists was also high, and a few, hoping to make the grade to political models, donated their private plots to the collective and opened new land in the hills.

About 30 percent of team members had private plots by the lake, so the team leader approached them individually, asking them to give the land to the collective. Yet for many families private plots were their only source of sugar, cooking oil, and vegetables, as well as fodder for their pigs. Years of hard work had made the land quite fertile, so most families resisted these initial pressures. After a month the holdouts were called in for individual meetings with team and brigade officials. Although peasants fear confrontations with political authorities, it took an average of three to four meetings, and in some cases six meetings, before the peasants acceded to these demands. While cadres called on peasants to learn from Dazhai, love the state, the collective, and Chairman Mao, most peasants saw the issue in personal economic terms. Two team cadres, who had worked long and hard on their plots, also felt it unfair to take the peasants' land. Knowing that the policy initiative was local, not national, the peasants resolved to resist cadre pressures. But two weeks of intense face to face confrontations forced all households to give in. The land reverted to the collective, and in the elections the following year the brigade rejected the nomination of the two dissenting cadres.

Although private plots had not been crucial for peasant welfare— a workpoint was worth over one *yuan* per day and many peasants received overseas remittances—they did make life more enjoyable. Peasants had also labored hard to improve the quality of their plots and fought to keep them. Still, local cadres, having decided to collectivize this land, refused to budge and buoyed by both a national and local radical environment pressured peasants to accept the cadres' decision.

Changing Policy Content

A common response to upper level pressures was to change the policy's content. This action could entail collectivizing less land than the upper levels demanded, collectivizing land other than the principal plots as a symbolic gesture, or collectivizing principal plots while allowing peasants to farm their own section of the now collectivized fields.

In two communes in Jurong County, Jiangsu Province, where private plots and work on them were collectivized, peasants still tended the original plots and received their output.

The fields, made up of small pieces of land in and around the larger collective fields in the hills, were basically worked collectively. The water was carried by everyone, collectively. The team took one day in the particular season to work the private plots. The team gave the seedlings for rice that were to be transplanted . . . Water, seeds, everything was collective. Time also was collective time. The private plot was planted only in rice or wheat, as were the collective fields, so we could work together on the private fields.

And while higher-level cadres driving along would see people working collectively on their land, each peasant "received the harvest from that part of the collective private plot that had originally been theirs. Essentially, the harvest belonged to individuals and the work was done collectively (*shouhuo gui geren, gongzuo wei jiti*)."[70] This way cadres ensured that all peasants grew grain in their private plots.

In Jiangpu County, Jiangsu Province, a leftist county Party secretary had limited household yard plots to 3.3 meters in both their front and back yards. But according to a commune leader in rural Nanjing, he and his associates "expanded the area. They [the county] wanted a one-to-one ratio, but we made it two-to-one. We also knew that [one particular brigade] did not do it well, but forget it. You open one eye and you close the other." Similarly, in 1968 officials in one of the poorest brigades in this commune had refused to limit private plots to .04 *mu*, as the commune had requested. Because private plots were crucial to a few teams, the secretary decided that a shift from .2 to .08 *mu* sufficed. Although commune officials were displeased, brigade leaders waited until the wind passed several months later and the external pressure decreased.

In some areas local cadres responded to pressures to restrict principal private plots by curtailing marginal plots, thereby demonstrating support for the policy wind. One brigade official outside Nanjing claimed to have resisted pressures in 1968–1969 for collectivizing private plots.

The work team stayed one year. They told us to take in the private plots, but we didn't do it. We took away marginal land, although after a while peasants planted it again. We knew, but the work team didn't. Also, we knew the peasants wouldn't like the restrictions on their private plots so we decided to take away .2 *mu* of land and leave everyone .1 *mu*. This way everyone was satisfied . . . We knew it would be acceptable. Everyone was willing to concede a little.

Conflict Avoidance

A third strategy involved avoiding conflict with the peasants, either by warning them of the impending policy, so they did not plant anything in their plots, or letting them harvest crops in the plots before collectivizing or restricting them. To ensure enough time to warn the peasants, the policy had to filter down slowly through the bureaucracy; but if the policy was a local initiative, sufficient time was not always available. In a brigade in Sichuan Province, 170 miles east of Chongqing, peasants had been cultivating marginal plots for several years. In 1973 the county or province decided to cut back on these plots. In summer 1973 the villagers were warned that come fall, marginal land would be collectivized. So after the summer harvest they let the plots lie fallow. In the fall, when the brigade secretary announced that the county wanted to limit "indiscriminate cultivation of waste land" (luan kai huangdi), no one complained.[71] An uncomfortable face-to-face confrontation over uprooting crops was avoided. Alternatively, some cadres let peasants harvest their plots before collectivizing them,[72] while others undercut peasant hostility by financially compensating them for crops still in the ground. Nevertheless, because the simplest way to avoid interpersonal conflicts was to implement the policy before peasants prepared for the next sowing, properly timing policy initiation, not just enforcing policy compliance, affected the success of the restrictions.

Negotiations

A common strategy was to negotiate with the peasants, seeking an outcome that was acceptable to both sides. While making concessions to peasant interests, local cadres could implement the policy and protect themselves from political recriminations. The outcome, however, undercut the goals of agrarian radicalism. In spring 1973, at a time of relative political quietude, a team in Qingyuan County, Guangdong Province, was ordered to increase its rice acreage.[73] Local leaders decided to halve the principal private plots and told the peasants of this decision at a meeting 20 days before spring planting. The peasants voiced no objections at the meeting but afterwards grumbled that the new plots were too small; not only did peasants raise fodder in these plots, but many men grew their own tobacco. That night many peasants went to the homes of team management committee members to complain about the loss of land and tobacco.

The team leader, who smoked, also favored a compromise, so within a few days about 20 people, including the management committee and some peasant representatives, met to discuss the problem. They still collectivized the private plots but peasants who smoked were allowed to clear .1 mu of hilly land for tobacco. A notice outside team headquarters told peasants which land could be cleared. Cognizant that the collective needed more grain—pressures to "take grain as the key link" had been intense in Guangdong Province in the early 1970s—peasants accepted this compromise, especially since the ones who smoked ended up with enlarged private plots. Moreover, collectivizing private plots to increase grain output occurred county-wide, so other team members could not complain either.[74]

Although the county issued the directive for increasing grain output, the political environment had not been intense. Demands for policy compliance, especially on grain policy, were fewer in 1973 than in the late 1960s. By articulating their interests outside the formal setting of the meeting and expressing only economic concerns, peasants avoided making it a political issue. Still, the policy was carried out. Perhaps because the policy's specific goal had been to produce more grain rather than restrict private plots, local leaders had been so willing to compromise.

The above negotiations were hardly a unique event. In spring 1973 a team in Jilin Province was informed that their private plots were to be cut back, making them the same size as in neighboring communes.[75] Concurrently, private plots were relocated, and the fertile land reverted to the collective. The peasants were also prohibited from growing cash crops in their yards. Since cash from private plots paid for marriages, new homes, and other expenses, some people spoke up at the meeting, particularly those who had larger plots. Still, they criticized the policy in economic terms, arguing that the collective already supplied too little grain and vegetables; without private plots life would get even more difficult.

The political team leader, a leftist, as well as local activists, Party members, and the resettled urban youth all supported the policy. The educated youth tried to persuade the peasants that they had to overcome their private viewpoint (*si you guan*) and bourgeois tendencies. But support for the restriction was limited. No national or local campaign generated a radical environment, and at least 70 percent of the peasants opposed the policy, while the other 30 percent did not care. Other team officials as well, including the team manager, opposed narrowing the plots. So a deal was struck. They decreased the size of the principal plots, which helped local officials avoid trouble with their superiors, but expanded the team's vegetable plot, and with it the peasants' vegetable supply. However, the following year the team planted melons in the vegetable plot, which they marketed. In the commune's eyes, a marketable surplus proved that the vegetable plot was larger than necessary, so the commune reduced it to the same size it had been before the restriction of the private plots.

Policy Evasion

Finally, some local cadres tried to evade restrictions entirely by implementing the form rather than the essence of the policy, creating the appearance of implementation while avoiding the deed for as long as possible. This is how in 1976 a brigade secretary in Jiangpu County, Jiangsu Province avoided collectivizing private tree seedlings and cutting back on the size of yard land. Aware that the policy was the idea of a leftist county secretary, who himself was responding to the intense political conflicts ensuing in Beijing in summer 1976, the brigade leader suspected that this local policy wind would blow by. Yet he protected himself by counting the trees, measuring the land, and reporting his progress at commune meetings. But he never collectivized the trees, never paid for them, and never narrowed the yard land. According to him, "we told the commune we had measured the area and had figured out how much to pay, but they never specifically asked if we did it." The commune secretary reported to the county that restrictions were proceeding smoothly, so he was safe. The peasants' and teams' economic interests were also protected. "It was crazy. It would have cost us 2,000 *yuan* to buy one team's trees, while for the whole brigade it would have cost us 20,000 *yuan*." When the policy was dropped several months later, things returned to normal.

This brigade secretary, a self-confessed rightist, who always favored the peasants' and his collective's interests over radical pressures and state interests, explained his behavior. "We listen a little more to the masses in our brigade. We look after their interest. We are a little to the right (*you qing*). It is partly due to being poorer."[76] Other brigades, however, whose leaders had been more responsive to the wind, lost a great deal of money. According to one leftist leader, no one cared for the trees after they were collectivized. Peasants wanted to be paid for the trees and for taking care of what had become collective property. "The trees died from drought and young children broke off branches. The loss was big. We gave the trees back one year later, and the teams had to pay for the loss. In [another brigade] they moved many of the trees, cut down others and the collective paid for all this itself. They then had to give the wood to the peasants so the collective loss was great."[77] While this official had implemented the policy, the former one had evaded it owing to the policy's high cost, the strength of local opposition, his natural tendency to protect peasant interests, and the fact that the wind might be short-lived. Yet had the pressure intensified, he was prepared to implement the policy immediately.

Conclusion

From 1960 on, peasants in many areas and local supporters of this radical policy were locked in a head-to-head battle over the control of land and private plots. And although they lacked sufficient central power to make it a formal policy, the radicals kept this issue very much alive at the local level. In 1968–1970, private plots in many parts of China were collectivized; in 1973–1974, marginal plots and opened barren land returned to collective control; and in 1975–1977, wealthier peasants were often prohibited from growing cash crops in their household plots.

Yet some peasants used every respite from radicalism to open barren land and marginal plots, or expand and secure their household yards. Even support from various sectors of the peasantry and local officialdom could not ensure the success of this radical policy; conversely, the lack of opportunity to market what was produced in the private plots did not deter the desire for private land. The average rural leader who implemented the policy to protect himself and his job, and who was concerned about his own and the peasants' economic interests, often had room to maneuver, particularly during less radical periods. Through a variety of stratagems, including diluting the policy's content, evading the wind entirely, or negotiating compromise solutions with peasants, leaders below the commune level responded to peasant opposition, undermined the radicals' policy goal, and helped maintain the peasants' tie to private land.

Following the 1978 Third Plenum, private control of land re-turned in force as did the opportunity to market its produce. Peasants again opened large tracts of barren land and some older peasants began to work full time on their private plots. By 1981 a team could divide 15 percent of its land for private plots, and combined with barren land, some peasants were farming as much private land as they had following Land Reform. When the introduction of house-hold contracts was completed in 1983, peasants had more control over larger tracts of land than at any time since before the cooperative movement of 1955. Agrarian radicalism had clearly failed to destroy the system of private plots in China and the peasants' tie to private property.

7

RESOURCE EXPROPRIATION
AND EQUALIZATION

DURING THE RADICAL decade rural officials, particularly commune and county cadres, used the opportunities generated by radical winds and the authority derived from their Party posts to transfer wealth, property, and labor from one unit to another. Through this process, cadres expropriated the resources of lower level units to strengthen their own bureaucratic sinecure and its political economy—their base of power and authority. The fusion of political and economic power in the rural bureaucracy, the lack of private property and clearly legislated property rights, and the historical tradition whereby the state expropriated the property of entrepreneurs, all facilitated this phenomenon. Although this policy, widespread during the Great Leap, was criticized by Mao in 1959 and in the 1962 *Sixty Articles*, rural officials did this frequently from 1968 to 1978 so that by the end of the radical era many county, commune, and brigade officials were in a far more powerful position than they had been ten years before.[1]

During the radical decade national elites demanded that localities mobilize peasant labor for massive farmland and water conservation projects. But rather than pay the peasants for their efforts, the state called on them to demonstrate a "communist spirit" and "mutual assistance" for neighboring units. These slogans, and the radical era's emphasis on greater equality, facilitated these transfers. Finally, the tenor of the times—its heavy ideological content and constant pressures to organize labor mobilization campaigns—heightened the cost of resistance. Under these circumstances, cadres could take resources with limited overt opposition.

This process, which the Chinese call "equalization and transfer" (*ping diao*), refers to the equalization of wealth among different units at the same level of the rural organizational structure—particularly brigades and communes—and the expropriation or transfer of resources, including labor, money, and machinery from teams and brigades to commune and county levels without fair compensation. While most team leaders and peasants did not oppose resource transfers among production teams, they deeply resented transfers across brigade lines, or up to the commune and county level. Still, brigade expropriation of team resources, which occurred mostly in 1968–1971, falls under the rubric of equalization and transfer.

The Nature of Equalization and Transfer

Generating the Wind

The impetus for equalization and transfer came less from Beijing than from commune and county cadres. Central supporters of radical policies never advocated this method to increase inter-unit equality, carry out inter-unit exchange, or strengthen the collective economy; but their desire to narrow inter-unit inequality, increase peasant concerns for the larger collective, and strengthen the collective economy at and above the brigade contributed to this phenomenon. More important, by invoking egalitarian slogans, by generating a massive mobilization of peasant labor—the so-called "high tides"— for field and water conservation projects, and by making participation in those projects a political issue, national leaders gave further impetus to this policy outcome.[2]

Demands for mobilizing high tides of rural capital construction work and the egalitarian messages filtering down from the center struck a responsive chord at the upper levels of the rural bureaucracy, as county and commune cadres used these opportunities to promote their own interests and initiate an even more radical policy. They manipulated calls to display a communist spirit during these projects to blow a "communist wind" of expropriation and egalitarianism as they had during the Great Leap.[3] This phenomenon occurred in Guangdong Province, where cadres were criticized for believing that only through "egalitarianism and indiscriminate requisitioning" could farmland capital construction work be carried out "in a big way."[4] And while Guangdong Province supported "cooperative projects" and the "communist style" (gongchanzhuyi fengge), a book published in 1979 argued that "we must never allow the idea of cooperation to be used to blow a 'communist wind'."[5]

Yet that is precisely what rural cadres throughout China did. They argued that transferring resources was in line with national goals of increasing inter-unit equality and strengthening the collective. They criticized peasants and team leaders who resisted the expropriation of their labor, capital, grain, or machinery for not demonstrating a communist spirit of concern for the greater collective good. They used coercion and Party pressures to silence opposition and mobilize immense amounts of resources for these projects. Once mobilized, the resources fell under their control, and they dictated how and where the resources were used. Even cadres who felt uncomfortable stealing from peasants were forced by grossly inflated quotas to use peasant labor without proper compensation. And although their teams' collective economy was the major loser, team leaders and peasants could not halt the process, even when they suffered a financial loss.

Labor Expropriation and the Creation of Rural Wealth

In a resource-poor society such as China, where capital for expanding collective wealth is limited, competition for control of labor among peasants, various levels of the state, and the collective bureaucracy was intense. Since rural China had received little state funding for decades,[6] labor was the most important resource for expanding the household or collective economy. Whoever controlled labor wielded real power, so the most critical resource rural cadres expropriated was the peasants' labor time.

By participating in collective projects, peasants "objectified" their "living labor" in agricultural land.[7] At little financial cost to the collective or the state, these projects increased crop output by reducing the probability of natural disasters and by improving conditions for introducing modern inputs.[8] Although peasants probably prefered to relax during the winter, produce marketable commodities at home, or do other work around their houses, Chinese leaders wanted to create more rural value—higher outputs, new factories, better roads—by mobilizing the peasants to work.

Hence a struggle ensued over the control of peasant labor. The *Sixty Articles* stipulated that peasants contribute 3 to 5 percent of their "basic labor days" to the collective in the form of unpaid or "obligatory" labor (*yiwu gong*), and for additional work peasants were to receive workpoints and a grain supplement while on the job site. Unless a team received payment or benefits for participating in a project, the extra workpoints paid to the peasants merely deflated the value of each workpoint, since the labor added nothing to the team's collective income. To the extent that this labor was then used to benefit levels other than the team, time and labor that could have been used for developing the team's economy paid for the expansion of the commune's wealth and its leader's power.

Two Types of Expropriations

In response to the Great Leap Forward's communist wind of equalization and transfer, the State Council stipulated that no inter-unit cooperation or labor allocation could occur without proper compensation.[9] Mao had complained that "those who 'blew a commmunist wind' were primarily county- and commune-level cadres, especially commune cadres who extorted things from production brigades and teams," and that local cadres "mistook collective ownership for ownership of the whole people."[10] The two types of expropriations that occurred during the Great Leap were: (1) "equalization"—the uncompensated movement of labor, money, or material among units at the same bureaucratic level; and (2) "transfer"—the uncompensated expropriation of lower level labor, money, or material by higher levels in the rural bureaucracy.

Responding to these problems, the 1962 *Sixty Articles* stipulated that all communes must manage inter-unit cooperation "in line with the principles of voluntariness and mutual benefit, as well as of exchange at equal value." Commune leaders were "prohibited to [sic] commandeer labor force, capital goods, or materials without compensation."[11] These key guidelines—voluntariness, mutual benefit, and equal exchange—were to govern all exchanges among rural collectives and between lower and higher levels of the rural bureaucracy. Peasants could refuse to work in unfair projects, join more willingly and with more enthusiasm in projects that were to their benefit, and still privately increase household incomes through sidelines and private plots. Moderate elites were convinced that without the right to refuse to work in projects that were not to their benefit, peasants would not participate willingly in future projects.[12]

Throughout the 1960s and 1970s, some commune officials responsible for field and water work tried to follow the guidelines and maintain good relations with local cadres and peasants, all the while expanding the scope of irrigated land by leveling fields, building reservoirs and dikes, and installing pipes. Some consulted and negotiated with brigade and team leaders before starting a new project. But the high tides in rural capital construction generated by inflated output quotas—measured by the amount of cubic metres of earth moved—made it almost impossible for middle-level cadres to follow these guidelines. According to Nickum, "a strict adherence to exchange at equivalent values has a dampening effect on inter-unit projects. One common reaction by higher administrative levels during times of 'upsurge' is to ignore the provision and to engage in 'equalization and transfer,' a 'leftist' error involving the unrequited transfer of resources from the haves to the have-nots."[13]

Exchanges of capital, material, and labor among units at the same level in the rural hierarchy, for which beneficiaries did not make a fair payment, occurred primarily during the first radical period of 1968–

1971, especially during Lin Biao's "flying leap" in winter 1969–1970. Of 12 criticisms of equalization and transfer in *People's Daily* in 1972–1973, nine referred to labor expropriation. This form of equalization occurred when projects were organized on so large a scale, and labor was mobilized from so many teams, that it was difficult to ensure mutual benefits for all teams from every project.[14]

A second type of equalization and transfer, motivated by cadre self-interest, involved transferring labor, capital, or material from teams or brigades to higher levels in the bureaucracy or the state. Peasants could be forced to build county or commune factories, but their teams received no compensation for the labor. A brigade might take over a successful factory built by a production team, or the county could impose a grain tax on teams and use that grain as the peasants' food supplement for participating in the project.[15] This way rural leaders expanded the resources they controlled or made teams contribute to field construction projects. By the late 1970s, the expropriation of money and material had become a major target of criticism (Table 10). In fact, in this later period the term "one equalization and two transfers" (*yi ping er diao*) was changed to "one equalization, two transfers, and three take in money" (*yi ping, er diao, san shou kuan*).[16]

Explaining the Local Response

Systemic Factors

A unit's location and its level of economic development helped determine whether its resources were expropriated. Where people lived affected whether they won or lost in the exchanges of labor. A commune secretary's contention that hilly units more often helped the teams on the plain with the diked fields was corroborated by county officials.[17] Fertile hilly areas which experienced rapid population growth had excess labor that could be mobilized for dike building and land leveling in the flatter plain areas.[18] As one brigade secretary

Table 10. References to equalization and transfer in the *People's Daily*, 1978.

Level criticized	Resource affected				
	Labor	Money	Material	No Data	Total
Brigade	3	3	3	0	9
Commune	5	6	6	0	17
County	5	7	3	1	16
District	2	1	2	0	5
Unclear	1	4	3	0	8
Total	16	21	17	1	55

remarked, "generally people go to the hilly areas [to get labor] because they have little land and lots of labor."[19]

Because middle-level cadres usually stuck to main roads on inspection tours, units away from the main roads were less likely to have their land leveled than units beside well-travelled ones. Furthermore, the need to create models and demonstrate a positive attitude towards rural capital construction projects and economic development made local officials favor land leveling where it was visible to all, rather than in distant, and often more needy, hilly areas. In a commune in Jiangpu County, all teams worked for free to "beautify" the land paralleling the main road running from the commune headquarters to the county seat.[20] A team leader in a brigade in rural Nanjing described a similar pattern: "Before there was no road to this village so when outside officials came to see the brigade they didn't come here to see us. Therefore the brigade leveled the land down by the road first. To level the land up here would have involved building terraced fields, but they are very expensive. We can't do it on our own, but we get no extra money from the brigade." And although the brigade built viaducts into the hills, it also leveled the land beside them. Since these irrigation canals traversed the plain for over a mile before rising into the hills, the land lower down was leveled first; but before the terracing could occur large projects were banned.[21] Xiyang County also spent much money fixing the road from the county seat to Dazhai and improving the units beside it.[22]

Because Dazhai had become famous for terracing its hills, the Dazhai movement made some hilly units the local focus of labor mobilization campaigns. A model brigade in Fujian Province was the beneficiary of commune-wide financial and labor assistance because, like Dazhai, it was in the hills.[23] But because terracing fields was so expensive and the returns were often limited, many communes gave all their assistance to one Dazhai model, leaving other hilly units to fend for themselves.

The province, district, or county where a unit was located affected the quantity of terraced fields that were constructed. One would expect that most such work was done in Shanxi, where the Dazhai campaign's influence was strongest. Similarly, Xiangtan District, Hunan Province, where Hua Guofeng had ruled, was a likely place for massive projects. In Jiangsu Province, where irrigation is critical, provincial leaders also strongly supported such projects.

Proximity to the brigade or commune headquarters increased the likelihood that a unit's resources would be expropriated. The closest brigade to a commune seat in Jiangpu County lost more land to the state and collective than any other brigade, both during the Great

Leap—when the commune gave collective land to the state-run tree farm and built a new reservoir—and in the 1960s and 1970s, when it built new factories on brigade land. Such events probably occurred nation-wide during both periods.

A unit's level of economic development also helps explain whether it was the victim of this policy wind. Equalization and transfer appears to have helped poorer teams, especially during brigade-run projects. In winter, a brigade secretary in suburban Nanjing used slack labor from the wealthier teams to help the poorer teams for several years. This wealthy brigade in turn assisted a poorer neighboring brigade, and the commune never intended that it should be repaid. In another Nanjing commune, stronger and richer teams received extra work during the second year of a dike-building project. Of 17 cases of equalization and transfer compiled in 1980–1981 from interviews and research in China, nine involved special help for poorer teams that was not repaid. Only three cases benefited rich teams unfairly. Brigade-organized mutual aid projects often benefited poor teams that were unable to complete their work, while outcomes of commune-run projects were more mixed.

The politics of the radical era precipitated this situation. A Nanjing brigade secretary, criticized by several villages during the early part of the Cultural Revolution for ignoring their economic development, organized major projects to help them from 1968 to 1972, after he returned to power. After 1974, when cadres needed to demonstrate high growth rates, poor teams with economic potential became good targets for collective-managed projects since they could yield high short-term improvements. Finally, the ideological emphasis on helping the poor catch up, which began in 1974 and continued during the 1975–1977 Xiyang County Movement, persuaded some brigades to give free labor assistance to their poorer neighbors.

After Hua Guofeng's September 1975 call on counties to help poor brigades catch up to average brigades in each county,[24] peasants in a wealthy brigade of approximately 3,000 people outside Jinan, in Shandong Province, reportedly "donated" 60,000 labor days in 1976, 30,000 days in 1977, and in 1978 planned to donate 10,000 days of work in poor neighboring brigades—all for free.[25] A brigade outside Qingdao, Shandong Province, gave "half conditional aid"; short-term assistance was for free, but if the period of assistance stretched out close to one year, they accepted repayment at slightly below the value of a work day in the unit they were helping. Rich units outside Shanghai also were repaid at less than the value of a workpoint in the benefiting unit, but commune officials stressed that their assistance was never for free.

Wealthy units were also the best target for county and commune leaders who expropriated peasant wealth in order to strengthen their own economies. They were often the only units who had resources to steal. When a commune in Qidong County, Jiangsu Province, responded to a county directive and paid back funds it had expropriated, it returned funds only to those in economic trouble, leaving the wealthier teams to carry the burden of expanding the commune's economy.[26]

Overall, radical policies of cooperation probably favored poorer teams. Undoubtedly it happened that when hilly teams helped valley teams fix dikes and level land, the poorer gave up opportunity costs and helped the richer teams. And when rich model units became the site of large construction projects, the rich got richer.[27] However, many policies favored helping poorer units, and if more than lip service was involved, they must have benefited.

Team Leaders' Attitudes

Team leaders most strongly opposed equalization and transfer because their units paid most heavily for them. The projects were often without benefits to the team's economy or productivity: its collective income did not increase, but the increased number of workpoints decreased each workpoint's value, suggesting to the peasants that team welfare was declining. A leader whose team's workpoint value dropped was rarely popular. Also, a team leader's personal income depended on team output; using team labor to benefit others hurt his income as well. Yet while team leaders were responsible for prodding peasants to participate in often unpopular projects, they, of all rural officials, had the least influence on this policy.

Team leaders resented the financial burdens imposed on their unit by these projects.

> In 1976 we sent many people to work on Xiaoxingwei . . . We lived and ate there. We paid 2,000 workpoints for that job. The food was paid by the team as well as the oil for cooking it and the grain. It was a big burden for us. The commune did not give us money for the earth that we moved . . . The problem was that for the units who did not benefit, there was no reward . . . We were poor before, and we spent too many workpoints. We have to be repaid. But for a team that does not benefit from the project and which does not get any payment, that is equalization and transfer.[28]

Another team leader, aware that paying workpoints hurt his team's economy, agreed that "when the team gives workpoints, the team is then the loser (*daomeile*). But if peasants don't get workpoints, they won't go." A team leader blamed commune-organized projects for taking too much labor, leaving his team no time for its own work. "The years that we spent building Xiaoxingwei meant that we couldn't level our own land. If not for that project, we would have finished much earlier." Another team leader, whose unit was the farthest in the brigade from the site of the reservoir, planned to send only a small work force—leaving time to dig their own pond—until he was admonished that "no one should place his own interest above the joint undertaking, because without everyone's help the project could not be completed." Some team leaders were upset even when they sent only one or two workers.[29]

Leaders in teams which relied on their peasants getting employment outside the collective to bolster the team's economy opposed labor expropriation. The quota of earth a team had to move depended in part or totally on the number of people eating collective grain. Since outside workers contributed to the collective's accumulation fund in return for cheap collective grain, they were included in the calculations determining team quotas.[30] But if they did not return to participate in the project, peasants in their teams would receive larger tasks than peasants whose teams had no outside workers. Team leaders then confronted a serious dilemma: force outside workers to return and lose their contributions to the collective, or let them work outside but face the wrath of the peasants whose tasks would be bigger. Also, to teams with many outside laborers it made a difference whether the calculations for quotas included the land to labor ratio or just the population. A team with little land but a large population, with many people working outside during the winter, resented commune projects which allocated the quotas only according to population. Their team's task would shrink if the land to labor ratio was also considered. One team which confronted this dilemma— quotas were based completely on population—argued with their leaders. But only in 1977 did the brigade switch to a ratio of people per *mu*. And although for many years they said that they would not participate, "we had no way of avoiding going . . . the commune gives tasks to the brigade, and they give us the task, so we had to do it well. If you didn't finish, you couldn't go home, and this would hurt our production. So we had to pull out entire families to go to the work site to get the job done."[31] With little land and a large population, they depended on outside work. Yet because tasks were divided solely on the basis of population, they had a bigger task than most other teams.[32]

Team leaders resented it when communes expropriated their land for commune enterprises. When a Nanjing commune built a brick kiln, several teams had to sell land to it. Although the commune agreed to employ some peasants in the kiln, based on the amount of land taken, one leader complained that his team had too few peasants even before the land was sold. Sending workers to the factory only aggravated their labor shortage. Team leaders also resented the lack of mutual benefits from larger projects. During the 1950s, as well as the 1960s and 1970s, when mutual aid teams or production teams exchanged labor and resources on their own, lack of reciprocity ended all inter-unit cooperation.[33] Without outside efforts, projects without mutual benefits would not have occurred. In a brigade in Jiangpu County, team leaders refused to work with one team leader who, they claimed, never reciprocated or shared with other teams.

Some team leaders demonstrated a form of "communist spirit" and willingly helped neighbors without repayment, but only for short-term assistance. In two cases, well-organized, well-disciplined teams sent hard-working, politically active peasants. As one informant suggested, "they sent the people with Dazhai spirit." In suburban Nanjing, southside leaders helped their poorer neighbors in the north for several years. Only after their villagers complained that this work prevented improvements in their own teams did leaders in the prosperous teams complain as well.[34]

Finally, only leaders in teams with chronic problems and deep-seated poverty supported inequitable exchanges. Leaders of poor teams in suburban Nanjing were pleased that the southside teams' help improved their standard of living, but they were intent on repaying them when the work finally shifted south.

Therefore, while beneficiaries of inter-team equalization supported this policy, and while short-term assistance generated less hostility than long-term mutual aid projects, team leaders unanimously opposed commune- and county-run projects. Their teams rarely benefited or received fair compensation; yet they had to pay workpoints which influenced the peasants' evaluation of their job performance. In the short run they could not always see how a project several miles down the road could help their team, yet these outside obligations forced them to shelve their own projects. Team leaders resented the establishment of commune enterprises on their land even when they were compensated for it. When they were not repaid, and the commune officials merely used their political power to expropriate the land, the hostility increased. Yet they could do little in the face of commune pressures on any of these issues. As one leader explained: "We had no way out. The commune Party committee put out a call. We had complaints about it. We were busy planting the wheat, so sending our own people was not good."[35] In the end, he sent people to participate.

Peasant Attitudes

Peasant attitudes towards conservation projects and labor expropriation were more complex than one might have expected. Strong oppposition arose because these projects cut into peasant sideline activities and leisure time.[36] As an informant from Jiangsu Province complained, "just when they should have had a little rest, it suddenly became busy."[37] Peasants with young children resented these projects because it often meant long walks home at lunchtime to feed their children. As one cadre recalled, those "who complained about this [project] had household work to do or children to take care of."[38] Young people who had not experienced the difficulties of rural life were less willing to help their poorer neighbors, while even those more willing to help could not maintain their support as the unrepaid assistance continued year after year.

Some peasants recognized that free labor on commune projects harmed their team's collective income, and even if they received workpoints, their household income might not increase. So peasants generally opposed commune projects, preferring county projects which paid money according to the amount of earth moved. When teams did not benefit, some peasants refused to work on a county-run project, while others simply did not work well.[39]

Still, some peasants willingly participated in these projects. A team leader recalled that peasants in his village did not complain about briefly helping a neighboring unit for free, but "only criticized the poor team for not getting its work done." Why did they help? "They saw that the soil was not producing anything, so they felt the need to help. It hurt their heart to see this situation."[40] Older people were most willing to help, as well as "energetic ones [who] had worked well at home and had done a good job organizing their own production."[41] Young peasants joined county projects principally for the extra money. During the radical years, when private economic activity was restricted, construction work was often the only way to expand household income. Large families in areas where household sidelines were sharply restricted were especially likely to send their children to participate in these projects. The grain supplement was also an attraction in poor areas.[42] Young bachelors who wanted to have a good time, escape their immediate surroundings, meet new people, make some extra money, or even look for a wife were most willing to go.[43]

Some peasants may have been extremely calculating. With little money to be made at home during the winter, peasants may have seen winter projects as a way to increase their share of the year-end distribution. Although unrequited projects devalued each workpoint, participating increased a family's share of the total number of workpoints distributed within the team. If only some peasants worked, participants increased their household's share of an unchanged pie. Similarly, peasants supported field and water conservation in areas where the vagaries of nature created yearly output fluctuations and in areas of impending or recent disaster.[44] Peasants received no compensation during emergencies, so they preferred projects which decreased the likelihood of local emergencies and paid workpoints and grain.

Peasants who opposed a project were usually forced to participate anyway. In the late 1960s, a team in Yunnan Province sent 10 percent of its labor, even though "people in our unit, which did not benefit from the road, didn't want to go. But they were afraid that it would show that they were selfish, so they didn't say anything. They didn't want to show that they did not have high political consciousness." They were particularly nervous because "at almost every commune meeting, the Party secretary gave someone a cap."[45] Similarly, a district secretary in Guangdong Province compelled peasants to contribute one *yuan* from their own pockets and work for nothing on a project. To ensure their "willing" participation, work teams placed intense pressure on the peasants, including monitoring their mail to areas outside the county.[46]

Thus individual peasants had financial incentives to participate even in inequitable projects. Some helped in the short run because they abhorred waste; others commiserated with their neighbors' poverty. Such peasants demonstrated what the radicals called fraternal or socialist concern. Young people participated for more selfish reasons, such as adventure and profit. Finally, some peasants wanted to increase their household food supply or income, although it weakened their collective. Most peasants, however, were mildly hostile to these projects, and since open expressions of opposition could generate political problems, they relied on passive resistance.

The Locus of Support

Although strong opposition existed below the brigade level, equalization and transfer meshed with the interests of county, commune, and even brigade officials. Political pressures to fulfill state-imposed quotas (in terms of cubic meters of earth dug), the need to prove that they were following the proper political line, and the desire to build model units led officials to expropriate resources. Some cadres, striving for equality, transferred labor from richer to poorer teams. However, many commune and county officials manipulated the radical environment and the "high tides" in rural capital construction to commandeer team labor, capital, and machinery and expand the collective economy they controlled. Finally, the way tasks and funds for field projects were allocated and the attitudes of rural bureaucrats and peasants support a structural explanation as to why commune leaders were the most common perpetrators of equalization and transfer. As a result, why the reform group's attacked the commune structure in the post-Mao era becomes clearer.

Political Explanations. County cadres generally supported field work, no matter what was involved in ensuring their success. From 1968 through 1972, military officers who controlled many county governments dutifully mobilized high tides in winter field work, demonstrating little concern for production teams, team leaders, or economic outcomes.[47]

To prove their political redness, county and commune officials sometimes expanded projects and cubic meter commitments beyond the quotas passed down by their superiors. According to officials at the Ministry of Water Conservation in Beijing, during the high tide generated by Hua Guofeng's 1976 Second Dazhai Conference, counties increased already excessive provincial demands. Yet 1976 was not unique. In 1970 a county in Guangdong Province increased its quota for cultivating barren land, sorely taxing commune capabilities.[48]

These political pressures led county water conservation officials to downplay inequitable contributions from different localities, calling them "mutual assistance."

> Before 1978 the hilly areas went to help the paddy areas more than the paddy areas helped the hilly areas. In our thoughts it was rather equal but not absolutely equal. If not equal, then it is a question of mutual assistance. This year you go to the paddy to build dikes and next year we go to the hills to build reservoirs. The hilly areas helped the paddy areas more, but we raised the idea of socialist cooperation.[49]

Yet in 1981, after equalization and transfer had been banned, these officials remained committed to organizing rural capital construction even if inequitable labor exchanges occurred. "This type of situation is an example of labor exchange. Only a few years later can you see the equality of it all. We will attempt to prevent equalization and transfer with all our energies, but we will persist in pressing for large scale cooperation." In their world, labor expropriation was part of the daily fare. "Mutual cooperation and equalization and transfer can never be separated (*wang wang bu neng fenkai*)."

Time Constraints. To minimize the effects of winter capital construction on production, cadres were expected to complete projects in one year or during one winter. As time ran short and fears arose that they would not finish, commune and brigade leaders resorted to equalization and transfer to fulfill their obligations. For example:

> In winter 1970, two brigades in Hsiao *Xian*, Anhui Province, began to build a dam and reservoir. Since the project was moving slowly due to a lack of workers, the commune Party committee transferred some 1,000 men from other brigades without either consulting the brigade leadership or giving reasonable remuneration to the production teams that provided the labor. The commune was criticized for not having respected the right of the production teams to make their own decisions and having engaged in "equalization and transfer." In a later project, labor allocations were made according to expected benefit.[50]

A brigade Party secretary recalled a time when in his brigade "needed to plant wheat quickly, so we had to get the project done quickly or it would affect the fall planting . . . But one brigade was not enough to get it done. We needed help."[51] The commune forced neighboring brigades to send laborers to finish the work faster.

Brigade secretaries sent laborers to help team leaders they had placed in power and to ensure that all teams finished their work in time. Team leaders spoke of the brigade's obligation to help them complete their projects or harvests in time once they became leaders of poor teams. Such short-term assistance, particularly to prevent ripe crops from rotting in the field, was rather common in rural China, but it rarely transpired without brigade intervention. Often teams with excess labor were prodded into helping "backward teams who have little labor and lots of land."[52] One brigade secretary who worried about his political future felt he had to ensure that the whole brigade, including the poorest team, finished in time. According to an informant, "The brigade leader had to do this. It was his job."[53]

Building Models. Creating models was important for political survival and advancement, but doing so on the cheap necessitated expropriating labor, capital, and equipment from teams and the long term investment of immense amounts of resources in the model unit. Thus building models almost always led to equalization and transfer. A brigade official in Jiangsu Province suggested that county water conservation officials supported equalization and transfer because they wanted to show how they had transformed his poor brigade into a rich one. They did this by leveling all the land along the road running to the commune headquarters.[54] Another county government went overboard in its zeal to build a national model. A former Shandong provincial official told how a county had taken one-third of the strong laborers from units all over the county to create one model:

"The south part of the county had a good water supply, but this unit was in the north. So the county decided to dig a canal 20 to 25 kms. long to bring water from the Xiaoqing River. Brigades in the entire county sent people to do it. They did not tell anyone publicly that the reason for the canal was to help this specific brigade, but in reality it was."[55] By creating one wealthy, provincial Dazhai model county officials hoped to divert attention from the county's overall poverty. By solving the brigade's water shortage they could also "show they were advancing and not standing still . . . This way they could make the county famous as well." All the county's money went to this project, and while the county paid for the teams' laborers and supplied grain, the amount was insufficient. Teams supplemented the project with their own grain.

Similarly, in Fujian Province leaders organized an entire commune to terrace fields and tunnel through a hill, à la Dazhai, to turn one brigade into a model. For a while this brigade was the district's most advanced unit in Learning from Dazhai. But when the commune could no longer feed all the workers, the teams refused to send more people, and work on the tunnel ceased.[56] Because peasants were not paid for their efforts and resources, they were impoverished in a few years; once they shifted their energies to the private sector, the model collapsed.

Some commune officials expropriated team labor to create monuments to themselves that would outlast their tenure in office. According to one informant from Jiangsu Province,

> Some cadres wanted to create monuments to themselves by directing peasants to dig new rivers to cover old ones. In 1958 our commune's first Party secretary asked the commune members to do good irrigation work, but it was good for only one to two years. In winter 1975–1976 the new vice-Party secretary asked the peasants to dig a new stream. But peasants who understood local conditions said there would be no benefit, that it would be useless after two to three years. Now they are right. Some young people said he wanted to build a new stream as a monument to himself . . . Whenever we saw the new stream we thought of him. Although he asked for opinions, the cadres told him what he wanted to hear. Now the stream is useless. I feel for the peasants whenever I see the river. They worked very hard in the winter to dig it up.[57]

Agricultural officials in Nanjing recognized this problem as well. "There is an expression that reflects some of the problems in water conservation work: 'When the secretary changes, the water projects are redone'."[58] This desire for immortality made the projects themselves more important than their economic costs or benefits.

Increasing Equality. Although in 1975 Hua Guofeng announced that helping poor units catch up to advanced ones was a criterion for Xiyang-type counties, few counties expropriated resources for this purpose. No bureaucratic machinery was established to implement or monitor this policy. Investigations in 1977 in Hebei Province revealed that no county had fulfilled Hua's requirements, although many had been declared Xiyang-type counties.[59] Excessive help to poor units alienated rich units on which the county relied for fulfilling grain quotas. According to one county official, his cohorts on the one hand "do want to promote equality. But on the other, the county has to rely on the richer grain-producing areas more, so it has to pay more attention to helping them out."[60] Falling short of their agricultural quotas was a far more serious problem than failing to narrow inequality, especially since the latter policy was not monitored. Hebei provincial agricultural officials also rejected the idea of using rural projects to help poorer units, while a county official from Guangdong Province stated that "in building large scale projects, the county does not take into consideration local wealth or poverty."[61]

However, brigade officials did transfer resources to help poorer teams. They were directly responsible for the welfare of the teams in their domain, so increasing inter-team equality was a powerful part of the "revolution within the revolution" during the radical era.[62] According to the Nanjing brigade secretary who sent labor from the southside to the northside teams to increase equality, it was unfair that the south was rich while the north lacked food to eat.[63]

The Issue of "First and Last." Shifting policy lines contributed to equalization and transfer. Historically, peak periods in rural capital construction were always followed by moratoria on new and large projects, as the stress shifted to coordinating (*peitao*) old projects. The 1957–1959 high tide was followed by the NEP of the early 1960s; Lin Biao's 1969–1970 mini-Great Leap was followed by Zhou's 1971–1973 moratorium; and 1974–1978 was followed by the total banning of commune projects in most localities. These impending freezes on commune-run projects led commune officials to try to repay units that had helped their neighbors before the moratorium set in. After all, output differentials created by these projects could influence inter-unit equality for five to ten years. Faced by such a forthcoming moratorium, a commune in Jiangpu County expropriated labor for a large project, although equalization and transfer had already been criticized nationally. To help one brigade improve its economy before the moratorium took effect, it was necessary to utilize labor from other brigades. Undoubtedly, similar problems arose across China in 1978–1980, if not in 1971–1972 as well.

Expanding Collective and State Wealth. To meet the demands placed on them in 1968–1978, county leaders tried to expand their financial resources. They needed money to carry out more projects than state allocations permitted. Of 47 *People's Daily* articles which in 1978 criticized rural bureaucrats for equalization and transfer, over 34 percent (16) blamed the county, mostly for taking labor and money from local units. In Hunan Province's infamous Xiangxiang County, the major target of criticism in July 1978, the bureaus of agriculture, water conservation, and forestry expropriated money and labor to build their own office buildings. Between 1974 and 1978 the county built 23 buildings for 1.8 billion *yuan*, using money from commune industries, and labor and land from the teams. To ensure enough grain for projects, the county water conservation office had instituted a water conservation tax of .033 kg. per hectare by which they expropriated 350,000 kg. of grain.[64] In Shulu County, Hebei Province, officials expanded industrial projects and put the profits in an "extra-budgetary fund" beyond the purview of state fiscal and planning authorities.[65] Some of this money may have been used for county-run projects. But counties that did not have extra budgetary funds could expropriate money and labor to create them.

A Bureaucratic Explanation of Expropriation

While county and brigade officials expropriated team resources and transferred them into their own domain, the county's position as the lowest level of the state bureaucracy gave it more funds to pay for projects than were available to the commune. Commanding a smaller area than the commune, the brigade was far more able to ensure equal labor exchanges. For these and other reasons—financial constraints, an inability to control the size of quotas it received, the scale and relative infrequency of the projects it ran, its position in the bureaucratic hierarchy, and the local perception of its role—the commune was the most important perpetrator of equalization and transfer.

The Commune's Financial Dilemma. Commune officials were given important economic tasks without the economic resources to fulfill them. Like the county magistrate of traditional China, who was responsible for the economic well-being of the rural population and the organization of water conservation projects to ensure that well-being, both the commune secretary and the traditional county magistrate received little or no financial support from the state to complete these tasks. County magistrates squeezed the local gentry, who in turn forced peasants to supply the necessary labor and resources without proper compensation.[66] Particularly after 1855, the vicissitudes of maintaining order in the face of declining imperial control forced county magistrates to seek new sources of funding besides the inelastic land tax.[67] From the mid-nineteenth century, magistrates and other county officials imposed brokerage taxes on commercial enterprises and unofficial surtaxes, excise taxes, and "special funds" on local gentry.[68] The gentry passed all these expenses onto the peasants.

Communes faced similar dilemmas. Although they controlled numerous resources in 1958, the 1962 transfer of ownership rights to the production team left the commune with political control over team and brigade economic activity, but with few economic resources. The only formal tax, the agricultural tax, was inelastic—it declined as a percentage of output from the 1950s—and it was passed onto the state. County funding for managing the commune's daily affairs was limited and often insufficient given the heavy demands imposed by the high tides in rural projects. Communes needed grain to supplement the peasants' rations in the arduous hours they spent on the project site and funds to reimburse teams for the labor hours they covered by paying workpoints.

But the communes had no funds to pay for these projects. County water conservation officials in Jiangsu Province differentiated between county- and commune-mananged projects, emphasizing that "there is no money for the agricultural field construction projects [commune-run projects]."[69] Although communes submitted reports to county water conservancy offices who authorized or rejected the projects, financial assistance, while always necessary, was not always forthcoming. And it usually only covered the material costs of running the projects.[70]

The military's need for funds in the late 1960s and early 1970s and the overall poor economy caused the state to raise the slogan of self-reliance. An official from Yunfu County, Guangdong Province recalled the problems this slogan caused his county after the Cultural Revolution.

> In the 1950s the state was investing in these large basic construction and water conservancy projects. But after the Cultural Revolution [post-1969] they raised the slogan of self-reliance. This was because the national economy had suffered during the Cultural Revolution, so the state didn't have the resources to invest in these projects. Also because of the Cultural Revolution, the basic levels were afraid to oppose the self-reliance slogan

and the policy of financing these projects themselves, because if you opposed it you could be accused of committing an error.[71]

And though the county did finance a portion of these projects, by 1972–1973 it did not have much money. So instead of paying for the projects, the county, which was "short of financial resources due to the disruptions of the Cultural Revolution," had no choice but to pass the burden along to the communes, which passed them onto the brigades, then to the teams, and finally to the team members.

When counties ran short of funds during 1968–1978, they passed the political responsibility for mobilizing the peasants to the communes. Another informant from Guangdong Province recalled that in 1970, "All these projects needed money but it didn't come from the county. The teams had to give money to the commune to pass on up. In some places each person had to give one *yuan*, while in other places they had to give more. Then the people did the work for workpoints but they didn't get money in return."[72] Peasants paid for this project with their funds and labor. Similarly, commune officials who received little county support rarely paid peasants for their labor, promising instead future assistance that was often not forthcoming.

The Problem of Expanded Quotas. Without funds, communes could simply have not organized any projects. However, during the radical era not only did they have to carry out projects, but the quotas expanded unreasonably while funding shrank dramatically, reaching proportions similar to the 1957 mass mobilization campaign. In 1969–1970 and again in 1975–1977, peasants were mobilized on a massive scale for large projects which the county expanded beyond already ambitious quotas, forcing localities to do more projects with less state assistance than at any time since the Great Leap. In winter 1970 when the new Party committee of Xiangxiang County, Hunan Province, called for a massive amount of capital construction work, officials in one commune transferred labor from several brigades, prodding them to "develop a little communist spirit."[73] In Nanjing the amount of earth moved (that is, the amount of labor expended) per *yuan* of state and local (city and lower) investment almost doubled from 1968 to 1969; after bottoming out in 1971 it rose again in 1972–1973, peaking from 1974 to 1977, with winter 1975–1976 being the highest year. In other words, Nanjing peasants were digging more but earning less (see Table 4).

The real problem for commune officials, however, were the larger quotas imposed by the county which forced them to run their own large-scale projects. One commune official spoke with some distress when he said that during "the 'ultra-leftist' period, we were told that the task we had planned to do was not enough. We then had to increase it."[74] The commune Party organization had to mobilize peasants commune-wide to participate, however unwillingly, in these projects. Nanjing city officials admitted that although commune leaders tried to resist the higher quotas, they persuaded the commune to expand its commitment.

The Dilemma of the Scale of the Projects. Large commune-managed projects occurred rather infrequently. Between 1968 and 1978 one of the three communes around Nanjing organized only one inter-brigade project, while the other two organized no more than five or six new projects between 1966 and 1979. Not only was it impossible to ensure that every participating brigade benefited from every commune-run project, but it was difficult to ensure that each participant got some benefit within a five- to ten-year radical phase. Thus in 1979, even after the state-declared moratorium, commune officials expropriated labor to repay the brigades that had helped others but had received no help themselves.

One commune official wanted to run a project that needed more labor than was available in the benefiting brigade, so when a large quota came down in 1974–1975 he mobilized the whole commune for this project. According to the commune official, they paid .40 *yuan* and gave them .13 kg. of grain as well for each cubic meter. "However, this was merely a supplement. We knew it wasn't the true value of the work they did and that it was just a living supplement."[75] However, a more reliable source who was involved in the project denied that the commune paid anything for the labor, supplying only a grain supplement. Although the commune leader justified this equalization and transfer by arguing that "all peasants are one household" (*tianxiade nongmin shi yige jia*), and that "people must have the spirit to help each other," he really had no choice.[76] Without funds, he had to transfer labor from the other brigades to complete the project. And without projects of this scale, he could not fulfill his quota.

Brigade officials, on the other hand, confronted less difficulty organizing inter-unit projects than did commune officials. Brigades were smaller; over a five-year span projects could benefit most teams in the brigade. Equality of contribution may not have been absolute, but equality is relative. Second, brigade leaders could organize mini-projects to respond to specific problems in their teams. One team that gave a lot of assistance could feel confident that it would be helped soon. Third, brigade-run projects apportioned labor responsibilities according to criteria which matched local conditions.

Commune-determined criteria could not match the interests of all brigades and teams.

Perceptions of Expropriation. Differences among county, brigade, and commune projects made team leaders feel less hostile to brigade projects than towards commune-run projects. Commune projects rarely, if ever, paid for team labor, while brigade projects occurred regularly and resolved local problems. And while team leaders did resent county projects, at least they got some money to pay for the workpoints they were giving out.

Brigade leaders, too, were more hostile to commune- than to county-run projects. According to one brigade secretary, "there is real equalization and transfer when the brigades help each other under commune leadership."[77] But county projects paid peasants for their work, took fewer laborers, and some money reached the teams' coffers, ensuring that county-run projects led to less expropriation. The brigade secretary continued:

> When the state runs a project they take only a few laborers. In 1979 there was a provincial project in Jiangning County called the Qin Huai River project. The state gave lots of money, .70 *yuan* per cubic meter. In one day you could make 2 *yuan*. You also got half a *jin* (.25 kg.) of grain for each cubic meter. The brigade sent 34 people. Half the income went to the team and half was kept by the individual . . . Sometimes in the Qin Huai River project the teams didn't take the money from the people. Also since they pulled out only about two or three people per team it wasn't so bad.[78]

This brigade secretary, however, resented all commune interventions in his brigade because for many years the commune had been taking his brigade's land.

Finally, peasants preferred county projects which paid in part for their labor over commune projects that paid nothing, regardless of how hard they labored. And while they sometimes had to sleep at county-run projects, while they could almost always walk home from commune projects, in the peasants' eyes commune projects were more exploitative than any other projects.

The People's Daily and Commune Culpability. While the brigade was the major target of the 1972–1973 *People's Daily* articles criticizing equalization and transfer (six of 12 articles), it was accused mostly of expropriating labor rather than money or resources (four of six articles). Yet much of this involved inter-village cooperative projects, and over time this labor may have been repaid. However, parties guilty of expropriations changed from 1972–1973 to 1978. In 47 references to specific bureaucratic levels in 1978, the *People's Daily* mentioned the brigade only nine times (19 percent; see Table 10). Close face-to-face relations among brigade officials, team leaders, and peasants made it difficult for brigade cadres to confiscate funds and material from the teams under its leadership.

The 1978 articles, however, mostly blamed commune and county officials. The shift from the Dazhai brigade—the 1960s and early 1970s model—to Xiyang County, and the concomitant increase in county responsibility for rural development, may explain the county's increased culpability. Nevertheless, *People's Daily* articles referring to four bureaucratic levels mentioned commune expropriations most often. According to the press, commune officials used this labor, money and material for rural projects and building collective enterprises.[79] Communes also took team funds from banks and team grain from grain stations, both of which were managed at the commune level.

Bureaucratic Interest. Some commune officials welcomed high tides in capital construction projects and the radical environment they created, for without them it was difficult to mobilize large numbers of peasants to complete projects that otherwise were too large to do in one year. At these times, commune leaders could defer lower-level criticism to higher levels or stifle it with political slogans. For example, the Jiangsu provincial commune that rebuilt dikes at the time of the 1976 Second Dazhai Conference had planned to take several years to complete the project. But Hua Guofeng's call for the whole country to "do agricultural field construction work in a big way" galvanized Party officials from the county up to commit themselves to larger quotas. So the commune Party committee decided to complete the entire project in two years and pressured all brigades to contribute many laborers, established labor emulation competitions, and compelled peasants to work hard and fast.

Under these conditions commune leaders could push the peasants around. To expand the dikes involved demolishing homes, but the families refused to move. So the commune Party committee, which could not pay for new homes, blocked the doorways of the homes with piles of dirt, forcing the peasants to move. After their homes were destroyed, these peasants lived in work sheds for three years until the county built them new homes. A brigade official recalled that since the project was based on a report by the commune to which the county had agreed, "they could take all the commune's labor to do this. The commune didn't give any money. They called all brigade secretaries to a meeting and told us to develop our 'communist spirit.' Once they say this you have no way to oppose it."[80] Every brigade had a daily quota of earth to move and peasants could not rest until it was done. And because there was a "hard" target for this job, and commune officials meticulously kept watch, brigade officials could not evade their quotas.

Conclusion

For over one hundred and fifty years a struggle has been waged over control of the limited resources in rural China. Although the state taxed some agricultural output, the distribution of surplus grain and funds and control over the land and labor producing it depended on the distribution of power in the countryside. For all their lofty ideals, proponents of agrarian radicalism failed to alter this basic constant of rural political and economic life. In fact, their attempt to radicalize the countryside—by strengthening the collective, increasing inter-unit equality, developing a communist spirit of inter-unit cooperation to transform peasant consciousness, and mobilizing peasants for high tides of winter capital construction—fell prey to this ongoing battle for control over the political economy of rural China.

The strong—the county and commune cadres—used the radical environment to steal peasant resources and strengthen the economic basis of their political power. Brigade leaders, more closely linked to the peasants, tried at times to increase inter-village equality; at other times they too expropriated peasant labor to strengthen their political and economic power base.

However, the major villains in this script were the commune cadres. From the outset, they were the least legitimate of all rural leaders. Unlike brigade secretaries who were enmeshed in the local environment, or county cadres who carried the clear imprimatur of state authority, commune cadres existed in a political and economic limbo out of which they tried for almost twenty years to escape. Managing a bureaucratic organization that as of 1962 had little function or purpose other than political power, these "new class elements" used the peaks in rural capital construction and the radical environment of the entire era to flex their political authority and expand the economic resources under their command.

While strengthening the commune's authority and economy was a primary goal of the radical leaders, the means employed for achieving that political and economic legitimacy only alienated the peasants and team leaders. No doubt a host of reasons drove commune leaders to force peasants to participate in these projects without proper compensation. But each expropriation of peasant labor and resources undermined the team leaders' ability to improve team income. And although team leaders were willing at times to help their poorer neighbors, their obligations to their team members and their own prestige demanded that they resist this policy. Yet while suffering the most, team leaders were least able to affect the political outcomes.

No doubt the collective projects and the development of rural small-scale industry improved the rural economy and peasant welfare. But by resorting to equalization and transfer to meet these goals, the commune undermined the very socialist consciousness and support for the commune system that were to result from this process. Commune cadres simply failed to use the economic and political power invested in their posts during the Great Leap Forward to advance the goals of the radical leaders. Instead they used the "fusion of political and economic power" in the People's Communes (*zheng she he yi*) to advance their own personal and bureaucratic interests. Their abuse of this authority made their control of both political and economic institutions the target of the post-1978 attack on the commune system. Still, having used the radical era to their own advantage, commune officials have weathered the newest onslaught on their power. Today they remain as powerful as in 1978. Even the reform group's decision in 1983 to split the political and economic functions of the rural People's Communes has done little to undermine the economic and political base of their control. Perhaps only the rise of private enterprises, competing companies, and powerful private families will really undermine their bureaucratic power.

8

THE MAKING OF
A NEW RURAL ORDER

FOLLOWING HIS return to power in July 1977, Deng Xiaoping criticized the radical agricultural policies, offering instead a more moderate policy line. This initial attack had little clear direction, except to expunge the radical developmental strategy that had influenced the rural areas for the previous ten years and to revalidate the *Sixty Articles'* compromise between the CCP and the peasantry.[1] Deng first reintroduced policies of the pre-Cultural Revolution era and only afterwards developed a new overall strategy to replace agrarian radicalism.

To carry out this major policy shift, Deng mobilized support at both the national and local levels. In Beijing, he refuted the epistemological basis of Hua Guofeng's political line, undermining its ideological stranglehold on the introduction of a new policy line. By forming a string of winning political coalitions, he methodically squeezed those supporters of Mao's policies who had benefited from the Cultural Revolution out of the Politburo. At the local level, Deng and his provincial allies reintroduced policies based on the *Sixty Articles* in several provinces in fall and winter 1977–1978. Relying on grassroots hostility to radicalism, they created a rightist wind that popularized the policy changes even before central leaders, still strongly influenced by proto-Maoists, formally accepted them. From July 1977 through December 1978 informal channels, such as the press, public speeches, provincial Party meetings, and word of mouth all helped mobilize latent opposition to the radical line. Similarly, Deng built a local constituency for "household contract farming" before national consensus was attained. However, unlike the radicals, whose policies never gained formal national support, Deng got his winning coalition to accept many of his policies formally once they became the focus of national debate. With strong national and local support, Deng undermined local opposition and ensured widespread compliance with the decollectivization and commercialization of the rural political economy that ensued in the 1980s.

Reforming Ideology and Policy

Agricultural Politics Before the Third Plenum

A month after Deng's return to the Standing Committee of the Politburo at the Second Plenum of the Eleventh Central Committee, newspaper articles criticized the radical developmental strategy. From early August to mid-October, the *People's Daily* initiated the first stage in the attack on agrarian radicalism with criticisms of equalization and transfer, restrictions of private plots and markets, developing the brigade economy, the Heertao Experience, and burdens on the incomes of production teams and peasants.[2] And while a November effort by Deng, Zhao Ziyang, and Wan Li to reintroduce piece rate labor was blocked by Hua Guofeng and Chen Yonggui, a December management and administrative symposium, run by the Central Committee's Agricultural and Forestry Department and attended by provincial representatives, called for reinstituting the *Sixty Articles* and increasing team autonomy. A *People's Daily* editorial supported this conference, and although "a leading member of the CC-CCP in charge of agriculture" criticized private plots and household sidelines and admonished against "hastily expressing opinions" given that "people are still discussing the policy question," the tide had begun to turn.[3] Articles in January and February reemphasized the private sector's positive role in the rural economy and obliquely called for resurrecting the *Sixty Articles* by using the slogan "carry out rural economic policy" (*luoshi nongcun jingji zhengce*).[4]

Provincial supporters of reform, particularly in Sichuan, Anhui, and Gansu provinces, intensified the winds of change. In December, *People's Daily* lauded Sichuan Province First Party Secretary Zhao Ziyang's role in introducing a provincial document that advocated distributing a larger percentage of collective income to peasants.[5] Similarly, in winter 1977, Beijing allowed suburban peasants to collect herbs, wood, and fodder in the mountains for the first time in many years, while the Party committee of Qidong County, Jiangsu Province, ordered county, commune, and brigade organizations to return the 19 million *yuan* they had expropriated from the teams to build factories.[6] On 3 February 1978 *People's Daily* reported that both Anhui (now under Wan Li) and Sichuan provinces had promulagated provincial documents in November 1977 and February 1978 respectively, which advocated the policies of the *Sixty Articles*.[7] On 23 March 1978 *People's Daily* reported that the Gansu Provincial Party Committee had taken a similar decision in early December 1977, and other provincial meetings on rural policy throughout winter 1977–1978 indicated a major shift in local agricultural policy.

March 1978 witnessed a major debate on the issue of "distribution according to labor." Wan Li's call in *Red Flag* for a "system of responsibility" (*zirenzhi*) for rural labor management and payment juxtaposed this concept to Dazhai workpoints and advocated that sub-team work groups be assigned specific tasks, quality levels, and time limits for finishing the job, with fixed numbers of workpoints for each task.[8] On 28 March 1978, Deng told "responsible people in the Political Research Office of the State Council" that he both supported their recent document advocating "payment according to labor" and opposed Dazhai workpoints.[9]

During spring 1978 reform winds from the provinces intensified as Hunan, Guangdong, and Guangxi provinces announced new policy documents which signaled that provincial conferences had discussed issues reflecting the *Sixty Articles*.[10] These documents culminated in the Movement to Study the Xiangxiang Experience, also known as the Movement to Lighten the Peasants' Burden, which was formally authorized by the Central Committee on 23 June 1978, promulgated by a Central Party directive, and officially heralded in a 5 July *People's Daily* editorial.[11] Ironically, Xiangxiang County is located in Xiangtan District, where Hua Guofeng had been district Party secretary, about 25 kilometers from Mao's birthplace in Shaoshan.[12] This document also revalidated the *Sixty Articles*, and by juxtaposing team sovereignty with commune and county "commandism," the reformers gave team leaders a stake in the reforms.

Pressures from Beijing and local needs to keep in step led provinces across China to respond instantaneously.[13] The State Council's July 1978 Rural Capital Construction Conference, while still calling for a high tide in rural capital construction, reflected a mix of policy lines by emphasizing improvements in existing projects rather than carelessly starting new ones. In line with the *Sixty Articles*, units were to ensure mutual benefit and voluntary participation. While calling for a communist style, the conference forbade expropriating team labor, material, and capital.[14] Nevertheless, only the December 1978 Third Plenum of the Eleventh Central Committee and its two draft articles on agriculture convinced local leaders to stop implementing radical policies.[15]

The Theoretical Debate

Before deepening the critique of specific radical policies, Deng needed to undermine the ideological basis of Hua's allegiance to Maoist voluntarism and concepts such as the primacy of class struggle, the threat of capitalist restoration, and great leaps to communism, as well as the epistemological roots of the radical developmental strategy.[16] Only after this debate succeeded in undermining Hua's rejection of a critique of leftism could Deng attack specific Maoist policies.

Seeking Truth From Facts. For both political and ideological reasons, Hua Guofeng, Wang Dongxing, and other members of their "whatever" faction argued that truth was based on "whatever" Mao had said and the policy line he had established, thereby placing a stranglehold on reform. Since Mao had removed Deng from his Party posts, Deng's return also depended on repudiating the slogan of the "two whatevers."[17] Thus in spring 1977 Deng and his allies criticized this slogan and instead resurrected Mao's slogan of "seeking truth from facts" (*shi shi qiu shi*),[18] according to which no a priori political line could determine policy; only policy outcomes could determine the correctness of a particular political line.[19] Formally adopting this slogan at the December 1978 Third Plenum meant that "taking class struggle as the key link" and "continuing the revolution under the dictatorship of the proletariat" were no longer unassailable dogmas. Moreover, reforms could not be rejected on their political orientation; if they improved the peasants' situation they should be followed. Economic outcomes replaced political slogans as the criteria of policy evaluation.

Voluntarism and the "Transition Through Poverty." The first ideological issue the reformers criticized was Mao's voluntaristic view of the relationship between the forces of production (that is, the level of economic development) and the relations of production (that is, the nature of ownership and the class system). According to Maoists, the relations of production determined economic development; changes in the relations of production could precede changes in the forces of production. Thus introducing socialist relations of production and communist political consciousness into a poor peasant society could facilitate leaps into higher stages of socialism and create "communist sprouts" and "new- born socialist things" that were the harbingers of the communist era.

A critique of this voluntarism in 1978 argued that peasants supported team, not brigade, ownership because their consciousness was determined by the lowly forces of production.[20] The Gang of Four had fallen prey to their "theory of transitions without condi- tions" (*wu tiaojian guodu lun*) and the "theory of the decisiveness of the productive relations" (*shengchan guanxi jueding lun*). Their belief that the relations of production could lead the forces of production, what Gouldner labeled the "critical Marxist perspective," was, according to Joseph, "criticized as the embodiment of the ultra-leftist theory of the 'transition in poverty'."[21] According to another critique, Lin Biao and the Gang of Four believed that "the faster the relations advance, the faster the forces of production will develop."[22] This support for advancing the relations of production and the transition through poverty had allowed poor teams to expropriate the wealth of the rich ones.[23]

Pro-Deng academics turned the critique of voluntarism into a forceful argument for economic development. Differentiating between the communist stage, developed socialism, and undeveloped socialism, and placing China in the stage of undeveloped socialism, Su Shaozhi argued that transitions to higher stages of socialism had to follow the strengthening of the socialist economy.[24] Since the communist era was not in sight, the laws of the socialist era, not laws based on speeding up the transition to communism, must be in effect.[25] The problem was not the fetters on rapid economic development imposed by the "tail of capitalism," but the constraints on development imposed by "deep-rooted remnants of feudalism."[26] Excessive concern with rapid, rather than steady, growth and criticism of the wrong fetters on development had undermined the economic development that might have occurred under socialism. Similarly, the impoverished countryside could not be the first line for any great leap into communism. Thereafter, future ideological debates focused on what Schram has called "putting economics in command."[27]

Rejecting Class Struggle. The reformers' second ideological target was Mao's belief in the persistence and wide scope of class struggle under socialism (*jieji douzheng kuodahua*), which the Gang of Four had argued was "the only motive force propelling socialist society forward."[28] Narrowing the scope of class struggle depoliticized policy decisions and created a less threatening social and political environment for most Chinese. Specifically, the reformers could now argue that bourgeois rights and spontaneous capitalist tendencies would not generate a capitalist restoration, and inequalities resulting from reopening rural trade fairs, expanding private plots, and reintroducing material incentives were no threat to socialism.[29] Constant criticism of capitalism, an important justification for the 1975 Bourgeois Rights Campaign, was inappropriate for socialist China. Most important, "spontaneous capitalist tendencies," which during political movements "have often been used as a club to show mercy to those who follow and to beat those who oppose," could no longer be manipulated to create a radical environment. People who "did more work on their private plot, did better in domestic sideline occupation, or took part in rural trade fairs several times," long labeled with "spontaneous capitalist tendencies," could now freely pursue private endeavors.[30]

Reformers also rejected the purported existence of ubiquitous class enemies in the countryside. These often innocent landlords and rich peasants, "chickens" who had been abused throughout the 1960s and 1970s to quiet peasant opposition to radical policies, had to be restored to society if the reforms were to succeed. In January 1979, class labels were removed from landlords, rich peasants and their offspring; in March 1979 "caps" of "anti-Dazhai elements" were removed; and in July 1979 people with "right opportunist" labels were also rehabilitated.[31] These actions showed both local cadres and peasant entrepreneurs that they would no longer be subjected to rightist labels if they implemented the reforms or pursued their private interests. In the end, the link of class struggle and economic development was totally rejected. The Third Plenum's announcement that "class struggle in the socialist period must succumb to the needs of developing the productive forces," forced Hua to concede that "class struggle is no longer the principal contradiction in our society."[32]

Decollectivizing and Commercializing Agriculture

Although the Third Plenum of the Eleventh Central Committee became the watershed for agricultural reform, numerous battles remained. Informal policy mobilization kept the pace of decollectivization in parts of rural China well ahead of formal policy guidelines; while reformers in Beijing fought to authorize one form of the responsibility system, they concurrently experimented with more decentralized forms in localities under their control. As soon as the opposition acceeded to one step on the path to decollectivization, new demands for another change arose from the localities, keeping up the pressure on the policy process in Beijing until collective agriculture was dismantled.[33]

The Third Plenum's decisions were critical for the process that followed. Primary among those decisions was an increase in the procurement prices paid by the state for the peasants' crops. Crops sold to the state under the compulsory sale (*zhenggou renwu*) increased by 20 percent, while surplus crop prices increased by 50 percent. Reformers were banking heavily on material incentives to improve the quality of peasant labor and to boost crop output. Remuneration based on output by work groups, with bonuses for overproduction, was accepted, but household quotas and distributing land to individuals were consciously prohibited.[34]

Yet immediately after the plenum, and under the watchful eyes of Zhao Ziyang and Wan Li, peasants not only expanded the scope of the forbidden household quotas, but five teams in Anhui's Qu County began experimenting with decentralized "household quotas with fixed levies."[35] The implementation of household quotas triggered serious debates which several editions of the March 1979 *People's Daily* carried. While one side opposed weakening the production team's role as the basic accounting unit, reformers argued that because individual production quotas were highly successful and popular in Anhui Province, they must be permitted.[36] Open opposition to the reforms, including an April 1979 "adverse current,"[37] forced Deng to publicly state that "it is necessary to enable every family to try its way and open more avenues for increasing production and incomes. It may be necessary to have farming groups or even individual peasants enter into contracts for a fixed quota."[38] When the September 1979 Fourth Plenum ratified the Third Plenum documents—now called the *New Sixty Articles*—which included household quotas for very remote regions, decollectivization achieved a major victory.

The February 1980 Fifth Plenum dramatically altered the political context of reform. Chen Yonggui and Ji Dengkui, members of the "whatever" faction who had resisted agricultural reforms at every turn, were purged. A shift in the locus of agricultural policy decisions from the Politburo, which Hua as Party chairman could influence, to the newly reestablished Secretariat run by Hu Yaobang, sharply restricted Hua's influence on the rural reforms. Moreover, the Fifth Plenum gave Wan Li, the agricultural reformer from Anhui Province, the Secretariat's portfolio for agriculture. The widespread introduction of household quotas began.[39]

Following nation-wide research trips in summer 1980 by over 100 staff members from the Central Committee and the State Agricultural Commission, the September 1980 Party Secretariat Work Conference, attended by first Party secretaries of all provinces, cities, and autonomous regions, issued Central Document No. 75.[40] This document, which accepted "household contracts with fixed levies," signaled the demise of collective agriculture in China as it had existed since the mid-1950s. All that remained was for the reformers to push the policy nation-wide.

During winter 1980–1981 Zhao Ziyang and Hu Yaobang travelled around the country—Zhao investigated the responsibility system and Hu looked at diversifying crop production—while the State Agricultural Commission under Wan Li also carried out its own investigation.[41] After their return, the Secretariat on March 30th proposed Central Document No. 13, the first step towards today's emphasis on commercializing Chinese agriculture. Peasants could now withdraw totally from collective agriculture and work full-time on their private plots. Peasants would soon be able to leave collective agriculture outright and grow economic crops or work on household sidelines outside the collective agricultural structure. While the battles would go on for several years, the cornerstone of a new agricultural system—household farming and the commercialization of Chinese agriculture—had been firmly established.

An Economic Evaluation of the Radical Strategy

While political factors explain part of the radicals' failure, immense economic and organizational problems also played a critical role in their overthrow. Their development strategy involved simultaneous and mututaly reinforcing transformations on three local fronts—organizational, psychological, and economic. Only in a condition of raised political consciousness would peasants support higher levels of socialist organization. Similarly, heightened consciousness and more tightly integrated rural organizations reinforced the labor mobilization and high levels of capital formation critical to the development strategy.

However, much of the strategy ran counter to various laws of economic development. The emphasis on grain self-sufficiency flew in the face of comparative advantage. Parts of Fujian, Shandong, and Guangdong provinces, which specialized in sugar cane, cotton and other cash crops, lost their comparative advantage and became impoverished.[42] In Jiangsu Province the added production costs of triple cropping of rice increased total output but bankrupted collectives.[43] Restrictions on trade owing to the emphasis on cellularity slowed economic growth.[44] Furthermore, though the voluntary formation of rural organizations is essential for successful rural development, limits on their horizontal interaction imposed by the ban on inter-regional trade undermined their utility.[45]

Organizational changes did increase capital formation, but strategies other than establishing brigade accounting and amalgamating teams would have generated less hostility among amalgamated units. The fact that many teams were united, split, united and then split again, could hardly have benefited agricultural development. For wet rice cultivation economies of scale have little utility; enlarging units simply complicated their management and created serious incentive problems.[46]

Although unifying teams and brigades, restricting comparative advantage, and limiting horizontal interactions may have limited regional inequalities, the radical strategy expanded other forms of inequality. The key determinant of income differences among households was not old social class, as the radicals argued, but the dependency ratio—the ratio of laborers to nonlaborers in each household—and the variation in the number of laborers among households.[47] For Four Families Brigade outside Nanjing, the strong relationship between number of laborers and collective income per household, when correlated collectively and within each team (.860), shows that smaller households and those with more dependents received less income from the collective sector.[48] These smaller households—with two or less laborers—also relied more on the private sector than the collective sector for their total income.[49] In this wealthier area restricting the private sector hurt families with two or less laborers more than larger families. And since larger families made more money from the collective, restricting private plots hurt families at the bottom of the income scale. Wherever this relationship holds across the country, restricting private plots and closing down related household sidelines simply made the already poor even poorer.

Similarly, while radical ideology called for narrowing the urban-rural gap, this gap increased under Mao. According to various calculations, the urban-rural ratio of two to one in the late-1950s reached three to one or even six to one by 1978.[50] Part of this unevenness grew from the radicals' prohibition on having peasants work in towns; the resultant overemployment in the countryside limited per capita income growth.

The attempt to build the rural economy through guerilla-style "swarming" had more negative than positive effects. While suggesting that agricultural growth during the Cultural Revolution era— excluding 1967–1968—was quite acceptable, Perkins argues that labor mobilization and accumulation added little to agricultural output.[51] Moreover, while Perkins and Yusuf argue that the use of labor mobilization significantly increased agricultural inputs in China, "the organization required for this achievement (such as communes, mass campaigns, and so forth) played such havoc with management and incentives that many of the benefits of increased inputs, both modern and traditional, were lost."[52] These economic problems undermined peasant labor enthusiasm and built support for rural reforms.

Finally, the radicals' strategy wasted opportunity costs. Grain production did keep pace with population growth; some forms of inequality were prevented; and rural capital construction created vast economic rents for future growth in output. But the impressive growth in output and incomes after 1978 show that an alternative approach to development was more productive and efficient. In fact, the reform strategy's ability to recoup many of these lost opportunity costs may explain its rapid adoption in most of rural China. Clearly the radical strategy had created opportunities for prosperity; but only by removing its economic and organizational fetters and increasing incentives were agricultural ouput and peasant incomes able to rise dramatically.

Undoing the Radical Strategy

Policy Transitions

As the reformers gained political ground, they undid specific policies implemented under the radical strategy. Successful changes in one policy facilitated changes in others, while the high growth rates in gross value of agricultural output (GVAO) and increased output for most crops in the early reform era helped the reformers win further policy concessions.

Post-Mao China moved rapidly towards lower stages of socialism. While the number of brigades nation-wide with brigade accounting peaked in 1978 at 66,712, or 9.5 percent of brigades in China,[53] national policy allowing localities to revert to team accounting precipitated a rapid decline in the number of units declaring themselves to have brigade accounting. In 1979 only 51,767 or 7.4 percent had brigade accounting, and in 1980 the number dropped to 42,429 or 6.0 percent. By 1981, the last year the Chinese reported this information, the number had shrunk further to 35,754 or 5.0 percent.[54] Pressures also arose to reduce the number of nonproductive brigade cadres who drew salaries without working in the fields; this probably increased the funds available to distribute to peasants at year-end.[55]

The shift to team accounting, which brought the relations of production—the level of ownership—into line with the backward level of productive forces, was only the first step toward reintroducing household farming. By 1981–1982 collectives had sold many of their assets—tractors and farm machinery—and auctioned off orchards and factories for long-term management contracts. While production teams persist today, "household contracts with fixed levies" (bao gan dao hu or da bao gan) were adopted throughout most of rural China by early 1983.[56]

Brigade and commune factories remain the only Great Leap policy innovation to have developed during both radical and reform eras. Although peasants and local cadres feared that weakening the collective economy would undermine collective enterprises,[57] the reforms expanded the quantity of small-scale enterprises. By expropriating resources and building extra-budgetary funds during the radical years, rural enterprises reaped benefits from the late-1970s decentralization of controls on capital and the freer rural economy that developed in the mid-1980s.[58] Tax breaks for new rural enterprises also helped. By 1985 rural enterprises produced almost one-third of China's total industrial output value and by 1987 they had surpassed the gross value of agricultural output.[59]

Criticizing equalization and transfer was a major task of the Xiangxiang Experience and the *New Sixty Articles*.[60] Unlike the conference held one year before, the July 1979 National Conference on Water Conservation Work allowed only small projects in connection with previous projects and banned all large new projects.[61] Writing in summer 1979, Wang Fenglin outlined the Central Committee's new criteria for evaluating field projects. "Don't look at how many people participated or how much earth or rock was dug; look instead at how much land is now irrigated, how much land with high and stable yields has become secure from droughts and floods; and the increase in grain production."[62] Since projects that could not be completed in one year or linked with other projects could not be started, local officials could not organize new projects.[63]

After 1978 peasants were allowed to open barren land and cultivate it as private plots, and because output from these plots was not taxable, peasants increased their private plots even as they received strips of collective land on which they had to pay taxes. Changes in the scale of private plots occurred quickly. In 1978 private plots comprised 5.35 million hectares of land or 5.7 percent of total cultivated land. Under the *New Sixty Articles*, private plots could be between 5 and 7 percent of total cultivable land.[64] By 1980 the total area of private plots had increased by 23.3 percent to 6.6 million hectares or 7.1 percent of cultivated land. In Sichuan Province private plots made up 9.5 percent of total area by 1980, although provincial guidelines in 1979 already allowed private plots to make up 15 percent of a team's cultivable land.[65] Finally, Central Directive No. 13 (1981) increased the size of private plots to 15 percent of arable land for all areas not dividing land to the household.[66]

As the reformers opened the system, private economic activity returned with a vengeance. In areas where restrictions were not tight in 1978, peasants quickly returned to many traditional handicraft activities.[67] Total output value of household sidelines rose 32.1 percent from 1978 to 1980, while the share of household sidelines in GVAO rose from 16 percent in 1978 to 18.9 percent by 1980.[68] Rural marketing underwent a similar transformation as the 33,302 trade fairs in 1978 increased to 36,767 in 1979, 37,890 in 1980 and 39,715 in 1981. Between 1978 and 1981, the total value of transactions in these rural markets doubled from 12.5 billion to 25.3 billion *yuan*.[69]

If ideology had blinded Chinese planners into overstressing grain self-sufficiency, they quickly recognized the need for a better balance between grain and economic crops. Soon after the 1978 Third Plenum, the structure of crop production in rural China changed. From 1978 to 1981, sugar cane production rose by 40 percent; tea production was up by 28 percent; cotton production increased by 37 percent; and oil bearing crops—peanuts, rapeseed and sesame—rose an amazing 95 percent.[70] These trends continued through 1985. At the same time, grain production did not suffer major repercussions from this structural change until 1985—there was a slight drop in 1980 following a record harvest in 1979—when for the first time since 1980, grain production fell dramatically.

For almost twenty years rural per capita income had not increased.[71] However, the 1979–1980 increase in procurement prices, as well as all of the above mentioned policies, particularly the expansion of the private sector, precipitated dramatic growth in peasant incomes. Total rural savings, 3.69 billion *yuan* in 1976 and 4.65 billion in 1977, reached 12.06 billion in 1980 and 16.96 billion in 1981.[72] Real per capita income rose rapidly—particularly when compared to the previous twenty years—from 137.5 *yuan* per capita in 1978 to 189.9 in 1981, a 40 percent increase in three years even when controlling for inflation.[73] Even while the collectives' share of rural wealth decreased, the collectives increased the percentage of yearly income they distributed to peasants. Accumulation rates by basic accounting units dropped accordingly, from 9.3 percent of 1978 total income to 6.55 percent of 1981 total income, while the proportion of collective income distributed to commune members rose from 52.6 percent in 1978 to 59.2 percent in 1981, attaining the same level as during the 1961 famine (Table 1).[74]

In 1979 *The Masses* (*Cunzhong*) announced that the unity of economics and politics (*zheng she he yi*), which lay at the heart of the People's Communes, was not good, and "all unfavorable situations must be changed."[75] At that time, Guanghan County, Sichuan Province, began experimenting with new organizational structures. Three economic joint companies—agricultural, industrial, and commercial—replaced the commune's economic functions and separated them from the commune's political components.[76] By 1980–1981 the commune was blamed for many problems that rural development confronted in the 1960s and 1970s. One Chinese source argued that the commune "is an organization for grasping political campaigns, for grasping administration, [and] using administrative techniques to manage production," which has "the power to intervene in the economic activities of the basic accounting unit, allowing it to expropriate team capital and labor without repayment, and force the teams to carry out economic measures in planting crops which betray objective laws."[77] Once the new State Constitution of 1982 announced the reestablishment of the township government, a major trademark of the radical developmental strategy—the People's Communes— which in 1958 had signified the withering away of the state, began to wither away.

Nevertheless, the separation of economic and political power at the commune level remains rather formalistic, as many commune Party secretaries became township Party secretaries, commune managers retained their management posts and the new companies came to be administered by members of the former commune Party committee. As private and collective sideline activity expanded, rural officials, as in the late nineteenth and early twentieth centuries, imposed illegal surtaxes on commercial exchanges and introduced transportation or *lijin* taxes as well. Others simply extorted money from hard working, newly prosperous peasants.[78] While this type of graft was criticized in the mid-1980s, power relations and the pattern of resource allocation allow cadres to persist in using their political or bureaucratic authority to increase their economic resources.[79]

Techniques of Implementation

Before the reforms were accepted at the national level, Deng and his allies generated their own policy winds by creating test points, attacking old models, organizing provincial conferences, mobilizing peasant support, and publishing articles in the national press. Their first attack on the radical strategy, the June-July 1978 Xiangxiang movement, had roots in unsanctioned reforms in Sichuan, Anhui, and Gansu provinces. However, peasant support for these policies also played a major role in introducing the reforms. While press reports of peasants forcing cadres to introduce the responsibility system or redistribute private plots may be exaggerated, the introduction of the reforms followed a pattern that reflected more commitment to the "mass line" than Mao or the radicals had demonstrated. According to a reliable Chinese source, Wan Li knew of the incipient decollectivization occurring in 1978 in Anhui and asked Deng Xiaoping how to deal with it; Deng's response was to let it be. Thus policies were tested and the "masses" were consulted before new reforms were introduced. However, after the new policies became official, the reformers grew impatient with local opposition.

In 1982–1983 they, like the radicals, succumbed to the everpresent tendency towards policy uniformity, what the Chinese call "one knife to cut all" (*yi dao qie*) and enforced nation-wide introduction of "household contracts with fixed levies" (*da bao gan*).

Horizontal Policy Winds. In fall 1977, over a year before the Third Plenum heralded the start of the reform program, villages in Anhui and Sichuan provinces introduced the responsibility system. Reports of test points in one locality spread by word of mouth to nearby counties and provinces and forced local cadres to implement the policy. Tangquan Commune is located across the Qu River from Qu County, Anhui Province. In spring 1978, when word of the experiments with household quotas crossed the river from Anhui, Tangquan's leaders, unbeknownst to officials and agricultural specialists in Nanjing who opposed household contracts, secretly used this technique for raising cotton. In 1980 they introduced household contracts with fixed levies into two villages, again without informing county officials. Similarly, brigade officials in Dalie Commune, Fujian Province, established household contracts with fixed levies in early 1980 when they heard about it occurring in Guangdong Province.[80] Pressure to implement the reforms often came from below, making the horizontal policy winds of the reform era far more powerful than those generated by the radicals.

Work Teams. Unlike radical era work teams, which forced peasants to adopt specific radical policies, work teams in the initial stages of the reform movement carried out serious rural investigations. Less driven than their predecessors by ideological commitments to a predetermined political line, these teams sought future directions for the reforms. Given that reforms often involve weakening existing controls and allowing new forms based on popular sentiment to emerge, many work teams allowed the peasants to guide the reformers.

Some work teams, responding to peasants' complaints, forced local cadres to stop implementing radical policies or stop resisting the reforms. In other instances work teams went into villages to ensure that policies, such as the removal of rural class labels, were implemented.[81] Moreover, when the state in 1981 demanded a link between income and output, and in 1982–1983 forced the adoption of household quotas, work teams probably enforced policy conformity. Reform era work teams also served as information conduits from the localities to the center, as they had before the radical era.

Press Reports. Two types of articles mobilized support for the reforms. "Letters to the Editor" in the *People's Daily* exposed instances of how local officials had used the previous decade's radical environment to prosper at the peasants' expense. These letters, whose numbers increased dramatically in the year after Deng's return to power,[82] undoubtedly galvanized some peasants into criticizing those inequities, while undermining cadre support for maintaining the radical line. Second, from 1978 to 1980, newspapers, particularly the *People's Daily*, were filled with investigatory reports which exposed local cadres who persisted in following the radical line. These "negative models" publicly embarassed local cadres who did not get in step with the new beat. As in the radical era, the press created fear among cadres who did not dance to the official tune.

Refuting Old Models and Creating New Ones. The reformers also attacked false models that had intimidated localities into implementing radical policies. Peasants in model units were allowed to express their anger at having been forced to live a lie,[83] while those units which had tried to emulate models could now overturn the policies. Leaders and units which had been punished or labeled for refusing to follow radical models were also liberated.

The focal point of this strategy was Dazhai, which was first attacked in October 1978 in a Hong Kong magazine controlled by the reformers. Initial criticism focused on how units had blindly followed Dazhai and suffered economically because of obedience to an inappropriate model. Dazhai "had its own historical reason and actual conditions" for adopting so many radical policies; whether other communes and brigades should follow its example "will be decided by the majority of their commune members. They need not follow suit. What is effective in Dazhai may not be effective in the other communes and brigades."[84]

As momentum for the reforms increased, Dazhai and Xiyang County were linked to important leftist errors. In November 1979, Dazhai was blamed for "expanding class conflict" in the rural areas, especially since being labeled "anti-Dazhai" carried class connotations during the radical era.[85] Deification (*shenhua*) of Dazhai and Xiyang County also made it difficult for villages to resist Dazhai's inappropriate policies.[86] Thus Dazhai had facilitated the creation of the radical environment which had helped spread the leftist line nation-wide.

By mid-1980, leaders in Dazhai and Xiyang County came under assault. A massive water project begun in 1975 in Xiyang County, called "moving west water east" (*xi shui dong diao*), was attacked, while in August 1980 Chen Yonggui, a member of the "whatever" faction and former brigade Party secretary of Dazhai, was formally blamed for many problems that developed in Dazhai and Xiyang County.[87]

However, reformers resorted to distortions in their own bid to defame Dazhai and undo its lingering influence on rural cadres. An early 1981 report stated that when Shanxi Province and Xiyang County elected representatives to their respective Twelfth Party congresses, no previous leaders of Dazhai had been elected. This fact reportedly demonstrated the bankruptcy of the radical line even in Dazhai and Xiyang.[88] However, a visit to Dazhai in July 1981 disclosed that both Chen Yonggui and previous Dazhai Brigade Party Secretary, Guo Fenglian, had been forbidden by Xiyang County's organizational bureau from standing for office.[89] Little wonder they were not reelected. Similarly, the errors of "moving west water east" were inflated.[90] According to its designer, the project took only 11 percent of the neighboring county's water, not 20 percent as *People's Daily* had argued. "Anyway," he argued, "they [the other county] are not controlling the water, so a lot of it simply runs off." While the critique was valid—investments of 15,000 *yuan* per hectare, final overall costs of 90 million *yuan*, an excessively large reservoir, and a grandiose viaduct instead of less expensive pipes—the project was not as evil as *People's Daily* had portrayed it. In typical Chinese fashion, the reformers tried to totally destroy all positive aspects of the previous line.

At the same time, the reformers created new models, the most noteworthy being Fengyang County, Anhui Province—for the responsibility system—and Guanghan County, Sichuan Province—for dismantling the commune. Just as tens of thousands of peasants had paraded through the hills of Dazhai and Xiyang County every day during the 1970s, thousands of cadres and peasants reportedly trekked to Fengyang County to bear witness to the miracles of the "responsibility system."[91] Moreover, the reformers, like the radicals, used these models to enforce nation-wide policy conformity. Although Fengyang County's poverty explained popular support for household farming—famine had occurred there as late as the mid-1970s—places where collective farming remained a rational economic choice were forced to shift to household farming during winter 1982–1983.[92] Once again, political logic overruled economic calculations in the introduction of new policies.

Opposition and Support for the Rural Reforms

Sources of Opposition

Popular opposition to one policy program need not translate into support for its replacement, even if the new policies differ dramatically from the rejected policy line. Thus as reforms moved from dismantling the radical system to instituting a new policy program, supporters and opponents shifted, and in some cases unpredictably.

The dilemma of the team leader was the most glaring. Initial criticism of equalization and transfer and "blind interference" by commune leaders increased his influence over production. That influence was virtually destroyed in 1981 by household farming, making team leaders major opponents of the reforms.[93] When it became clear that decentralizing team management—so critical to the reformers' developmental program—assaulted the team leader's power, the leaders either "locked horns" and resisted the policy, or adopted a laissez-faire attitude and abdicated their posts.[94] These early supporters of the reform program became major blocks to introducing more decentralized responsibility systems.

The reverse holds true for many brigade secretaries. One entire thrust of the radical strategy—brigade accounting, expanding the brigade's economy, or strengthening the militia which became the brigade secretary's coercive tool—increased the brigade Party secretary's control. Of all rural actors, he and the commune secretary benefited most from the radical strategy. Thus brigade leaders, particularly from units which had expanded their economic infrastructure during the radical years, initially opposed the responsibility system. Yet after 1981 they gained from the decision to divide collective assets among households. Many gave relatives and friends, if not themselves, preferred access to valuable collective goods that were often sold at deflated prices.[95]

From a systemic perspective, strongest opposition to the reforms came from wealthy units which had "learned from Dazhai" and had built strong nonagricultural bases of prosperity. Peasants in these wealthy units, who feared the reforms would undermine the brigade factories which offered them escape from the drudgery of field work and funds to supplement village economies, initially were unsupportive of these reforms.[96] However, as brigade enterprises flourished under the new system, increasing incomes in wealthy areas, this opposition abated.

Specific radical policies, such as collective private plots, were not overturned without serious opposition. Peasants received benefits from collectivized private plots without working on them. While they may have opposed their initial collectivization, they also opposed their decollectivization.[97] Press reports show that peasants who received a fair share of the produce from the collectivized private plots were less assertive in demanding that the plots be redivided.

Many commune and county officials opposed the moratorium on

field and water conservation projects. While some admitted that it was wrong to expropriate resources, they knew these projects were critical to rural development and that it was impossible to complete them without some redistribution of resources. The right of teams to resist participating in projects from which they would not benefit made it difficult for commune leaders to organize enough labor to complete many projects.

Fear of renewed polarization and increased inequality galvanized serious opposition to the new reforms. Some peasants and cadres supported protectionist policies—investigations, taxes, forced investments, and banquets—which restricted the private pursuit of prosperity and forced rich peasants to share their new-found wealth.[98] But concerns about polarization, first raised in 1980, have persisted, as peasants express concerns that exploitation will return. Based on a "fear that polarization will occur and that a new bourgeoisie will arise," some local cadres "set limits for outstanding production teams and have forbidden them to exceed those limits."[99] A peasant outside Nanjing argued that "if you divide the land you will have polarization. Landlords and capitalists will return. Collective socialism is good. Chairman Mao is good. We do not want to move off Chairman Mao's road."[100] In summer 1981, outside Fuzhou in Fujian Province, a commune official, upon returning from a county-level meeting at a suburban test point for individual responsibility systems, asked: "Do you think that the policy will lead to polarization between rich and poor?" His tone suggested that he feared it would.[101] And although Vice-Premier Wan Li wondered in 1983 "why should the Communist Party be afraid of people prospering? . . . The Communist Party should be adept at leading the people to create wealth while avoiding polarization,"[102] concern over polarization grew so intense that Central Document No. 1 (1986) directly addressed it. What appeared as a leftist critique of the reforms remains today a contentious issue and major source of opposition to the reforms, demonstrating support for continued egalitarianism.

Strategies of Evasion

Cadres employed various strategies to evade the reforms. Some refused to promulgate the new directives from Beijing. Uninformed peasants were in no position to push for the reforms. In Henan Province, when Liaohe Commune's leaders failed to inform peasants about the Central Directive on the Xiangxiang Experience, the provincial Party secretary sent work teams to this commune. Popular enthusiasm then forced the issue on the commune's agenda.[103]

Similarly, some units in Jiangsu Province had not explained Central Document No. 75 to the peasants by spring 1981.[104]

Cadres reinterpreted the policy's content in ways that mobilized opposition. In March 1981 a county south of Nanjing announced that poorer hilly areas could institute household quotas. On returning from this meeting, a brigade official reportedly asked peasants on the street if they wanted to work the land "on their own." One person said that "they blew a wind," implying that they triggered a massive panic among the local community. When team leaders discussed implementing household quotas, even the brigade's poorest team resisted.

Cadres also altered the policy's content, introducing only the form of the reform, but never making a major change. When pressure to link income to output intensified in early 1981, making task rates unprogressive, a Nanjing brigade leader increased efficiency by introducing a new link between income and inputs. These long term task rates showed that he was improving labor accountability without instituting output quotas, the precise policy he wanted to avoid. Other cadres, who formally announced a shift to household quotas, found ways to maintain brigade control over agricultural inputs or crop types, although in form the peasant households had decision making authority. Other strategies included "strategic retreats."[105] Or in the early stages of the reforms, when policy dictated that areas relying on state grain had to introduce household farming, some cadres found ways to deny that their units were totally dependent on state aid.[106]

Support for the Reforms

Opponents to reforms notwithstanding, strong rural support existed for many of the changes. Expanding private plots was a popular policy, particularly where uncultivated hilly land was plentiful. Lifting restrictions on household sidelines allowed peasants to increase household incomes, as did the shift from grain to cash crops. Most important, once national policy offered them an out, peasants in poor areas of China demonstrated little support for keeping the collectives. Press reports from 1979–1980 described peasants confronting county and commune officials with faits accomplis which they could not undo without calling out the troops. In summer-fall 1981 peasants in many parts of China dismantled collective property and withdrew from collective agriculture in such a massive wave that policy makers introduced contracts to ensure that peasants met their collective responsibilities.[107] This local support meshed with pressures from the reform faction, squeezing middle level bureaucrats who opposed the responsibility system and other reforms. While national pressure was critical in spreading the responsibilty system during fall-winter 1982–1983, most support for the policy before that was spontaneous.

Conclusion: A New Vision of Rural Development

Having overthrown the radical developmental strategy, the reformers created the economic and organizational basis for a new rural developmental strategy. During the early 1980s the reform faction was uncertain as to the future line it would follow. However, favoring horizontal rather than vertical economic interaction, they decided to dismantle the commune's vertical command structure and advocated increased inter-unit and inter-regional commercial exchange. As long as peasants did not totally disregard the state's interests, their pursuit of family economic interests would lead to general prosperity. The countryside had suffered disastrous losses in opportunity costs by ignoring comparative advantage; thus reformers advocated that households and newly formed economic associations (*jingji lianheti*) seek market specialization.

Central Documents No. 1 of 1983 and 1984 clarified the direction of change and demonstrated a somewhat coherent developmental strategy. The primary organizational framework for this new strategy is the household and various economic units, including economic associations and township and brigade enterprises run in a cooperative profit-sharing spirit. Rather than force peasants to join collectives, the reformers hope that demands for economies of scale and capital formation will trigger an economically rational shift to real cooperatives and cooperative farming. By allowing subleasing of farmland, they hope that specialized households will till larger plots of land. Peasants are even to buy shares in Supply and Marketing Cooperatives to ensure that these agencies of state dictatorship of the 1960s and 1970s behave in the best interests of the peasants who own them.

Regional specialization has ended the era of self-reliance, while economic diversification has replaced the overemphasis on grain. Households and economic associations are to produce purposefully for the market, according to their skills, local conditions, and local resources, utilizing their comparative advantages. Increased commercial exchange among units and regions and a vibrant rural market are seen as the ticket to rural prosperity. Excessive numbers of underemployed laborers who plagued agricultural production are expanding a previously moribund service sector, particularly in transportation and commercial exchange. According to the strategy, by the year 2000 over 70 percent of peasants will leave agriculture and work in rural factories and the growing service and commercial sectors.

Modernization is to develop naturally and not be imposed by the state from above. Peasants, possessing economic incentives to increase household productivity, are expected to seek modern technological improvements that mesh with local conditions. Education becomes a necessary tool for improved farming and prosperity. However, if farming persists along the present lines of numerous scattered strips, mechanization is likely to falter.[108] Nevertheless, reformers hope peasants will hire agro-technicians to introduce new agricultural techniques and technologies, as will the growing rural industrial sector.

By introducing economic contracts, the reformers hope both to regulate the economy and ensure that laws replace political commandism as the basis of interaction among cadres and peasants. Peasants are to be protected from the arbitrary decisions of higher-level bureaucrats; otherwise, they will be unable to pursue their economic interests.[109] But if they sign a contract, they are bound by its legal strictures. Above all, peasants are to be spared the threats and coercion that characterized agrarian radicalism. In the more relaxed, legalistic environment they are expected to expand rural production.

The new purpose of rural development is not to attain higher stages of socialism or prevent a capitalist restoration, but to increase the amount of resources produced in the rural areas and the per capita income of the average peasant, without privatizing land or creating enormous inequalities. As the rural areas develop and prosper, they are expected to become more closely entwined with the urban economy, both as a supplier for urban consumers and as a robust market for urban technology, skills, and industrial products. Through this integration and growth, rural and urban living standards are to increase, light industry is to develop, thereby increasing consumer satisfaction and foreign exports, state coffers are to fill, and the modernization and prosperity of China is to occur. Whether this new vision of a "socialist commodity economy" will be attained is unclear; however, these new reforms swiftly moved China eons away from the radical vision that was agrarian radicalism.

CONCLUSION:
THE FAILURE OF
AGRARIAN RADICALISM

> People like to say: Revolution is beautiful, it is only the
> terror arising from it which is evil. But this is not true. The
> evil is already present in the beautiful, hell is already
> contained in the dream of paradise. . . .
>
> Milan Kundera

THE LESSONS OF agrarian radicalism in China are clear. When
ideologues try to change the world, the one they build falls short of
their dreams. The gap between vision and reality is particularly acute
for contemporary radical Marxists who try to transform poor rural
societies into utopias. The source of their failure is also clear. Marx's
vision was based on the revolution occurring in an advanced indus-
trialized society, with a highly developed economy; socialism was to
be established simply by overthrowing the bourgeoisie, not by
state-directed development programs. Moreover, society's process of
capitalist modernization was to have already destroyed the petty-
bourgeois peasant and his private property mentality, leaving only
the collectivist mentality of the socialized factory worker.

But in reality, at the time of the revolution economic modernization had not yet occurred in China. With capitalism still in its incipient
stage, the influence on ideology of China's peasants and the values of
their society remained widespread. It fell to the radicals to build
socialism, transform peasants into proletarians with collectivist values, and then move the new society into communism. Fulfilling this
task proved impossible.

The new society created burgeoning resistance to radical demands for continued social change. Popular hopes for economic
development, accompanying needs for specialization, and the creation of institutions to manage the production of material goods
placed a high priority on social stability. Peasants, forced under
socialism to donate to the collectives the land they received during the
capitalist agrarian reform, maintained their attachment to the private
sector and their family unit; motivated by economic rather than
ideological concerns, their loyalty to the new regime depended
almost totally on improvements in the standard of living, not on the
attainment of some communist utopia. At the same time, vested

interests generated by economic development, rural cadres who were the state's critical weapon for social change, and social forces which were benefiting from the postrevolutionary pattern of resource distribution worked publicly and behind the scenes for political and social demobilization. Finally, there was no popular outburst of enthusiasm for continuing revolutionary changes, particularly from the countryside; nor could one occur, since building socialism on the peasant's backs needed the creation of a powerful Party-State and powerful cadres, who feared that spontaneous behavior might oppose continued social change or the extant distribution of power and economic resources, in favor of the prerevolutionary society.

Revolution Versus Modernization

In their efforts to maintain the revolution, and at the same time promote the economic development needed for attaining the communist utopia, Mao's radical supporters confronted a universal dilemma. As Chinese society settled into fixed patterns of social, economic, and political behavior, ideological concerns were displaced by material ones; and while change persisted, its direction—towards Thermidor—was antithetical to the radicals' drive for communism. Convinced of the historical necessity and inevitablity of their goal, these radicals sought to give new impetus to the revolution in order to narrow this ever-widening gap between social reality and the millennium.

But the question remained: how to transform peasants into proletarians? How to end their tie to traditional values and private property? How to maintain their support for the regime and at the same time move society closer to communism? Prisoners of their own Maoist ideology, with its theory of the continuing revolution, the radicals saw social change in only one direction—movement to higher stages of socialism. All other changes were rejected. Thus the radicals' solution was to turn the collective farms into socialist workshops with ownership by all the people; to imbue the peasants with Maoist concepts of selflessness and exhort them to resist attachments to the private sector; and to mobilize them for massive work projects to promote agricultural development. In part, the idea of paying peasants equally for their labor—albeit paying women 20 percent less—reflected an attempt to proletarianize the peasantry.

But the ideology of revolution, with its call for a communist spirit, failed to stir a social class that perceives the world and pursues life in line with its own rational economic interests. Unlike ideologues whose minds blend fiction with reality, portraying the world in a more idealized form, peasants saw only the reality around them.

Promises of wealth, equality, participation, personal well-being, and liberation from domination by man and nature failed to materialize. Instead, they were forced to set aside their personal and familial needs and their desire for a better life in the name of some greater collective good to which they had difficulty relating, and which often gave little in return.

Picture the average Chinese peasant of the 1960s and 1970s. His food consumption and per capita income had not increased since the mid-1950s; even the variety of foods he ate had narrowed. Society, he was told, was on the brink of a revolutionary breakthrough to prosperity, yet he was still using the same technology as his great-grandfather. And even where modernization had begun, minor changes in the weather could have destroyed the modicum of economic security he had begun to enjoy. No wonder China's peasants cared little about attaining communism or continuing the revolution, even had they understood what these concepts meant.

While Maoist vocabulary was pro-peasant, radical policies were clearly anti-peasant, fuelled by an anti-modernization mentality that saw economic development as the antithesis of revolution and was dedicated to the destruction of the peasant class. And while Maoist values implanted in the late 1960s may have generated extra-family loyalties among some peasants, demands for economic sacrifices in the name of supra-village ties caused peasants in the 1970s to turn inward and again seek private interests. Under these circumstances, China's peasants could not change in the way the radicals wanted. As rational actors they responded to each policy's incentives, not their ideological implications. Clearly Mao and the radicals had erred in their belief that ideological transformations could occur separate from social reality or that peasant mentality could be transformed into proletarian consciousness amidst poverty.

On the other hand, Deng's post-Mao reforms have shown that the peasantry may disappear faster through the modernizing impetus of rural industrialization and commercialization. Today peasants are leaving agriculture by the millions; some as entrepreneurs, the majority joining the proletariat as workers in rural factories. One part of the Party's mission may yet be fulfilled and through measures far more popular with the peasantry and more in line with their economic interests. Even inequalities among most peasants may contract as more standardized factory salaries replace the inequitable incomes determined by varying resource endowments of the agricultural cooperatives. Modernization, not revolution, may solve many of the problems inherited from Marx.

State-Society and the Nature of Elite-Mass Relations

The social engineering necessary to bring about the radical vision furthered the gap between the peasants and radical state leaders. In their own view, the radicals were fighting for the life of the revolution. Political struggle was a cause and a crusade—not a vocation. Each policy dispute was one act in a class war for the future of humanity. The goal was to overcome petty-bourgeois resistance and persuade local cadres and peasants to support the battle for their own liberation. The need to impose a new world on a hesitant peasantry seemed to justify vicious treatment of all enemies and the use of terroristic tactics.

Yet salvation for the peasants came at the price of their imprisonment. Their new world made them serfs to a state that expropriated their surplus value for urban industrial development—in which peasants were forbidden by residency permits (that is, pass laws) to take part—and made them coolies for rural cadres who dominated the local political economy. Peasants were exhorted to fight selfishness and continue to struggle against invisible class enemies, but even their free time was spent strengthening a voracious state and its collective sector, which consumed all the peasant had and all he produced. And yet any resistance involved possible violent reactions.

The state-centered policies coming from Beijing were partly the result of a meshing of the two policy lines that worked at cross-purposes throughout this period, each struggling to control the policy process. Advocates of the bureaucratic line saw strengthening the state bureaucracy and central control over stable economic development as the ultimate goal of government. The rural bureaucracy, including the collective, was the agent of that development, but within that state control some limited room existed for private economic activity. On the other hand, even as radical policies attacked bureaucratic self-interest, the radicals' search for utopia justified local cadre use of strong-armed tactics. This way, their attack on the overall political system, which weakened the links between the state and local collectives, combined with their demands for local self-sufficiency, fostered the growth of powerful collectives or "independent kingdoms" ruled by local cadre autocrats. Finally, the radicals' attacks on the private sector and support for development through moral incentives further strengthened the hand of cadres who sought to pull all rural resources under their own command.

All these aspects of the radical program strengthened the power of the collective vis à vis the state and the peasants. The mixed message from Beijing came down in the form of Dazhai campaigns, whose basic content was an ideological drive to raise peasant consciousness and ensure peasant support for putting the interests of the collective and the state before their own. Yet as Bertram Silverman noted in analyzing Cuba's experience of the late 1960s, development by moral incentives or "social consciousness" readily dissolves into economic development through compulsion.[1] In the Chinese case, the peasants were the target of that coercion.

Closing the private sector put all peasant labor at the disposal of collective production. Peasants, forced to return from the towns where they could have made some money, worked instead on the collective, receiving only an increasing share of a decreasing pie. Even peasant household fertilizer became the property of the collective. All winter leisure time went into improving the land and increasing its output. The proportion of the collective's income going to the peasants was restricted; even as peasant collectives earned more, peasants got less. Moreover, the collective produced little that peasants wanted, excluding grain which was sold to the state at state-determined prices. In many ways the degree of peasant exploitation was quite remarkable.

The radicals' emphasis on each locality's economic self-reliance reinforced the tendency towards "closed peasant communities"[2] and strengthened village defenses against unwanted state intrusions. To control the direction of social change, the radicals needed to penetrate the villages and enter people's courtyards and homes. However, their narrow view of acceptable social change conflicted with village corporate interests, pushing economically self-reliant villages with strong intra-group solidarity to resist state financial and political pressures. Indeed, the state's efforts to intrude increased the power of local cadres. As agents of an aggressive state and its radical leadership, they often were able to pursue their own, rather than the state's, interests. So long as they could fulfill state-imposed quotas, which transferred rural wealth to the cities, and convince the radicals that they were moving in a progressive direction—which they did through policy formalism—they were relatively free to expand the collective's interests and with it their own power.

Finally, the radicals had also hoped that peasants would respond with voluntaristic enthusiasm to this series of policies that attacked peasant interests, sought to destroy them as a class, and offered them few benefits of urban existence. However, fearful that spontaneous rural development would go against their world view, the radicals tried totally to dominate the direction of rural change, thereby undermining peasant support. This dilemma—Mao's desire that the masses move spontaneously in the direction he preferred—is a critical problem for all efforts at mass social change. It became a major contradiction during the radical decade. Not surprisingly, no peasant outbursts of revolutionary zeal followed calls for imminent economic or ideological transformations. Yet peasants also had few opportunities for expressing dissatisfaction, thereby increasing their alienation and their dependency on passive resistance, personal approaches to local officials, and the good will of more compassionate local leaders. This situation also increased the power of the rural cadres. In all, peasants remained oppressed by local elites and the Party-State that was to bring about their emancipation, and frightened of expressing their anger at this unjust situation.

Today leaders in Beijing have willingly relinquished even more central authority and in return peasant society has responded with enthusiasm and a burst of economic development. Peasants are more actively involved in local initatives, local decisions, and local change, while the recession of terror has allowed them to resist cadre misbehavior more actively. And as local characteristics and attitudes were the most convincing explanations for variations in local responses to radical impulses, today these differences are having an even wider impact as reformers in Beijing recognize that they can lead rural China only through a form of guided development.

Rural Cadres Under Agrarian Radicalism

While the radical era's stress on collective economic development and the radical environment's validation of coercive techniques both benefited rural cadres, incessant policy shifts in post-1949 China created a nightmare for them as well, as followers of one line became targets of the next one. The Great Leap's local critics were castigated during the 1959 Anti-Rightist Campaign, and many cadres were mistreated during the Socialist Education Campaign of 1963–1965. But deciphering the changing policy winds was no easy task. The messages from Beijing have almost always been mixed, with different leadership groups sending out their own messages; only during brief and often extremely dangerous periods have the messages been clear and consistent.

But after 1968, the cost of errors increased again, as economic decisions were once again placed under the microscope of political evaluations. With each new campaign, villages all over China became hosts to campaign work teams, which, after taking control, often discovered that cadres were the source of whatever problem they were investigating. Many targets were purged; in a few instances cadres were killed. To decrease the possibility of erring, rural cadres had to respond to the radical message and avoid getting caught on the wrong end of the political spectrum.

In this insecure environment it was best not to be a cadre; yet for those who were, a clean slate, loyal local allies, good political connections, and extreme caution were the best ticket to survival. Cadres sought to expand their economic base and the size of their factional network. Lower-level officials established ties with higher level bureaucrats who could protect them during political unrest. Finally, most cadres eschewed economic risk-taking that was not in line with the radical strategy, and since investments on the margin and economic entrepreneurship are the engine of rapid economic development, the pace of economic growth was ploddingly slow.

Mao had hoped to ensure that a policy's ramifications vis à vis the struggle for socialism and communism became the primary measure of its validity. Instead, each policy's political ramifications for the cadres, not the revolution, became the chief determinant of local decisions. Moreover, because radical messages often warned cadres to avoid certain forms of behavior, the result was a coterie of cautious, risk-evading, self-centered cadres, who spent most of their time trying to avoid the political ramifications of each new campaign that swept down on them from Beijing.

Implementing Agrarian Radicalism: Blending Form and Reality

The events described here differ dramatically from any current model of a totalist state. The supreme leader was in his waning years. The so-called "unified" Party was so sharply split that few formal policy directives could emerge; instead, different factions sent out their own messages. The local Party was in the process of reconstruction. No doubt, efforts to penetrate and control all aspect of rural life, which peaked in spring 1968 and ended with Lin Biao's death in 1971, greatly affected rural economic and political life. But local factional battles and inconsistent messages from Beijing—due to conflict within the Communist Party—made consistent policy implementation an elusive goal.

The feedback elites received about local conditions and the extent of local policy implementation had little to do with local realities. Frightened cadres knew that their bureaucratic superiors wanted to hear reports which conformed to the ideal portrait of the Chinese peasant as painted in the ideologically tinted novels, films, and press reports generated by the radicals. So cadres who disagreed with unpopular policies often employed elaborate strategies and established superficial conformity. They became masters of deception and worked with the peasants in the face of radical attacks on private interests. Together they created a grand performance of "radical rural China."

Heavy reliance on models, propaganda, and forced implementation contributed to the false portrait of radical popular support. Most model units received support unavailable to others. Although they were only examples to which others could strive, constant reportage on how models were fulfilling the goals of each campaign—when they too were falsifying statistics or forging their qualifications—began to blur the distinction between present and future. Since most official reports relied either on work teams—which visited progressive units or forced backward ones to conform—or on undocumented reportage by local leaders, the depth of popular support fell far short of the apparent level of support.

To what extent did Mao and the radicals really know that this portrait was false? Could the radicals, sheltered in *Zhongnanhai*, within the gates of the Forbidden City, have accepted the idealized portrayal of the collectivist Chinese peasants of Dazhai, Xiyang County, Sandstone Hollow, and a myriad of other model units as a true reflection of rural China? No doubt, they knew of the strong resistance that confronted their policies. After all, they believed that omnipresent class enemies would fight to the death to prevent further socialist development. They also knew that agricultural development was slow and that peasant incomes had not increased.

Perhaps they simply didn't care. Like radicals worldwide, these Chinese leaders' emphasis on the *quxiang*, or direction of change, and their inherent hostility to spontaneous mass movements, made them far less interested in the overall status of peasant life in rural China than in the "communist sprouts" they were tending in their model countryside. After all, these sprouts formed the roots of the coming millennium. But if in fact they did know the true conditions in rural China, how damning a criticism it is to recognize that the man Edgar Snow once described as extraordinary because of "the uncanny degree to which he synthesized and expresses the urgent demands of millions of Chinese, and especially the peasants,"[3] could take private plots from hungry peasants, demand collective capital formation while peasants had no money for household amenities, or expand grain production that left peasants in even wealthy areas with no cooking oil.

Mao, Radicalism, and the Demise of Collectivization

China was and remains poor, and most peasants in Maoist China were involved in a daily struggle to fill their bellies. Under those conditions, few could relate to organizations outside their family or their immediate work group when they offered few financial rewards. Yet Maoism's priority was continuous revolutionary fervor, not rapidly expanding personal incomes. As a result, Mao Zedong bears ultimate responsibility for the failed radical attempt to transform rural China and establish a stable collective system. By blaming the failures of the Great Leap Forward and the Socialist Education Movement on locally entrenched "vested interests" and nationally empowered "capitalist roaders," Mao expanded the targets of class struggle and introduced it into all corners of Chinese society. Detached as he became from reality, Mao created an enormous gap in the late 1960s and early 1970s between the values of the state and society, while at the same time his image, aphorisms, and cryptic messages generated the radical environment which the state used to try to impose its will upon society. Ideology also led Mao to politicize the entire decision-making process, undermining rational policy evaluation at both the national and local level. The outcome was waste: an overemphasis on grain, the strangulation of the marketing system, and the creation of terraced hillsides and waterworks which often added little to society's well-being.

Mao's radical program precipitated the demise of collectivized agriculture, once the hallmark of his rural policy. Convinced that limited collectivization would permit the rebirth of capitalist farming, Mao pushed for higher levels of collectivization. And believing that voluntaristic leaps of consciousness could surmount restrictions imposed by the material world, he emphasized moral, rather than material, incentives. Both these strategies alienated peasants from the collective structures in which they lived and undermined their support for the radical program.

Restrictions on private income did generate some peasant concerns for the collective, since its revenues determined most of each family's income. But the method of remunerations failed to differentiate between strong and weak workers or the skilled and the unskilled. This "intrinsic anti-incentivism" led to slow economic growth within the collective, while extrinsic factors—such as prices, grain quotas, and market limitations—further undermined the collective's economy.[4] Moreover, for collectives to succeed, peasants must join them voluntarily, and internal decision making must occur within a democratic forum.[5] That collectivization occurred involuntarily is clear, but had peasants been actively involved in its internal decision making, they might have developed stronger attachments to the collective.

However, the thrust of agrarian radicalism, with its distrust of peasant spontaneity and its demand for constant change led to intense pressures from above for peasants to accept policies antithetical to their perceived interests. Where cadres did not succumb to these pressures, they still used the collective system to impose their will on local society and expand their own political power. And even where local cadres worked for the peasants' interests, personal ties, not formal bureaucratic obligations, made them resist the radical program. Ironically, by pushing peasants to form larger accounting units which downplayed material incentives and undermined democratic procedures, Mao and the radicals weakened the collective road which was at the heart of their developmental strategy. Moreover, they created widespread peasant antipathy towards any form of collectivization which today undermines reformist efforts to reestablish more voluntary forms of rural cooperation.

Agrarian Radicalism's Heritage and the Future of Rural China

Monumental tasks faced the post-Mao leadership. While disaster was not at hand, key economic indicators, such as the marginal returns on labor and capital, had been declining for many years. Peasant entrepreneurship had to be resurrected if significant growth was to occur. Rural cadres' arbitrary power had to be curbed, while at the same time they had to be persuaded to use their skills to advance private and collective prosperity. Finally, leaders in Beijing needed to establish a more reliable system to monitor the implementation and impact of these rural developments. Only in this way could they adjust policies to meet the needs or responses of peasant society.

Yet if the reformers were to learn from the radicals' failure, they had to know that they could not instantaneously build their new world on top of the old. Nor could they arbitrarily decide the future path of rural China and expect the peasants willy-nilly to follow suit. A decade or more of radical policies had left their mark. Between 1978 and 1983, a coalition of national-level reformers and peasants in poorer areas weakened the bonds of the collective system, enabling peasants to more freely pursue their own economic interests. While rural cadres at all levels strongly resisted the reestablishment of household farming, by 1983 over 95 percent of rural families controlled a piece of land and the authority to determine what to do with most of it. The reformers used price increases, introduced in 1978–1979, as incentives for the peasants to work hard, and agricultural output soared. Along with it, rural per capita income more than doubled in five years.

Beginning in 1983, the leaders intensified the depth of the rural reforms. Some peasants, acting as independent units, turned to nonagricultural endeavors, such as animal husbandry, fishery, forestry, transportation, and household sidelines. Residents in small rural towns established private businesses or subcontracted collective businesses and began competing openly with Supply and Marketing Cooperatives and other collective rural enterprises. Beginning in 1984, peasants in parts of China left the land in large numbers, expanding the urban population that Mao had tried to suppress.

Nevertheless, the heritage of the radical era has played its role. Rapid increases in agricultural output reflect economic rents built up during a decade of winter field and water conservation projects. Rural industries, developed both through the expropriation of peasant resources and legitimate investments, have grown dramatically, so that the 1983 formal demise of the People's Communes masks continuing influence by township and county officials who manage many factories, particularly in wealthy areas. Today rural enterprises make up almost 20 percent of China's GNP, and they are playing an expanding role in China's foreign trade. Supply and Marketing Cooperatives are still expected to play the major role in supplying peasants with consumer and agricultural goods and in purchasing peasant produce, even though competition with private businesses is intense. At the village level, many cadres have become entrepreneurs relying on contacts and skills developed during the radical era to dominate the newly commercialized, rural economy. Even the state's grain quotas have persisted, albeit in a new form, to ensure sufficient grain for national needs.

Yet problems continue on the horizon. Weakened rural collectives accumulate less capital; so rural investment in agriculture is lagging, as peasant entrepreneurs spend their profits on nonagricultural endeavors. The irrigation system in some areas has begun to collapse for lack of collective support. Regional disparities, supressed by the radicals' constraints on comparative advantage, are growing, as coastal areas are geographically and financially better situated to take advantage of new domestic and international market opportunities. And concerns about intra-regional and even intra-village income polarization continue to be voiced at the local and national levels. Finally, rural cadres continue to use their political and economic power to try to dominate the rural peasant community, and with political campaigns unlikely in the future, they may feel more secure in doing so.

Mao and the radicals sought their utopian transformation of the countryside for the purpose of putting these issues to rest. However, their methods, as much as their goals, undermined those efforts. Their strategy constrained national economic development and kept the peasants immersed in poverty. But the concerns that they tapped—about economic and social justice and the creation of a rural welfare net; about abuses of power by rural cadres and the creation of a new, self-centered ruling stratum; and about the inequitable distribution of opportunities and skills both within and across regions—all reflected real peasant concerns. As the rural reforms proceed today, these issues have reemerged as the state has shifted its overall emphasis to development instead of utopia. Clearly the reforms have brought widespread economic growth and some real prosperity to a recently impoverished countryside. But the future of rural China and the rural reforms may depend on whether Deng and his supporters are any more successful in solving these social issues than was Mao and other supporters of radical agricultural policies.

ABBREVIATIONS
APPENDIX
NOTES
BIBLIOGRAPHY
INDEX

ABBREVIATIONS

BR - Beijing Review (called *Peking Review* until 1979)

CB - Current Background (Hong Kong: U.S. Consulate General)

China Group - Reports on Rural People's Communes, unpublished data set (compiled by Fredrick Crook, P.O. Box 23291, Washington, D.C.)

CNS - China News Summary (Hong Kong)

CQ - China Quarterly

FB - Foshan bao (Foshan Report) (Stanford: Hoover Institution)

FBIS - Foreign Broadcast Information Service—China: Daily Report (Springfield, Va.: National Technical Information Service)

HQ - Honggi (Red Flag) (Beijing)

JFRB - Jiefang ribao (Liberation Daily) (Shanghai)

JJYJ - Jingji yanjiu (Economic Research) (Beijing)

JPRS - Joint Publication Research Service (Springfield, Va.: National Technical Information Service)

MECA - Zhongguo nongye dashiji, 1949–1980 (Major Events in Chinese Agriculture; Beijing: Nongye chubanshe, 1982)

MECE - Zhonghua renmin gongheguo jingji dashiji, 1949–1980 (Major Economic Events in the PRC; Beijing: Shehui kexue chubanshe, 1984)

RMRB - Renmin ribao (*People's Daily*) (Beijing)

SCMP - Survey of China Mainland Press (Hong Kong: U.S. Consulate General, 1950–1977)

SPRCM - Survey of People's Republic of China Magazines (Hong Kong: U.S. Consulate General, 1950–1977)

SWB–FE - Survey of World Broadcasts—Far East (Reading, England: British Broadcasting Service)

XXYPP - Xuexi yu pipan (Study and Criticism) (Shanghai)

APPENDIX

TYPES OF PRIVATE PLOTS

The following describes the seven types of private plots that existed in 1968–1978.

1. *Principal Private Plots.* During the 1955 cooperative movement peasants received from 2 to 5 percent of the collective's land on a per capita basis for use as private plots.[1] The 1962 *Sixty Articles* allowed each team to divide 5 to 7 percent of its cultivated land as private plots, but by 1965 Burki found that the average of the ten communes he studied was 7.5 percent of cultivable land.[2] The size and distribution of these principal private plots were to be readjusted every few years to ensure that population changes did not generate inequitable holdings; however, this readjustment rarely occurred.

2. *Household Yard Plots.* Where the population was not too dense, peasants built walls around their homes and planted crops in their yards. This land was close to their homes, so peasants protected these crops more vigorously than crops grown on "marginal land" (see below). Although the *Sixty Articles* did not discuss this type of plot, it became important to some households, particularly when private plots were reduced or collectivized.

3. *Marginal Land Plots.* Referred to as "five" or "ten sides land" (*wu bian di* or *shi bian di*), these plots pertain to land beside roads, lakes, fields, rivers, hills, homes, or any small piece of fallow land that peasants planted. This type of plot, unlike land in front and behind people's homes, could not be walled in, so it was more vulnerable to theft and confiscation than land within people's yards. Definitions of "marginal land" varied across China. According to Blecher, informants from Guangdong Province called land around the homes, including the inner courtyard, *wu bian di*.

4. *Opened Barren Land Plots.* Peasants and collectives were authorized to clear and plant areas surrounded by hilly land, dried up river beds, and any other barren land, and where this was done on a private basis it became the peasant's private plot. According to the *Sixty Articles*, "fractional wasteland may be opened up under a unified programming [sic]."[3] The only stipulation was that privately managed land, including barren land, could not exceed 15 percent of cultivated land.

5. *Fodder Field Plots.* This land was divided among households according to the number of pigs each family raised.[4] However, very few informants had such fields; they depended more on their principal private plots to supply food for pigs and fowl.

6. *Vegetable Plots*. These plots, also not discussed in the *Sixty Articles*, were established either in units which grew grain in their principal private plots or where the principal plots were collectivized. Since most of China had been compelled to grow as much grain as possible in 1968-1978, this land supplied peasants with their only source of vegetables. According to one informant from Jiangsu Province, peasants in his collective received less than one-tenth of a *mu* or .0067 of a hectare as vegetable plots.

7. *Collective Private Plots*. Although this designation may appear a contradiction in terms, most localities that collectivized private plots distributed some or all of the produce to the peasants for free, as if they still managed the plots. Although the land had essentially been collectivized, collectivized private plots were not subject to taxes or the "unified purchase" (*zhenggou renwu*), and what crops were grown was determined by the team.

NOTES

Introduction

1. Crane Brinton, *Anatomy of a Revolution* (New York: Prentice Hall, 1965).

2. Richard Lowenthal, "Development vs. Utopia in Communist Policy," in Chalmers Johnson, ed., *Change in Communist Systems* (Stanford: Stanford University Press, 1970): 33–116.

3. Jonathan Kelley and Herbert S. Klein, *Revolution and the Rebirth of Inequality* (Berkeley: University of California Press, 1981).

4. Sheila Fitzpatrick, *The Cultural Revolution in Russia, 1928–1931* (Bloomington: Indiana University Press, 1978).

5. Carmelo Mesa-Lago, "Ideological Radicalization and Economic Policy in Cuba," *Studies in Comparative International Development*, vol. 5, no. 10 (1969–1970): 205.

6. For a discussion of information asymmetry see Terry M. Moe, "The New Economics of Organization," *American Journal of Political Science*, vol. 28, no. 4 (November 1984): 761; for leakage of authority see Anthony Downs, *Inside Bureaucracy* (Boston: Little, Brown, 1967): 134–136.

7. Merilee S. Grindle, ed., *Politics and Policy Implementation in the Third World* (Princeton: Princeton University Press, 1980).

8. Samuel L. Popkin, *The Rational Peasant* (Berkeley: University of California Press, 1979).

9. For a discussion of hegemony see Antonio Gramsci, *Selections from Prison Notes* (London: Lawrence and Wishart, 1971), and James C. Scott, *Weapons of the Weak* (New Haven: Yale University Press, 1985), chap. 8.

10. James C. Scott, *The Moral Economy of the Peasant* (New Haven: Yale University Press, 1976).

11. Thomas P. Bernstein, "Problems of Village Leadership after Land Reform," *CQ*, no. 36 (October-December 1968): 1–22.

12. Maurice Meisner, *Mao's China: A History of the People's Republic* (New York: Free Press, 1977). For the political debates leading up to the Great Leap, see Roderick MacFarquhar, *The Origins of the Cultural Revolution*, vol. 2., *The Great Leap Forward, 1958–1960* (New York: Columbia University Press, 1983). For the local response see David and Elizabeth Crook, *The First Years of Yangyi Commune* (London: Routledge and Kegan Paul, 1979).

13. On excessive grain procurements see Thomas P. Bernstein, "Stalinism, Chinese Peasants and Famine: Grain Procurements during the Great Leap Forward," *Theory and Society*, vol. 13, no. 3 (May 1984): 339–378. For the wind of exaggeration, see William Hinton, *Shenfan* (New York: Random House, 1983).

14. See Byung-joon Ahn, "Adjustments in the Great Leap Forward and Their Ideological Legacy, 1959–62," in Chalmers Johnson, ed., *Ideology and Politics in Contemporary China* (Seattle: University of Washington Press, 1973).

15. "Regulations on the Work in the Rural People's Communes (Revised Draft)" (hereafter cited as *Sixty Articles*), in *Issues and Studies*, vol. 15, no. 10 (October 1979): 93–111, and vol. 15, no. 12 (December 1979): 106–115.

16. Under the collective system peasants received workpoints for their labor, based on the time they worked or the task they performed. A production team's yearly net income, divided by the total number of workpoints distributed that year, generated a workpoint value. Every peasants' yearly income from the collective was based on that value times the number of workpoints they received that year. With brigade accounting the process was similar, except that calculations were based on the brigade's net income and the total number of points given out in the brigade.

17. Paul J. Hinniker, *Revolutionary Ideology and Chinese Reality: Dissonance under Mao* (Beverly Hills: Sage Library of Social Research, no. 47, 1977).

18. Richard Levy, "New Light on Mao," *CQ*, no. 61 (March 1975): 95–117, and Mao Zedong, "Reading Notes on the Soviet Union's Political Economics," *JPRS*, no. 61269-2 (20 February 1974): 247–313.

19. Joseph W. Esherick, "On the 'Restoration of Capitalism': Mao and Marxist Theory," *Modern China*, vol. 5, no. 1 (January 1979): 41–78. For the Chinese argument see "On Khrushchev's Phony Communism and Its Historical Significance for the World," *Peking Review*, no. 29 (17 July 1964).

20. For a description of peasants withdrawing entirely from collective agriculture and opening private businesses, see Gu Hua, *A Small Town Called Hibiscus* (Beijing: Panda Books, 1983). Some who stayed on the farms signed "household contracts" with the collectives to meet fixed production quotas, whereby each household's agricultural output on fixed strips of collective land determined the household's income. See Fredrick W. Crook, "Chinese Communist Agricultural Incentive Systems and the Labor Productive Contracts to Households: 1956–1965," *Asian Survey*, vol. 13, no. 5 (May 1965): 470–481. For reports on the reemergence of superstition and religious activities see C. S. Chen and Charles P. Ridley, *Rural People's Communes in Lien-chiang* (Stanford: Hoover Institution Press, 1969).

21. Richard Baum, *Prelude to Revolution: Mao, the Party, and the Peasant Question, 1962–1966* (New York: Columbia University Press, 1975).

22. The only discussion to date of this policy is Barry Naughton, "Industrial Policy During the Cultural Revolution: Military Preparation, Decentralization, and Leaps Forward," in William A. Joseph, Christine P. W. Wong, and David Zweig, eds., *New Perspectives on the Cultural Revolution* (forthcoming).

23. See Shanxi Provincial Party Committee, "Guanyu quansheng nongye xue Dazhai jingyan jiaoxun de chubu zongjie" (Preliminary Summation of the Lessons and Experiences of the Provincial Movement to Learn from Dazhai in Agriculture), 24 August 1980, in CC-CCP Rural Policy

Research Office's Material Office, ed., *Nongcun jingji zhengce huibian, 1978–1981* (Compendium of Agricultural Economic Policies), vol. 1 (Beijing: Nongcun duwu chubanshe, 1982), pp. 114–127. For an analysis of this theory see John B. Starr, *Continuing the Revolution: The Political Thought of Mao* (Princeton: Princeton University Press, 1979).

24. Robert C. Tucker, "The Deradicalization of Marxist Movements," *American Political Science Review*, vol. 61, no. 2 (June 1967): 343–358.

25. Alvin Gouldner, *The Two Marxisms* (New York: Oxford University Press, 1980).

26. Michael Walzer, *The Revolution of the Saints* (Cambridge, Mass.: Harvard University Press, 1965).

27. James A. Gilison, *The Soviet Image of Utopia* (Baltimore: Johns Hopkins University Press, 1975).

28. Robert M. Bernardo, *The Theory of Moral Incentives in Cuba* (University, Alabama: University of Alabama Press, 1971).

29. James A. Malloy, "Generation of Political Support and Allocation of Costs," in Carmelo Mesa-Lago, ed., *Revolutionary Change in Cuba* (Pittsburgh: University of Pittsburgh Press, 1971).

30. John H. Kautsky, "Revolutionary and Managerial Elites in Modernizing Regimes," *Comparative Politics*, vol. 1 (July 1969): 441–467, and Thomas A. Baylis, *The Technical Intelligentsia and the East German Elite* (Berkeley: University of California Press, 1974). In this study I employ Solinger's "three-lines" approach, which sees a marketeer, bureaucratic, and radical strategy of development. See Dorothy Solinger, *Chinese Business under Socialism* (Berkeley: University of California Press, 1985). For Kautsky the bureaucratic and marketeer line would both fall in the category of "modernizers."

31. Stalin's defeat of Bukharin allowed for the shift leftward in Soviet policy, while Castro's 1968 attack on Escalante and other members of the top Cuban leadership fueled the political mobilization for the "revolutionary offensive." See Mesa Lago, "Ideological Radicalization and Economic Policy in Cuba," p. 209.

32. Jiang Qing, "Speech at the National Conference on Learning from Tachai in Agriculture (Summary)," *Chinese Law and Government*, vol. 10, no. 1 (Spring 1977): 12–16.

33. *FBIS* (20 December 1976): E9–11.

34. Ann Fenwick, "The Gang of Four and the Politics of Opposition: China, 1971–1976" (Ph.D. diss., Stanford University, 1984).

35. This interpretation comes from Roderick MacFarquhar, personal communication.

36. Although Solinger's schema breaks Chinese elite "tendencies of articulation" into three approaches throughout this era, the political spectrum had shifted so far to the left that no leader could articulate the "market" or laissez-faire tendency. See Solinger, *Chinese Business under Socialism*.

37. William A. Joseph, *The Critique of Ultra-Leftism in China, 1958–1981* (Stanford: Stanford University Press, 1984), p. 142–75.

38. Only during the winter and spring of 1976–1977—when Hua Guofeng dominated central decisionmaking organs—could some of their more radical policies be advocated through formal channels.

39. Fenwick, "The Politics of Opposition."

40. See Chapter 2 for a discussion of the various models.

41. In the China field, studies which come closest looked at the ties between the radical elites and the local Red Guard factions during the Cultural Revolution, and at Mao's attempt to circumvent the Party in 1955 and mobilize local support for rapid collectivization. See Hong Yong Lee, *The Politics of the Chinese Cultural Revolution* (Berkeley: University of California Press, 1978), and Parris H. Chang, *Power and Policy in China* (University Park: Pennsylvania Press University, 1975).

42. A Chinese friend reported this story. See also Chen Jo-hsi, *The Execution of Mayor Yin* (Bloomington: Indiana University Press, 1974), especially the story entitled "Chairman Mao Is a Rotten Egg," and B. Michael Frolic, *Mao's People* (Cambridge, Mass.: Harvard University Press, 1980).

43. A critical reanalysis of Stalin's purges, based on local documents, suggests that the pattern of local politics—the purges—was due to political conflict over local issues. Stalin's actions merely created an environment conducive to local leaders' using terror to resolve differences with political rivals. See J. Arch Getty, *Origins of the Great Purges* (New York: Cambridge University Press, 1985).

44. For a discussion of the concept of policy "content" see Merilee S. Grindle, "Policy Content and Context in Implementation," in Merilee S. Grindle, ed., *Politics and Policy Implementation in the Third World* (Princeton: Princeton University Press, 1980), pp. 3–34.

45. For the general theoretical argument supporting the use of a structural approach to political culture see Kenneth Jowitt, "An Organizational Approach to the Study of Political Culture in Marxist-Leninist Systems," *American Political Science Review*, vol. 68 (September 1974): 1171–91. A fine application of this approach to Chinese politics is Susan Shirk, *Competitive Comrades* (Berkeley: University of California Press, 1982).

46. An excellent discussion of the formal and informal ways peasants pursue their political and economic interests is John P. Burns, *Chinese Peasant Political Participation* (Berkeley: University of California Press, 1988).

47. For a thorough discussion see David Zweig, "Form and Content in Policy Evasion: The Cultural Revolution in the Countryside, 1968–1978," paper presented at the conference on New Perspectives on the Cultural Revolution, Harvard University, 15–17 May 1987. See also Chapter 4 herein.

48. A valuable economic critique of the radical program, particularly its rejection of comparative advantage, is Nicholas P. Lardy, *Agriculture in China's Modern Economic Development* (Cambridge: Cambridge University Press, 1983).

49. Jonathan Unger, "Collective Incentives in the Chinese Countryside: Lessons from Chen Village," *World Development*, no. 6 (1978): 583–601.

50. David Zweig, "Opposition to Reform in Rural China," *Asian Survey*, vol. 23, no. 7 (July 1983): 879–900.

1. Agarian Radicalism Defined

1. See Alvin Gouldner, *The Two Marxisms* (New York: Oxford University Press, 1980).

2. Li Dazhao shared Mao's passion for action and faith in the power of

the masses. See Maurice Meisner, *Li Ta-chao and the Origins of Chinese Marxism* (Cambridge, Mass.: Harvard University Press, 1967).

3. Stuart R. Schram, *The Political Thought of Mao Tse-t'ung* (New York: Praeger, 1972), p. 135.

4. Gouldner, *The Two Marxisms*, p. 33.

5. Ibid., p. 34.

6. Marx argued that if the German petty bourgeoisie wanted to stop the revolution at the bourgeois stage, "it is our task to make the revolution permanent . . . until the proletariat has conquered state power." See "Address of the Central Committee to the Communist League," March 1850, in Karl Marx and Friedrich Engels, *Selected Works* (Moscow: Progress Publishers, 1950), p. 102, cited in Maurice Meisner, *Mao's China: A History of the People's Republic* (New York: Free Press, 1977), p. 206.

7. See Gouldner, *The Two Marxisms*, p. 230, and Mark Selden "Cooperation and Conflict: Cooperative and Collective Formation in China's Countryside," in Mark Selden and Victor Lippit, eds., *The Transition to Socialism in China* (Armonk, N.Y.: M. E. Sharpe, 1982), p. 36. This predated China's position that People's Communes could form the basic building block of communist society.

8. See Parris H. Chang, *Power and Policy in China* (University Park: Pennsylvania State University Press, 1975), p. 9; Editor, "The Conflict between Mao Tse-t'ung and Liu Shao-ch'i over Agricultural Mechanization in Communist China," *Current Scene*, vol. 6, no. 17 (October 1, 1968): 1–20, and Selden, "Cooperation and Conflict," p. 66.

9. Meisner, *Mao's China*, p. 148.

10. Cited in Rhoads Murphey, *The Fading of the Maoist Vision: City and Country in China's Development* (New York: Methuen, 1980), p. 24.

11. Mao Zedong, "Report to the Second Plenary Session of the Seventh Central Committee of the Communist Party of China," in Mao, *Selected Works* (Beijing: Foreign Languages Press, 1969), vol. 4, p. 374; and "Talk at the First Plenum of the Ninth Central Committee of the Chinese Communist Party" (April 28, 1969), in Stuart R. Schram, ed., *Mao Tse-tung Unrehearsed: Talks and Letters, 1956–1971* (Harmondsworth: Penguin Books, 1975), p. 288.

12. Karl Marx, "The Eighteenth Brumaire of Louis Napoleon" in Robert C. Tucker, ed., *The Marx-Engels Reader*, 2nd ed. (New York: W. W. Norton, 1978), p. 608.

13. Michael Duggett, "Marx on Peasants," *Journal of Peasant Studies*, vol. 2, no. 2 (January 1975): 159–182.

14. Oscar J. Hammen, "Marx and the Agrarian Question," *American Historical Review*, vol. 77, no. 3 (June 1972): 679–704.

15. Meisner, *Mao's China*, p. 115. Two articles which see Maoist China as this form of "oppressive despotism" are Tang Tsou, "Back from the Brink of Revolutionary-'Feudal' Totalitarianism," and Edward Friedman, "The Societal Obstacle to China's Socialist Transition: State Capitalism or Feudal Fascism," in Victor Nee and David Mozingo, eds., *State and Society in Contemporary China* (Ithaca: Cornell University Press, 1983), pp. 53–88, 148–174.

16. Seweryn Bialer, "Leninism and the Peasantry in the Russian Revolutions," paper presented at the SEADAG Rural Development Seminar,

Savannah, Georgia, May 1974. I am grateful to the author for sharing this unpublished work, and to Tom Bernstein who told me about it.

17. Benjamin Schwartz, *Chinese Communism and the Rise of Mao* (Cambridge, Mass.: Harvard University Press, 1979), p. 191.

18. Schram, *The Political Thought of Mao Tse-t'ung*, p. 252.

19. Ibid., p. 59.

20. Murphey, *The Fading of the Maoist Vision*, p. 25.

21. Jerome Chen, "The Development and Logic of Mao Tse-t'ung's Thought," in Chalmers Johnson, ed., *Ideology and Politics in Contemporary China* (Seattle: University of Washington Press, 1973), p. 107, and Jerome Chen, *Mao and the Chinese Revolution* (London: Oxford University Press, 1965), p. 156.

22. While Mao saw peasants as his major constituency—for him they were the masses—when Liu Shaoqi referred to the masses, he meant the workers. See Lowell Dittmer, *Liu Shaoch'i and the Chinese Cultural Revolution: The Politics of Mass Criticism* (Berkeley: University of California Press, 1974), p. 180.

23. This quote appeared in Jan Myrdal and Gun Kessle, *China: The Revolution Continued* (New York: Vintage Books, 1970), pp. 68–69.

24. Chen Boda, "Zhongguo nongyede shehuizhuyi gaizao" (The Socialist Reform of Chinese Agriculture), in *Chen Boda wenji, 1949–1967* (The Collected Essays of Chen Boda) (Hong Kong: Lishi ziliao chubanshe, 1971).

25. "Central Committee Resolution on Some Questions Concerning the People's Communes, 10 December 1958," in Robert Bowie and John K. Fairbank, eds., *Communist China, 1955–1959: Policy Documents with Analysis* (Cambridge, Mass.: Harvard University Press, 1962).

26. Maurice Meisner, *Marxism, Maoism and Utopianism: Eight Essays* (Madison: University of Wisconsin Press, 1982), p. 69.

27. Mao Zedong, "Reading Notes on the Soviet Union's Political Economics," *JPRS*, 61269-2 (20 February 1974): 247–313.

28. Jurgen Domes, *Socialism in the Chinese Countryside* (Montreal: McGill-Queen's University Press, 1980).

29. Tang Tsou, "The Cultural Revolution and the Chinese Political System," *CQ*, no. 38 (April-June 1969): 63–91.

30. Alfred Meyer, *Leninism* (Cambridge, Mass.: Harvard University Press, 1957).

31. Bialer, "Leninism and the Peasantry."

32. Meisner, *Marxism, Maoism and Utopianism*, p. 60.

33. Mao Zedong, in *Mao Zedong sixiang wan sui* (Long Live Chairman Mao's Thought) (Hong Kong: Po Wen Book Co., 1969), pp. 333–334.

34. Chin Wan, "On Transition in Poverty," *JFRB*, 5 December 1978, in *FBIS*, no. 236 (7 December 1978): E9–12.

35. Chin, "On Transition in Poverty," and Xu Dixin, "Lun qiong guodu" (On the Transition Through Poverty), *JJYJ*, no. 4 (1979): 2–7.

36. V. I. Lenin, *Left-Wing Communism: An Infantile Disorder* (Beijing: Foreign Languages Press, 1970), pp. 5–6.

37. Joseph Levenson, *Confucian China and Its Modern Fate* (Berkeley: University of California Press, 1968).

38. Prerevolutionary class enemies served as scapegoats when local problems arose for which the cadres themselves might have had to accept responsibility. Richard Kraus, "Class Conflict and the Vocabulary of Social Analysis in China," *CQ*, no. 69 (March 1977): 54–74.

39. Roderick MacFarquhar, *The Origins of the Cultural Revolution: Contradictions among the People* (New York: Columbia University Press, 1974), p. 268.

40. John B. Starr, *Continuing the Revolution: The Political Thought of Mao* (Princeton: Princeton University Press, 1979), p. 112n42. See also Chen Boda, "The Struggle between the Proletarian World View and the Capitalist World View," in *Chen Boda wenji.*

41. Mark Selden, ed., *The People's Republic of China: A Documentary History of Revolutionary Change* (New York: Monthly Review Press, 1979), p. 499.

42. See "Is Yugoslavia a Socialist Country?" and "On Krushchev's Phony Communism and its Historical Significance for the World," *Peking Review*, no. 39 (27 September 1963) and no. 29 (17 July 1964). According to Friedman, Mao's anti-revisionism developed earlier from opposition to Tito and Yugoslav socialism rather than from an anti-Soviet posture. Edward Friedman, "Maoism, Titoism, and Stalinism: Some Origins and Consequences of the Maoist Theory of Socialist Transition," in Selden and Lippit, *The Transition to Socialism,* pp. 159–214.

43. Graham Young and Dennis Woodward, "From Contradictions among the People to Class Struggle: The Theories of Uninterrupted Revolution and Continuous Revolution," *Asian Survey,* vol. 18, no. 9 (September 1978): 912–933.

44. As Starr points out, the shift from "uninterrupted revolution" to "the continuing revolution" necessitated positive action on the part of revolutionaries and the masses to maintain the destabilization of the social system and ensure the revolution's prolongation and the ultimate transition to communism. See Starr, *Continuing the Revolution,* p. 304.

45. According to Joseph, "Since class struggle was, in the ultra-left view, the essence of the relations of production, and the relations of production were the essential locus of historical change, it logically followed that class struggle should be touted as the most important factor in ensuring progress towards communism during the transition period." William A. Joseph, *The Critique of Ultra-Leftism in China, 1958–1981* (Stanford: Stanford University Press, 1984), p. 212.

46. "It tacitly recognized unequal individual endowment and their [the holders' of bourgeois rights] productive capacity as natural privileges. It is therefore a right of inequality, in its content like every right." Karl Marx, "Critique of the Gotha Programme," in Tucker, *The Marx-Engels Reader,* p. 530.

47. Zhang Chunqiao, *RMRB,* 13 October 1958.

48. See "Duida A. B. Saningria he B. F. Wenshener liang tongzhi de jiduan piyu" (Several criticisms of "A Reply to Comrades A. B. Sanina and B. F. Vinshire"), *Mao Zedong sixiang wan sui,* p. 122.

49. Interview with Gong Yuzhi, Cambridge, Mass., summer 1985.

50. Yao Wenyuan, "On the Social Basis of the Lin Piao Anti-Party Clique," *HQ,* no. 3, (1975): 20–29.

51. Yu Lin County Theoretical Group, *Shehuizhuyi jiti suoyouzhi* (The Socialist Collective Ownership System) (Nanning: Guangxi People's Publishing House, 1976), p. 69.

52. Ibid., p. 70.

53. Gouldner, *The Two Marxisms*, pp. 124–125.

54. According to Fagen, the Sierra Maestre's legacy for Cuba's revolutionary elite was "voluntarism, egalitarianism and ruralism," qualities that reflect agrarian radicalism. See Richard R. Fagen, "Cuban Revolutionary Politics," *Monthly Review* (April 1972): 27. See also Carmelo Mesa-Lago, "Ideological Radicalization and Economic Policy in Cuba," *Studies in Comparative International Development*, vol. 5, no. 10 (1969–1970): 203–216. Pol Pot firmly believed that because of the revolution's "purity and cleanliness," revolutionary violence could be used to skip stages. As soon as it took power, the Khmer Rouge abolished all private property. Elizabeth Becker, *When the War Was Over* (New York: Simon and Schuster, 1986).

55. Meisner, *Marxism, Maoism and Utopianism*, p. 163.

56. Franz Schurman, *Ideology and Organization in Communist China* (Berkeley: University of California Press, 1968), p. 49.

57. According to Cohn, one critical component of millennialism is a belief in the immediacy of salvation, "in the sense that it is to come both soon and suddenly." Norman Cohn, *The Pursuit of the Millennium* (London: Temple Smith, 1970), p. 13.

58. Mao Zedong, "Talk at an Enlarged Central Work Conference," in Schram, *Mao Tse-tung Unrehearsed*, p. 173.

59. An alternative perspective on this radical strategy would emphasize the state's role in extracting resources, especially grain, from the countryside, while minimizing the input costs to agriculture. This perspective has merit, yet the radicals remained highly suspicious of state bureaucrats; moreover, even though Mao's actions created a highly centralized bureaucratic state, his purpose and that of the radicals was to develop a decentralized economic and political system based on mass mobilization and widespread, mass political participation. The state-centric model was more an outcome than a goal of the radical strategy, owing in part to policy compromises among various factions. See Chapters 2 and 3.

60. Soviet Marxism also posits that the transition from socialism to communism involves destroying the collective property system. See James A. Gilison, *The Soviet Vision of Utopia* (Baltimore: Johns Hopkins University Press, 1975), p. 80.

61. See the Beidahe Resolution, "Central Committee Resolution on the Establishment of People's Communes in the Rural Areas, August 29, 1958," in Bowie and Fairbank, *Communist China*, pp. 454–456.

62. Xu Dixin, "Lun qiong guodu," pp. 2–7.

63. Chen Yonggui, "Thoroughly Criticize the 'Gang of Four' and Bring About a New Upsurge in the Movement to Build Tachai-type Counties throughout the Country," speech to the Second National Conference on Learning from Tachai in Agriculture, 20 December 1976, in *SPRCM*, no. 910 (7 February 1977): 79.

64. See *Renmin gongshe zai yuejin* (People's Communes Are Advancing) (Shanghai: Renmin chubanshe, 1974), pp. 57–64; and "Fazhan dadui jiti

jingji, cujin nongye da shang kuai shang" (Develop the Brigade's Collective Economy, Promote the Rapid Development of Agriculture), *XXYPP*, no. 10 (1975): 7–11.

65. In a study of Cuba, Silverman noted a similar dilemma. "Since all socialist revolutions have occurred in relatively backward economies, an inevitable contradiction exists between the organizational forms held to be most consistent with communist goals and the capacity to establish such an economic organization." Bertram Silverman, "Economic Organization and Social Consciousness: Some Dilemmas of Cuban Socialism," in June Nash et al., eds., *Ideology and Social Change in Latin America* (New York: Gordon and Breach, 1977), p. 238.

66. Robert M. Bernardo, *The Theory of Moral Incentives in Cuba* (University, Alabama: University of Alabama Press, 1971). According to Malloy, "the combination of mobilization and moral stimuli could be viewed as a functional adaptation to the realities of an economy that had to restrict its consumption and increase its production; a policy designed for a situation of scarcity in which material incentives are no longer available or are considered too expensive." James A. Malloy, "Generation of Political Support and Allocation of Costs," in Carmelo Mesa-Lago, ed., *Revolutionary Change in Cuba* (Pittsburgh: University of Pittsburgh Press, 1971), p. 39.

67. Castro, too, believed in the power of human will and consciousness and utilized a similar strategy in the late 1960s. See his May Day 1971 speech on creating matter from consciousness, in Bernardo, *The Theory of Moral Incentives*.

68. "Transformation of Small Production Is a Long-Term Task of the Dictatorship of the Proletariat," *RMRB*, 17 August 1975.

69. As late as the 1970s, some radicals still believed that the old exploiting classes had strong ties to the private sector and preferred to see its expansion. See Yu Lin County, *Shehuizhuyi de jiti suoyouzhi*, pp. 47–48.

70. Ibid., p. 49.

71. Mao Yuanxin, Mao's nephew, who was influential in Liaoning Province, tried to propagate the experience of Heertao Commune, Zhangwu County, in that province. See *RMRB*, 9 May 1976, p. 1. For a criticism of this policy by the Party secretary of Zhangwu County, see *RMRB*, 21 October 1979, p. 2.

72. *RMRB*, 24 November 1968, p. 3; Martin K. Whyte, "The Tachai Brigade and Incentives for the Peasants," *Current Scene*, vol. 7, no. 16 (15 August 1969); and Jonathan Unger, "Remuneration, Ideology and Peasant Interests in a Chinese Village, 1960–1980," in William L. Parish, ed., *Chinese Rural Development: The Great Transformation* (Armonk, N.Y.: M. E. Sharpe, 1985), pp. 117–140.

73. In the Cuba of the 1960s "emulation commissions" were established to evaluate individual labor contributions for moral rewards. Robert M. Bernardo, "Moral Stimulation and Labor Allocation in Cuba," in Irving L. Horowitz, ed., *Cuban Communism* (New Brunswick, N.J.: Transaction Books, 1981), pp. 185–218.

74. Being close to a city was seen as making a unit vulnerable to "capitalist tendencies." *RMRB*, 3 June 1973, p. 2.

75. Thomas P. Bernstein, *Up to the Mountains and Down to the Countryside* (New Haven: Yale University Press, 1977).

76. According to Donnithorne, the cellular nature of the economy after the Cultural Revolution may have increased local control over resources and local efforts to expand that resource base. Audrey Donnithorne, "China's Cellular Economy: Some Economic Trends since the Cultural Revolution," *CQ*, no. 52 (October–December 1972): 605–619.

77. In 1969 teams were under severe pressure to establish local grain reserves to ensure that in the event of war each locality would be prepared to fend for itself. Jean C. Oi, "The Struggle over the Harvest and the Politics of Local Grain Reserves," in Randolph Barker and Beth Rose, eds., *Agricultural and Rural Development in China Today* (Ithaca: Cornell University Program in International Agriculture, 1983), pp. 97–119.

78. Mei Fanquan, "How to Increase China's Cotton Production," *RMRB*, 1 January 1982, p. 3.

79. Lardy estimates that while 3.4 percent of total grain produced was transferred among provinces in 1953–1956, that figure was down to 1.5 percent in 1965 and 0.1 percent in 1978. Nicholas P. Lardy, *Agriculture in China's Modern Economic Development* (Cambridge: Cambridge University Press, 1983), p. 51. Only inter-county transfers occurred in the late 1960s and 1970s. Ibid., p. 167.

80. The Chinese expression was *chaoguo dazhai, zenme xue dazhai?*

81. Data collected in 1980 from communes in Jiangsu show that collective accumulation peaked in 1976, whereas in the commune Butler studied accumulation peaked during the Cultural Revolution and began to drop in the 1970s. See Steven Butler, "Field Research in China's Communes: Views of a 'Guest'," in Anne F. Thurston and Burton Pasternak, eds., *The Social Sciences and Fieldwork in China* (Boulder: Westview Press, 1983), p. 112. This model fits Cuba's experience, where the moral-incentive economy also led to high rates of capital formation. See David Barkin, "Cuban Agriculture: A Strategy of Economic Development," in Irving L. Horowitz, ed., *Cuban Communism*, 4th ed. (New Brunswick, N.J.: Transaction Books, 1981), p. 64.

82. Michel C. Oksenberg, "Policy Formulation in Communist China: The Case of the Mass Irrigation Campaign, 1957–1958" (Ph.D. diss., Columbia University, 1969). Also see James E. Nickum, "Labour Accumulation in Rural China and Its Role since the Cultural Revolution," *Cambridge Journal of Economics*, no. 2 (1978): 273–286.

83. "In the course of farmland capital construction, the collective concept and sense of organization and discipline of the peasants are greatly enhanced, and they think more of the collective and show greater zeal in building socialism." Hua Guofeng, *Let the Whole Party Mobilize for a Vast Effort to Develop Agriculture and Build Tachai-type Counties throughout the Country* (Peking: Foreign Languages Press, 1975).

2. Policy Winds

1. For a discussion of the structure of elites and the importance of elite integration, see Robert D. Putnam, *The Comparative Study of Political Elites* (Englewood Cliffs, N.J.: Prentice Hall, 1976).

2. Even early Western studies of administrative behavior rejected ideal rational-choice models. See Herbert A. Simon, "A Behavioral Model of Rational Choice," *Quarterly Journal of Economics*, 69 (February 1955), and

Charles Lindblom, "The Science of Muddling Through," *Public Administration Review* (Spring 1959).

3. The most important approaches include competition or bargaining among coalitions (Fox), opinion groups (Chang), factions (Nathan, Pye), "policy tendencies" (Solinger), "Mao in command" (Oksenberg), and a combined factional-coalitional model (Winckler). See Galen Fox, "Campaigning for Power in China" (Ph.D. diss., Princeton University, 1978); Parris H. Chang, *Power and Policy in China* (University Park: Pennsylvania State University Press, 1975); Andrew Nathan, "A Factional Model for CCP Politics," *CQ*, no. 53 (January-March 1973): 34–66; Lucien Pye, *The Dynamics of Chinese Politics* (Cambridge, Mass.: Oelgeschlager, Gunn and Hain, 1981); Dorothy J. Solinger, *Chinese Business under Socialism* (Berkeley: University of California Press, 1984); Michel C. Oksenberg, "Policy Making under Mao, 1949–1968: An Overview," in John M. H. Lindbeck, ed., *China: Management of a Revolutionary Society* (Seattle: University of Washington Press, 1971): 79–115; and Edwin Winckler, "Dimensions of Agricultural Policy: Hebei, Jiangsu and Guangdong in the 1970s," paper presented at the Conference on Rural Bureaucracy in China, SSRC-ACLS Joint Committee on Contemporary China, Chicago, 26–30 August 1981.

4. Fox, "Campaigning for Power." On network building by the Gang of Four, see Ann E. Fenwick, "The Gang of Four and the Politics of Opposition: China, 1971–1976" (Ph.D. diss., Stanford University, 1984), pp. 220–234. According to Fenwick (p. 567), factional ties reached down from the center to the county. See also John Wilson Lewis, "Political Networks and Policy Implementation in China," Occasional Paper of the Northeast Asia–United States Forum on International Policy, Stanford University, March 1986. For center-provincial factional ties see Dorothy J. Solinger, "Politics in Yunnan Province in the Decade of Disorder," *CQ*, no. 92 (December 1982): 628–662, and Keith Forster, "The 1974 Campaign against Lin Biao and Confucius in Zhejiang," *CQ*, no. 107 (September 1986): 433–462.

5. William A. Joseph, *The Critique of Ultra-Leftism in China, 1958–1981* (Stanford: Stanford University Press, 1984), pp. 142–144.

6. Solinger, *Chinese Business under Socialism*, pp. 60–86, and her edited book, *Three Visions of Socialism in China* (Boulder: Westview Press, 1984). Her concept of policy tendencies is borrowed from Franklyn Griffiths, "A Tendency Analysis of Soviet Policy-Making," in H. Gordon Skilling and Franklyn Griffiths, eds., *Interest Groups in Soviet Politics* (Princeton: Princeton University Press, 1971), pp. 335–377.

7. Winckler, who begins from the perspective of factions not policy tendencies, argues that five factions—Party radicals, military radicals, regional moderates, state socialists, and market socialists—have competed for power since 1968, each possessing a "pure policy tendency" on agricultural development. See Winckler, "Dimensions of Agricultural Policy."

8. See *RMRB*, in *FBIS*, 15 August 1977; James E. Nickum, "Labour Accumulation in Rural China and Its Role since the Cultural Revolution," *Cambridge Journal of Economics*, no. 2 (1978): 273–286; and David Zweig, "Agrarian Radicalism in China, 1968–1978: The Search for a Social Base" (Ph.D. diss., The University of Michigan, 1983), pp. 246–247.

9. Jurgen Domes, *China after the Cultural Revolution: Politics between Two Party Congresses* (London: C. Hurst, 1976).

10. 10. Robert Scalapino, "The CCP's Provincial Secretaries," *Problems of Communism*, vol. 25 (July-August 1976): 18.

11. Kenneth Lieberthal, with James Tong and Sai-cheung Yeung, *Central Documents and Politburo Politics in China* (Ann Arbor: Michigan Papers in Chinese Studies, no. 33, 1978).

12. Fenwick, "The Politics of Opposition," p. 562. Similarly, Ploss considers "divergent outlooks" to have been a source of the conflict between Malenkov and Khrushchev. Sidney Ploss, *Conflict and Decision-Making in Soviet Russia: A Case Study of Agricultural Policy, 1953–1963* (Princeton: Princeton University Press, 1965), p. 58.

13. Pye, *Dynamics of Chinese Politics*, p. 10.

14. Lowell Dittmer, "The Bases of Power in Chinese Politics: A Theory and an Analysis of the Fall of the 'Gang of Four'," *World Politics*, vol. 26, no. 1 (October 1978): 26–60.

15. "Democratic centralism" prohibits publicly airing personal views after a Party decision has been taken. An excellent discussion of the breakdown of Party norms in China is Fredrick Tiewes, *Politics and Purges in China* (Armonk, N.Y.: M. E. Sharpe, 1979).

16. Jiang Qing, "Speech at the National Conference on Learning from Tachai in Agriculture (Summary)," *Chinese Law and Government*, vol. 10, no. 1 (Spring 1977): 12–16.

17. Chang, *Power and Policy in China*.

18. Stephen A. Quick, "The Paradox of Popularity: 'Ideological' Program Implementation in Zambia," in Merilee S. Grindle, ed., *Politics and Policy Implementation in the Third World* (Princeton: Princeton University Press, 1980); and Arturo Valenzuela, *The Breakdown of Democratic Regimes: Chile* (Baltimore: Johns Hopkins University Press, 1982). My thanks go to Forrest Colburn for the second source.

19. Lucian W. Pye, *Asian Power and Politics: The Cultural Dimensions of Authority* (Cambridge, Mass.: Harvard University Press, 1985).

20. William L. Sheridan, *The Nazi Seizure of Power* (Chicago: Quadrangle Books, 1969). I am indebted to Bill Fisher, who introduced me to this book.

21. Carl Riskin, "Introduction," in Solinger, *Three Visions of Socialism*, p. 4.

22. The only exceptions were a 1967 document which criticized expanding private plots and a 1977 meeting on Dazhai, hitherto unknown in the West, which called on 10 percent of rural China to shift to brigade accounting. See *MECE*, pp. 592–593.

23. "CCP Central Committee Directive Concerning the Question of Distribution in the Rural People's Commune (Zhongfa 1971)," no. 82, 26 December 1971, in *Issues and Studies*, vol. 9, no. 2 (November 1972).

24. A "horizontal" wind occurred in 1977–1978 when test points for household quotas in Anhui became known in Nanjing. Local leaders who did not like this policy ignored it; supporters tried it. See David Zweig, "Peasants, Ideology, and the New Incentive Systems: Jiangsu Province, 1978–1981," in William L. Parish, ed., *Chinese Rural Development: The Great Transformation* (Armonk, N.Y.: M. E. Sharpe, 1985), pp. 141–163.

25. I drew my sense of the radical environment from Unger's "milieu of activism." See Jonathan Unger, "Collective Incentives in the Chinese Coun-

tryside: Lessons from Chen Village," *World Development*, no. 6 (1978): 583–601.

26. Union Research Institute, *The Case of P'eng Te-huai* (Hong Kong: Union Research Publication, 1968), p. 3.

27. By what Sheridan calls "perpetual campaigning" the Nazis politicized issues, polarized populations, and spurred on radicalism in preparation for their early 1930s seizure of power; Sheridan, *The Nazi Seizure of Power*, pp. 40, 135.

28. *Zhejiang ribao* (Zhejiang Daily), 29 November 1978, p. 3.

29. Ibid.

30. *RMRB*, 9 May 1976.

31. *RMRB*, 21 January 1979, and Hong Kong interview, 1980.

32. Wang Fenglin, "Yao shifen shenzhongde duidai nongcun renmin gongshe jiben hesuan danweide guodu wenti" (We Must Certainly Handle Carefully the Problem of the Transition of the Basic Accounting Unit of the Rural People's Communes), in *Zhongguo nongye jingji xuehuide yici xueshu taolunhui lunwen xuanluo* (A Collection of Articles from the First Academic Conference of the Chinese Institute of Agricultural Economics) (Beijing: Nongye chubanshe, 1979), pp. 351–364, and Rural Nanjing interview, 1981.

33. Edward Friedman, "The Politics of Local Models, Social Transformation and State Power Struggles in the People's Republic of China: Tachai and Teng Hsiao-p'ing," *CQ*, no. 76 (December 1978): 873–890.

34. Hong Kong interview, 1980.

35. Rural Nanjing interview, 1981.

36. Norma Diamond, "Model Villages and Village Realities," *Modern China*, vol. 9, no. 2 (April 1983): 163–181, and Hong Kong interview, 1980.

37. Diamond, "Model Villages and Village Realities," p. 177.

38. In Chinese the slogan was *Gesheng zuzhi nongye zhanxian lingdao tongzhi fenpi fenqi qu Dazhai canguan xuexi*. Interview at Nanjing Agricultural Work Office, 1981.

39. Shanxi Provincial Party Committee, "Guanyu quansheng nongye xue Dazhai jingyan jiaoxun de chubu zongjie" (Preliminary Summation of the Lessons and Experiences of the Provincial Movement to Learn from Dazhai in Agriculture), 24 August 1980, in CC-CCP Rural Policy Research Office's Material Office, ed., *Nongcun jingji zhengce huibian, 1978–1981* (Compendium of Agricultural Economic Policies), vol. 1 (Beijing: Nongcun duwu chubanshe, 1982), pp. 121–122.

40. Unger, "Collective Incentives."

41. For the Three-Anti's Campaign, see Hong Kong interview, 1980. When an official of the National Supply and Marketing Co-op Association went to Heertao in 1976 to prevent officials there from "killing the market," he was critized and chased away. Rural Nanjing interview, 1981. For an argument that opposing brigade accounting left one open to a charge of rightism in 1976, see *RMRB*, 10 February 1978 and 10 January 1979.

42. Rusticated youth interview, Nanjing, 1981, and Hong Kong interview, 1980.

43. Rusticated youth interview, Beijing, 1981.

44. Tang Tsou, Marc Blecher, and Mitch Meisner, "Policy Change at the

National Summit and Institutional Transformation at the Local Level: The Case of Tachai and Hsiyang County in the Post-Mao Era," *Select Papers from the Center for Far Eastern Studies*, no. 4 (University of Chicago, 1979–1980), pp. 241–392.

45. Wang, "Yao shifen shenzhongde duidai."

46. Marc Blecher interview in Hong Kong of a county official from Guangdong Province (hereafter cited as Blecher interview). I am grateful to Blecher for sharing this interview with me.

47. Michel Oksenberg, "Policy Formulation in Communist China: The Case of the Mass Irrigation Campaign, 1957–1958" (Ph.D. diss., Columbia University, 1969), chap. 13.

48. An extensive discussion of horizontal versus vertical authority in the Chinese bureaucracy is A. Doak Barnett, *Cadres, Bureaucracy and Political Power* (New York: Columbia University Press, 1965), p. 73.

49. Interview, Ministry of Water Conservation, Beijing, April 1981.

50. Interview, Nanjing Municipality Rural Work Office, 1981.

51. A point made privately by Richard Lowenthal.

52. Joseph, *The Critique of Ultra-Leftism*, p. 50.

53. Richard Madsen, *Morality and Power in a Chinese Village* (Berkeley: University of California Press, 1984).

54. See *FBIS*, no. 250 (24 December 1968), p. C6, cited in The China Group. In 1970–1971 leadership changes around Long Bow Village occurred in 21 urban Party committees, 11 commune Party committees, 47 general branches, and 711 basic branches. William Hinton, *Shenfan* (New York: Random House, 1983), p. 178.

55. According to one report, 10 of 15 brigade secretaries in one location were labeled capitalist-roaders and dismissed, and 476 of 923 team cadres were also dismissed. See *SWB-FE*, 5699/BII/15 (22 December 1977) and *SWB-FE*, 5706/BII/6 (6 January 1978).

56. Lewis, "Political Networks."

57. Gao Yuan, *Born Red* (Stanford: Stanford University Press, 1987).

58. Interview with county water conservation officials, rural Nanjing, 1981, and Blecher interview.

59. Hong Kong interview, 1980.

60. *FB*, 11 July 1974, p. 2.

61. Hong Kong interview, 1980.

62. Local cadres mobilized the more conservative youths to stop rural power seizures by Red Guards and participate in what Nee calls Red Guard bashing. Victor Nee, "Between Center and Locality: State, Militia and Village," in Victor Nee and David Mozingo, eds., *State and Society in Contemporary China* (Ithaca: Cornell University Press, 1983), pp. 223–243.

63. Richard Madsen, "Harnessing the Political Potential of Peasant Youth," in Nee and Mozingo, *State and Society*, p. 254.

64. Ibid. p. 254.

65. According to John P. Burns, "Chinese Peasant Interest Articulation: 1949–1974" (Ph.D. diss., Columbia University, 1978), p. 277, "campaign work teams" were less likely to listen to local opinion and more likely to impose national goals than "non-campaign work teams."

66. Hong Kong interview, 1980. Much of my information on work teams comes from two informants who participated in work teams during the radical decade.

67. Abrogating leadership functions was more common in "test points" than in other units visited by campaign work teams. Burns, "Chinese Peasant Interest Articulation," p. 277.

68. Interview with Chinese professor who had participated in these campaigns, Nanjing, 1980.

69. According to a Hong Kong interview, it was this way in Guangxi Province. A 1981 report on work teams said that cadres had to stay for four months. *Shanxi ribao*, 29 November 1981, pp. 1, 3.

70. Hong Kong interview, 1980.

71. Hong Kong interview, 1980.

72. For ways the Gang of Four used the media to contact their factional network see Fenwick, "The Politics of Opposition," p. 224.

73. Ibid., pp. 231–232, and *FBIS*, no. 60 (29 March 1977): E1–9.

74. Hong Kong interview, 1980. During the Criticize Deng Xiaoping Campaign the radicals sent preteens into the poster compound at Beijing University and then made a movie, hoping to demonstrate the campaign's popularity. David Zweig, "The Peita Debate on Education and the Fall of Teng Hsiao-p'ing," *CQ*, no. 73 (March 1978): 140–158.

75. Hong Kong interviews.

76. *FB*, 7 April 1974 and 18 September 1974. I am grateful to Steven Mosher for sharing these papers with me.

77. On the relationship between factional conflicts and media distortions see Pye, *Dynamics of Chinese Politics*, pp. 10–11.

78. Hong Kong interview, 1980.

79. Hong Kong interview, 1980.

80. Liang Heng and Judith Shapiro, *Son of the Revolution* (New York: Alfred Knopf, 1983), p. 161.

81. See Thomas P. Bernstein, *Up to the Mountains and Down to the Villages* (New Haven: Yale University Press, 1977), and Stanley Rosen, *The Role of Sent-Down Youth in the Chinese Cultural Revolution*, China Research Monograph no. 19 (Berkeley: University of California, Berkeley Center for Chinese Studies, 1981).

82. Anita Chan, Richard Madsen, and Jonathan Unger, *Chen Village: The Recent History of a Peasant Community in Mao's China* (Berkeley: University of California Press, 1984).

83. Hong Kong interview, 1980.

84. *FBIS*, no. 252 (27 December 1968): C6, in The China Group.

3. Periodization

1. For an outline of major agricultural events from 1966 to 1978, see Table 3.

2. William A. Joseph, *The Critique of Ultra-Leftism in China, 1958–1981* (Stanford: Stanford University Press, 1984).

3. The figure shows that 1968–1969 was a radical period. The 1971 peak,

the result of criticisms of private plots, household sidelines, and markets, does not correspond well with the politics of the period; however, Figure 2, which depicts the rightist trends, shows that the radical strategy was already being strongly criticized by mid-1971. The 1975 peak is due to similar criticisms during the Bourgeois Rights Campaign. Yet the leftist trend clearly continued through 1976.

4. Nicholas R. Lardy, *Agriculture in China's Modern Economic Development* (Cambridge: Cambridge University Press, 1983), p. 19.

5. Fang Yan, *RMRB*, 25 May 1979.

6. Hu Qiaomu, *RMRB*, 6 October 1978.

7. Data from State Statistical Bureau, *Zhongguo tongji nianjian, 1984* (Chinese Statistical Yearbook) (Beijing: Zhongguo tongji chubanshe, 1984), p. 138.

8. *RMRB* editorial, 10 November 1966.

9. In Chen Village of Guangdong Province, which is not in the suburbs, Red Guard attacks in January 1967 caused all brigade cadres to quit. The PLA had to move in to maintain order. See Anita Chan, Richard Madsen, and Jonathan Unger, *Chen Village: The Recent History of a Peasant Community in Mao's China* (Berkeley: University of California Press, 1984), pp. 126–129.

10. *FBIS*, no. 250 (24 December 1968): C6, in China Group.

11. Rural Nanjing interview, 1981.

12. Jurgen Domes, *Socialism in the Chinese Countryside* (Montreal: McGill-Queen's University Press, 1980), p. 64.

13. Han Ke-chuan, "Recent Developments in Rural Communes on the Chinese Mainland," *Issues and Studies*, vol. 5, no. 8 (May 1969): 7.

14. A report from Anhui Province described winter 1967 as a period of "anarchism," during which peasants in Youxi County cut and sold collective trees. See *FBIS*, no. 21 (31 January 1969): C11–12, in China Group. Nanjing cadres admitted that "in the years 1967–68, during the chaos of the Cultural Revolution, people opened up a lot of marginal land." Rural Nanjing interview, 1981.

15. Baum suggests that in the summer of 1966 restrictions on private plots were under way. Richard Baum, "The Cultural Revolution in the Countryside: Anatomy of a Limited Rebellion," in Thomas W. Robinson, ed., *The Cultural Revolution in China* (Berkeley: University of California Press, 1971), pp. 367–476. On 29 December 1967 *RMRB* reported that private plots had been restricted in Shandong. But these were sporadic events.

16. *RMRB* and *JFRB* joint editorial, 9 April 1968.

17. *Zhejiang ribao*, 29 November 1978, p. 3.

18. Interview at the Agricultural Economics Research Institute of the Chinese Academy of Social Sciences, 28 April 1981. Beyond knowing that it occurred at a small conference in Shanghai, no Chinese official seems to have the exact date or location of this speech.

19. *RMRB*, 4 May 1968, 16 June 1968, and 26 June 1968.

20. *SCMP*, no. 4176 (13 May 1968): 29–30, in China Group.

21. *RMRB*, 29 March 1971.

22. *RMRB*, 27 September 1968. See also Central Intelligence Agency,

Directorate of Intelligence, Intelligence Report, *Policy Issues in the Purge of Lin Piao* (November 1972), p. 44.

23. Colina McDougall, "The Cultural Revolution in the Communes: Back to 1958?", *Current Scene*, vol. 7, no. 7 (1968). See also Wang Fenglin, "Yao shifen shenzhongde duidai nongcun renmin gongshe jiben hesuan danweide guodu wenti" (We Must Certainly Handle Carefully the Problem of the Transition of the Basic Accounting Unit of the Rural People's Communes), in *Zhongguo nongye jingji xuehuide yici xueshu taolunhui lunwen xuanluo* (A Collection of Articles from the First Academic Conference of the Chinese Institute of Agricultural Economics) (Beijing: Nongye chubanshe, 1979), pp. 351–364. Han Ke-chuan too cites many restrictions on reclaimed land in October 1968. Several critiques of "ultra-leftism" published in 1971 dated these leftist excesses to the winter of 1968. See *RMRB*, 14 November 1971, p. 1; 26 December 1971, p. 3; and 4 June 1972, p. 1.

24. *RMRB*, 7 December 1968; 3 February 1969, p. 4; and interviews in Hong Kong, 1980, and rural Nanjing, 1981.

25. *RMRB*, 24 November 1968. For calls for shifting the control of state-run schools to the brigade, see *RMRB*, 14 November 1968.

26. In one Jiangxi Province commune, 30 brigades were condensed into 13, and 323 teams into 116. McDougall, "The Cultural Revolution in the Communes," p. 5.

27. *RMRB*, 17 January 1969.

28. Ibid.

29. Thomas P. Bernstein, *Up to the Mountains and Down to the Villages* (New Haven: Yale University Press, 1977), p. 32.

30. Michel Oksenberg, "The Fall of the Cultural Revolutionaries," paper presented at the Harvard East Asia Conference on the PRC, Cambridge, Mass., 3–5 January 1983, p. 27.

31. Budget outlays changed by almost 5 percent. Ronald G. Mitchell and Edward P. Parris, "Chinese Defense Spending, 1965–1978," in *Allocation of Resources in the Soviet Union and China*, Joint Economic Committee, U.S. Congress (Washington, D.C.: Government Printing Office, 1979), pp. 67–71.

32. Dennis Woodward, "Rural Campaigns: Continuity and Change in the Chinese Countryside—The Early Post-Cultural Revolution Experience (1969–1972)," *Australian Journal of Chinese Affairs*, no. 6 (1981): 97–124.

33. Oksenberg, "Fall of the Cultural Revolutionaries," p. 31.

34. Jurgen Domes, *China after the Cultural Revolution: Politics between Two Party Congresses* (London: C. Hurst and Co., 1976), p. 61n2. Hong Kong reported a great flying leap during the winter of 1969–1970. *JPRS*, 49822, no. 89 (12 February 1970): 1–2. While some provinces had spoken of a "new flying leap" in early 1969, the phrase was repeated with greater frequency at the end of the year in Hunan, Qinghai, Guangzhou and Heilongjiang provinces. *CQ*, no. 38, p. 185, and no. 41, pp. 171–172.

35. See CIA, *Policy Issues*, p. 35.

36. "The Opinion Concerning the Government Purchase and Distribution of Food and Oil in 1969," issued by the Revolutionary Committee of Mung-lien County in Yunnan, *Issues and Studies*, vol. 7, no. 4 (January 1971). This document was a province-wide order from the Provincial Revolutionary Committee and the Kunming Military Region.

37. See Zeng Qixian, "Comments on Consumption and Savings," *Social Sciences in China*, no. 4 (1983): 158.

38. When it began in November 1969 in Jiangxi Province, it was called the Four Anti's Campaign. See Woodward, "Rural Campaigns," and C. P. Chang, "The 'One Blow and Three Anti' Movement in Mainland China," *Issues and Studies*, vol. 6, no. 11 (August 1970): 12–13.

39. We know little about this campaign, and while Fenwick argues that it was a "demobilization campaign"—it led to the arrest of leftists and Cultural Revolution activists—it probably helped local military leaders. See Ann E. Fenwick, "The Gang of Four and the Politics of Opposition; China, 1971–1976" (Ph.D. diss., Stanford University, 1984), p. 130.

40. In Nanjing municipality 36.5 percent more cubic meters of soil were turned during capital construction projects that winter than in the previous year, and the amount of labor expended in these projects increased by 53 percent. Data collected from the Nanjing Agricultural Office, spring 1981. See Table 4. See also James E. Nickum, "Labor Accumulation in Rural China and Its Role since the Cultural Revolution," *Cambridge Journal of Economics*, no. 2 (1978): 280.

41. Between August and December 1969, six *RMRB* articles criticized peasants for using marginal land, which is precisely the kind of land that would be incorporated into collective fields during rural capital construction projects.

42. Data collected from *Zhongguo nongye nianjian* (Chinese Agricultural Yearbook), 1980, 1981, and 1983 (Beijing: Nongye chubanshe).

43. The Cultural Revolution Small Group was abolished, and the May 16th Group was accused of "ultra-leftism" and investigated. Leftists in Shanxi, Shandong, Heilongjiang and Guizhou provinces lost their posts as well. Philip Bridgham, "The Fall of Lin Biao," *CQ*, no. 55 (July-September 1973): 432.

44. CIA, *Policy Issues*, p. 45.

45. *CNS*, no. 347 (26 November 1970).

46. *MECA*, p. 135.

47. This conference met in Xiyang County, home of the Dazhai Brigade, in a preparatory session on 25 June 1970 and then in three formal sessions running from 25 August to 5 October. Only on 11 December was the State Council Report on the Northern Districts Agricultural Conference published. See *MECA*, pp. 136–137.

48. *MECE*, p. 468.

49. For support for the policies of the *Sixty Articles* see ibid. However, the Gang of Four undercut the moderating impact of the conference. Yu Guoyao, "Wo guo nongye jingji wentide yidian renshi" (Understanding Problems in our Country's Agricultural Policy), *HQ*, no. 5 (1980): 28–30.

50. *RMRB*, 17 June 1970, and Domes, *Socialism in the Chinese Countryside*, p. 70.

51. *RMRB*, 15 August 1970.

52. *CNS*, no. 347 (November 26, 1970).

53. Domes, *Socialism in the Chinese Countryside*, p. 71, and "The Secret Draft of the Revised Constitution of the People's Republic of China (1970–

1971)," in Winberg Chai, ed., *Essential Works of Chinese Communism* (New York: Bantam Books, 1972), pp. 513–520.

54. For Shanxi Province see *CNS*, no. 347 (26 November 1970). For Yunnan provincial documents see "Minutes of the Yunnan Provincial Conference on Rural Work (Draft)," 24 December 1970, *Issues and Studies*, vol. 7, no. 2 (November 1971). For Guangxi and Hunan provinces see *CNS*, no. 347 (26 November 1970), and no. 348 (3 December 1970).

55. Parris Chang, "Who Gets What, When and How in Chinese Politics: A Case Study of the Strategies of Conflict of the Gang of Four," *Australian Journal of Chinese Affairs*, no. 2 (July 1979): 28.

56. Galen W. Fox, "Campaigning for Power in China During the Cultural Revolution Era, 1967–1976" (Ph.D. diss., Princeton University, 1978), p. 183.

57. Robert A. Scalapino, "The CCP's Provincial Secretaries," *Problems of Communism*, vol. 25 (July–August 1976): 18–35; and Fox, "Campaigning for Power," p. 182. Roderick MacFarquhar told me that agricultural reforms following Lin's political demise might have represented a payoff to the regional military leaders.

58. Fenwick, "The Politics of Opposition," pp. 149–150.

59. CC-CCP Central Committee, "Directive Concerning the Question of Distribution in the Rural People's Communes, Zhongfa No. 82 (26 December 1971)," in *Issues and Studies*, vol. 9, no. 2 (November 1972).

60. A new county committee in Shandong Province attacked the leftist trends that had been developing in their county. *RMRB*, 10 January 1972, p. 1.

61. For reports on Menglian County of Yunnan Province and Tian'an County of Hunan Province, see *RMRB*, 7 April 1974, p. 2. For Panyu County see *FB*, 18 September 1974, p. 3.

62. This occurred in Jiangning County, Jiangsu Province, and in Chen Village, Guangdong Province. See Anita Cham, Richard Madsen and Jonathan Unger, *Chen Village: The Recent History of a Peasant Community in Mao's China* (Berkeley: University of California Press, 1984).

63. See *HQ*, no. 3 (1979): 37.

64. The proportion of total income of the People's Communes distributed to peasants did not rise in 1972, although the collectives made little money that year. Overall, from 1973 to 1976 the proportion of total income from the People's Communes distributed to the peasants dropped (see Table 2).

65. Higher levels of the collective could take team funds "under the conditions of not influencing the team's expansion of reproductive capacity," but no mention was made of influencing peasant incomes. *MECE*, p. 489.

66. *RMRB*, 18 March 1972.

67. *Resolution on Certain Questions in the History of Our Party since the Founding of the People's Republic of China* (Beijing: Foreign Languages Press, 1981), p. 38.

68. Joseph, *Critique of Ultra Leftism*, p. 142.

69. Fenwick, "The Politics of Opposition," pp. 205, 241.

70. Lowell Dittmer, "Cultural Revolution and Cultural Change," in Godwin Chu and Francis L. K. Hsu, eds., *Moving a Mountain: Cultural Change in China* (Honolulu: University Press of Hawaii, 1979), p. 222.

71. See Yang Rongguo's *RMRB* article of 7 August 1973.

72. Domes, *Socialism in the Chinese Countryside*, makes this argument.

73. Interestingly, four of the five articles appeared in December 1973–January 1974. See *RMRB*, 7 December 1973, p. 3; 11 December 1973, p. 2; 4 January 1974, p. 4; 7 January 1974, p. 3; and 5 August 1974, p. 2.

74. In the fall and winter of 1973 private plots were restricted in Sichuan and Guangdong provinces respectively. In winter 1973 some teams were amalgamated in Jilin Province. Hong Kong interviews, 1980.

75. For Shanxi and Hebei provinces see *RMRB*, 27 February 1975, p. 3, and 10 December 1974, p. 3. Gansu Province reported that the emphasis on politics, which waned in 1971–1973, was rekindled in 1974. *RMRB*, 12 July 1975.

76. *RMRB*, 31 March 1979.

77. Rural Nanjing interview, 1981.

78. *RMRB*, 12 December 1976, and *Kunming Radio*, 15 December 1973.

79. Hong Kong interview, 1980.

80. Interview with university professor, 1980.

81. *FB*, 4 April 1974 and 28 September 1974.

82. Hong Kong interviews, 1980.

83. Chen Yonggui, "Thoroughly Criticize the 'Gang of Four' and Bring About a New Upsurge in the Movement to Build Tachai-type Counties throughout the Country," speech to the Second National Conference on Learning from Tachai in Agriculture, 20 December 1976, *SPRCM*, no. 910 (7 February 1977): 64–82.

84. *MECE*, pp. 565–566.

85. *RMRB*, 3 February 1975, 4 February 1975, 10 February 1975, and two articles on 27 February 1975.

86. *RMRB*, 14 February 1975.

87. Zhang Chunqiao, *On Exercising All-Round Dictatorship over the Bourgeoisie* (Beijing: Foreign Languages Press, 1975). See also *HQ*, March 1975.

88. In Shaanxi Province in May-June 1975 local officials took away "some legal aspects of the rural economy." *FBIS*, no. 166 (26 August 1975): M2–3.

89. Chi Yan, *HQ*, no. 4 (April 1975), in *SPRCM*, nos. 819–820 (28 April–5 May 1975): 31–37; *HQ*, no. 5 (May 1975), in *SPRCM*, nos. 823–824, 27 May–2 June 1975): 13–19; and Cheng Yue, *HQ*, no. 6 (June 1975) in *SPRCM*, nos. 827–828 (30 June–7 July 1975): 10–13.

90. *FBIS*, no. 126 (30 June 1975): L2–4.

91. *Guangming ribao* in *JPRS*, 70685, no. 417 (24 February 1978): 46.

92. Fenwick, "The Politics of Opposition," p. 241.

93. David Zweig, "The Peita Debate on Education and the Fall of Teng Hsiao-p'ing," *CQ*, no. 73 (March 1978).

94. Jiang Qing, "Chiang Ch'ing's (July 2, 1975) Letter to the Delegates Attending the CCP-CC All-China Conference on Professional Work in Agriculture," *Issues and Studies* (October 1975): 86–87.

95. Jiang Qing, "Speech at the National Conference on Learning from Tachai in Agriculture (Summary)," *Chinese Law and Government*, vol. 10, no. 1 (Spring 1977): 16.

96. Speech by Wang Mingshen to the Second National Dazhai Conference, in *FBIS*, no. 245 (20 December 1976): E9–11.

97. Hua Guofeng, *Let the Whole Party Mobilize for a Vast Effort to Develop Agriculture and Build Tachai-type Counties throughout the Country* (Peking: Foreign Languages Press, 1975).

98. *FBIS*, no. 60 (29 March 1977): E8.

99. Ministry of Agriculture and Forestry Mass Criticism Group, "Two-Line Struggle around the First National Conference on Learning from Dazhai in Agriculture," *HQ*, no. 1 (January 1977).

100. "Ministry Mass Criticism Group Exposes Crimes of 'Gang of Four' in Undermining Agriculture," *Xinhua News Agency*, English, no. 6817 (26 November 1976): 4–6.

101. David S. G. Goodman, "The Shanghai Connection: Shanghai's Role in National Politics during the 1970s," in Christopher Howe, ed., *Shanghai* (Cambridge: Cambridge University Press, 1981), pp. 125–152.

102. In the winter of 1975–1976, 130 million people worked on capital construction projects with more turning out than ever before for winter field work in Hebei, Shandong, Anhui, Henan, Guangdong, Jiangxi, and Xinjiang provinces. *Xinhua Press Release*, 12 March 1976. I am grateful to Ross Munro for this citation.

103. See Tang Tsou, Marc Blecher, and Mitch Meisner, "Policy Change at the National Summit and Institutional Transformation at the Local Level: The Case of Tachai [Dazhai] and Hsiyang [Xiyang] County in the Post-Mao Era," *Select Papers from the Center for Far Eastern Studies*, no. 4 (Chicago: University of Chicago, 1979–1980), pp. 241–392.

104. According to Fox, at most 5 of 29 provincial leaders supported the radicals. Fox, "Campaigning for Power," p. 306.

105. Fenwick, "The Politics of Opposition," pp. 415–435, was the first study to discuss this important conference.

106. *FBIS* (29 March 1977): E6.

107. *Issues and Studies*, October 1977.

108. Chen, "Thoroughly Criticize the Gang of Four."

109. *FBIS*, no. 245 (20 December 1976): E9–11, and Chen, "Thoroughly Criticize the Gang of Four."

110. Lu Yang, *HQ*, no. 4 (April 1976), in *SPRCM*, nos. 867–868 (20–26 April 1976): 69–75.

111. *RMRB*, 9 May 1976, and *MECE*, pp. 565–566.

112. *FBIS*, no. 127 (30 June 1976): K4–6.

113. See *FBIS*, no. 118 (17 June 1976): H1–2; no. 120 (21 June 1976): K5–6; no. 124 (25 June 1976): H1–3; and no. 126 (29 June 1976): K2. Many of these articles reported meetings of Chen Yonggui with visitors to Dazhai. (Other articles not cited are available.)

114. *FBIS*, no. 60 (29 March 1977): E6.

115. Hong Kong interviews, 1980.

116. Rural Nanjing interview, 1981.

117. Rusticated youth interviews, Beijing and Nanjing, 1981.

118. These restrictions occurred in Fujian, Jiangsu, Jiangxi, and Guizhou provinces. Hong Kong interview, 1980, and *RMRB*, 18 January 1979, p. 2. Officials in Menglian County, Yunnan Province, cut back on the size of private plots that had been expanding since 1971. Hong Kong interview, 1980.

119. Pressures building since May 1976 in Sinan County, Guizhou Province, prompted 174 brigades to adopt brigade accounting in August 1976. *RMRB*, 10 January 1979. According to officials at the Agricultural Economics Research Institute of the Chinese Academy of Social Sciences, many transitions to brigade accounting occurred in 1975–1976.

120. Chen, "Thoroughly Criticize the Gang of Four," p. 71.

121. In 1976 peasants in Jiangpu County believed that Mao was grooming Zhanq Chunqiao for Party chairman. Rusticated youth interview, Nanjing, 1981.

122. Li Chengrui, "An Analysis of China's Economic Situation," *JJYJ*, no. 1 (1984): 23–31.

123. Chen, "Thoroughly Criticize the Gang of Four."

124. By January 1977, 260 brigades in Sinan County, Guizhou Province, moved to brigade accounting, while in 1977, a vegetable brigade outside Xining, Qinghai Province, did the same. See *RMRB*, 10 January 1979, and *Qinghai Daily*, 19 June 1979, p. 2.

125. The former restrictions occurred in Jiangpu County, Jiangsu Province; for the latter restrictions, which occurred in Wuxing County, Zhejiang Province, see *RMRB*, 31 May 1978.

126. Interviews in Hong Kong, 1980, and rural Nanjing, 1981.

127. Chen Yonggui, *HQ*, no. 10 (1977), in *SWB-FE*, 5641/B11 (15 October 1977): 1–9.

128. *MECE*, p. 582.

129. *SWB-FE*, 5641/B11, pp. 10–12.

130. *MECE*, pp. 592–593.

131. *RMRB*, 11 December 1977, editorial. This editorial probably heralded the conference, for it called for accelerating agricultural development and contained over 30 references to Dazhai.

132. *MECE*, pp. 592–593.

133. Wang Enmao, "Thoroughly Expose and Criticize the Gang of Four, Conscientiously Learn from Dazhai and Strive to Develop Agriculture in Our Province at High Speed," Report to the Second Jilin Learn from Dazhai in Agriculture Conference, 28 January 1978, in *FBIS* (23 February 1978): L16. Even the title of the talk matched the major themes of the December conference.

134. Figure given in a lecture at the Economics Department of Nanjing University in 1981.

135. *RMRB*, 4 January 1979 and personal interviews.

136. "Which is Bigger, the County Party Committee or the Constitu-

tion?" in Hugh Thomas, ed., *Comrade Editor: Letters to the People's Daily* (Hong Kong: Joint Publishing Co., 1980), pp. 41–46.

137. This movement was officially heralded in a *RMRB* editorial of 5 July 1978. The Central Document for the campaign, entitled "Zhonggong zhongyang zhuanfa zhonggong Hunan sheng Xiangxiang xianwei guanyu renzhen luoshi dangde nongcun jingji zhengce, nuli jianqing nongmin buheli fudande jingyan" (Transmission by the CCP-Central Committee of Hunan Province's Xiangxiang County's Party Committee on the Experience in Earnestly Implementing the Party's Agricultural Economic Policy and Energetically Lightening the Peasant's Unfair Burden), in *Zhongguo baike nianjian, 1980* (Chinese Yearbook; Beijing: Zhongguo da baike quanshu chubanshe, 1981), p. 337, included all the policies of the *Sixty Articles*.

138. In October 1978 cadres accused peasants who cut grass in their spare time of following the capitalist road. Xu Lu, *Renmin gongshede zizhuquan he suoyouzhi* (The Rights of Sovereignty and Ownership in the People's Communes) (Guangzhou: Guangdong renmin chubanshe, 1979), pp. 19–20.

4. The Local Response

1. An extremely useful definition of political culture, which suggests variations from level to level, is Kenneth Jowitt, "An Organizational Approach to the Study of Political Culture in Marxist-Leninist Systems," *American Political Science Review*, vol. 68 (September 1974): 1173.

2. Richard Madsen, *Morality and Power in a Chinese Village* (Berkeley: University of California Press, 1984). Scott argues that peasant participants in revolutionary movements have their own perceptions; their "revolution in the revolution" dictates the final revolutionary form. James C. Scott, "Revolution in the Revolution: Peasants and Commissars," *Theory and Society*, vol. 7, nos. 1 and 2 (January–March 1979): 97–134.

3. James C. Scott, "Protest and Profanation: Agrarian Revolt and the Little Tradition," pt. 2, *Theory and Society*, vol. 4, no. 1 (Spring 1977): 1.

4. Philip Converse, "The Nature of Belief Systems in Mass Publics," in David Apter, ed., *Ideology and Discontent* (London: Free Press, 1964), p. 213, argues that only 4 percent of Americans saw ideological connections between different policy issues and had constrained belief systems. Even American support for lofty ideals of justice and equality waned considerably when confronted by specific policies derived from these goals. James W. Prothro and Charles M. Grigg, "Fundamental Principles of Democracy," *Journal of Politics*, vol. 22 (1960): 279–294.

5. For Egyptian peasants, "general abstract principles were better understood when embodied in concrete policies and forms." Iliya Harik, *The Political Mobilization of Peasants* (Bloomington: Indiana University Press, 1974), p. 185.

6. Victor C. Falkenheim, "Rational-Choice Models and the Study of Citizen Politics in China," *Contemporary China*, vol. 3, no. 2 (Summer 1979).

7. James C. Scott, "Peasant Revolution: A Dismal Science," *Comparative Politics*, vol. 9, no. 2 (January 1977): 231–248.

8. Samuel L. Popkin, *The Rational Peasant* (Berkeley: University of California Press, 1979). For applications to China, see Falkenheim, "Rational-Choice Models," and John P. Burns, "Chinese Peasant Interest Articulation" (Ph.D. diss., Columbia University, 1978).

9. Vivienne Shue, *Peasant China in Transition* (Berkeley: University of California Press, 1980), p. 321.

10. James C. Scott, *The Moral Economy of the Peasant* (New Haven: Yale University Press, 1976).

11. R. David Arkush, "'If Man Works Hard the Land Will Not Be Lazy': Entrepreneurial Values in North Chinese Peasant Proverbs," *Modern China*, vol. 10, no. 4 (October 1984): 473.

12. Madsen, *Morality and Power*, p. 61.

13. Yuji Muramatsu, "Some Themes in Chinese Rebel Ideologies," in Arthur F. Wright, ed., *The Confucian Persuasion* (Stanford: Stanford University Press, 1960), pp. 241–267. The Taiping's document, "The Land System of the Heavenly Dynasty," promised that "if there is land, it shall be shared by all to till; if there is any food, clothing, or money, these shall be shared by all. In this way, all places will share the abundance equally, and will be equally well-fed and clothed." Vincent Y. C. Shih, *The Taiping Ideology* (Seattle: University of Washington Press, 1967), p. 81.

14. Shih, *The Taiping Ideology*, p. 80. See also Elizabeth J. Perry, *Rebels and Revolutionaries in North China, 1845–1945* (Stanford: Stanford University Press, 1980), p. 73.

15. Scott, "Revolution in the Revolution," pp. 120–123.

16. See Mao's 1948 speech cited in *JFRB*, 15 October 1981, in *FBIS* (21 October 1981): K1–3.

17. Mao's speech at Zhengzhou, 27 February 1959, translated by Pierre Perrolle, *Chinese Law and Government*, vol. 9, no. 4 (Winter 1976–1977): 10–44.

18. Martin K. Whyte, "The Tachai Brigade and Incentives for the Peasant," *Current Scene*, vol. 7, no. 16 (15 August 1969); and Peter Nolan and Gordon White, "Socialist Development and Rural Inequality: The Chinese Countryside in the 1970s," *Journal of Peasant Studies*, vol. 7, no. 1 (October 1979): 3–48.

19. According to Foster, peasants see inequality in zero-sum terms: one peasant's prosperity means a loss for the rest. George Foster, "Peasant Society and the Image of the Limited Good," in May N. Diaz, George M. Foster, and Jack H. Potter, eds., *Peasant Society: A Reader* (Boston: Little, Brown, 1967). See Chapter 8 below for the impact of the fear of polarization on post-Mao reforms.

20. Michel Oksenberg, "Local Leaders in Rural China, 1962–1965: Individual Attributes, Bureaucratic Positions and Political Recruitment," in A. Doak Barnett, ed., *Chinese Communist Politics in Action* (Seattle: University of Washington Press, 1969), p. 175.

21. One informant said that county and district officials who participated in his 1974 work team "were really afraid of a small group getting rich and the gap increasing as Marx said it would . . . So when they saw peasants getting rich they wanted to cut back on that." Hong Kong interview, 1980.

22. *RMRB*, 16 January 1979, p. 2, and 1 February 1980.

23. Wang Qinzu, "Learn from Dazhai to Continue the Revolution," in Hua Guofeng, ed., *Let the Whole Party Mobilize for a Vast Effort to Develop Agriculture and Build Tachai-type Counties throughout the Country* (Peking: Foreign Languages Press, 1975), p. 56.

24. Stuart R. Schram, "To Utopia and Back: A Cycle in the History of the Chinese Communist Party," *CQ*, no. 87 (September 1981): 423.

25. See Mao's "Talks at the Beidahe Conference," in Roderick MacFarquhar, ed., *Mao at High Tide* (forthcoming), p. 364.

26. Franz Schurmann, *Ideology and Organization in Communist China* (Berkeley: University of California Press, 1968), p. 49.

27. The idea of autonomy versus control comes from Philip A. Kuhn, "Local Self-Government under the Republic: Problems of Control, Autonomy and Mobilization," in Fredrick Wakeman, Jr., and Carolyn Grant, eds., *Conflict and Control in Late Imperial China* (Berkeley: University of California Press, 1975), while the dichotomy between penetration and participation comes from Philip A. Kuhn, "Political Development: Is There a Chinese Approach?" Edward H. Hume Memorial Lecture, Yale University, 1983.

28. Kuhn, "Local Self-Government," p. 282.

29. Mao Zedong, *Miscellany of Mao Tse-tung Thought, 1949–1968*, vols. 1 and 2, in *JPRS*, 61269-1-2 (20 February 1974), p. 214.

30. Comments by Jack Gray, cited in M. Stiefel and W. F. Wertheim, *Production, Equality and Participation in Rural China* (London: Zed Press, 1983), p. 123.

31. Kuhn, "Local Self-Government," p. 259, and Philip A. Kuhn, "Local Taxation and Finance in Republican China," in Susan Mann Jones, ed., *Select Papers from the Center for Far Eastern Studies*, no. 3 (University of Chicago, 1978–1979), pp. 128–129.

32. Kuhn, "Local Taxation and Finance," p. 100.

33. Victor Nee, "Between Center and Locality: State, Militia and Village," in Victor Nee and David Mozingo, eds., *State and Society in Contemporary China* (Ithaca: Cornell University Press, 1983), p. 236.

34. William L. Parish, "China—Team, Brigade, or Commune?" *Problems of Communism*, vol. 25, no. 2 (March-April 1976): 51–65.

35. Christine Wong, "Material Allocations and Decentralization: The Local Industrial Sector in the Post-Mao Reforms," in Elizabeth Perry and Christine Wong, eds., *The Political Economy of Post-Mao Reforms in China* (Cambridge, Mass.: Council on East Asia, Harvard University, 1984), pp. 253–278.

36. For a discussion of such factional networks, see Gu Hua, *A Small Town Called Hibiscus* (Beijing: Panda Books, 1980), and Liu Binyan, "People or Monsters," in Perry Link, ed., *People or Monsters* (Bloomington: Indiana University Press, 1983).

37. Allen H. Barton, "Determinants of Leadership Attitudes in Socialist Society," in Allen H. Barton, Bogdan Denitch, and Charles Kadushin, eds., *Opinion Making Elites in Yugoslavia* (New York: Praeger, 1973), p. 242.

38. Similarly, members of the Nazi Party "were trapped. They were now under party discipline and had to aid in the whole process." Party cells kept them under constant surveillance, making them more insecure, "for if they were ever expelled from the NSDAP, they would be marked men." William S. Sheridan, *The Nazi Seizure of Power* (Chicago: Quadrangle Books, 1965), p. 235.

39. County and commune control over village political life increased in Chen village after 1971. See Madsen, *Morality and Power*, p. 212. See also Marc

Blecher and Mitch Meisner, "Administrative Level and Agrarian Structure: The County (W)As Focal Point in Chinese Rural Development Policy," in Gordon White and Jack Gray, eds., *China's New Development Policy* (London: Academic Press, 1983).

40. During the radical peak of 1968–1970 (and perhaps as early as the Socialist Education Movement of 1964–1965), morally pure cadres, less embedded in long-standing social networks, often replaced older leaders, who were tightly entwined with the post–land reform elite. See Madsen, *Morality and Power*, p. 65.

41. Ibid.

42. A. Doak Barnett, with Ezra Vogel, *Cadres, Bureaucracy and Political Power* (New York: Columbia University Press, 1965).

43. Interview with officials from a county water conservation bureau in Jiangsu Province, 1981.

44. Blecher and Meisner, "Administrative Level and Agrarian Structure."

45. According to Butler, team and brigade leaders could not ignore county directives. Steven B. Butler, "Conflict and Decision-Making in China's Rural Administration, 1969–1976" (Ph.D. diss., Columbia University, 1980), p. 228.

46. Cited in Victor C. Falkenheim, "Decentralization and Control in Chinese Local Administration," in Donald Nelson, ed., *Local Politics in Communist Countries* (Lexington: University of Kentucky Press, 1980), pp. 191-210.

47. William L. Parish and Martin K. Whyte, *Village and Family in Contemporary China* (Chicago: University of Chicago Press, 1978), p. 38.

48. Butler, "Conflict and Decision-Making," p. 220.

49. On machinery see Jon Sigurdson, *Rural Industrialization in China* (Cambridge, Mass.: Harvard University Press, 1977). In 1975 a Nanjing commune gave its poorest brigade a small factory, which in 1986 remained its sole source of industrial employment and income. A wealthy commune in Nanjing's suburbs loaned machinery worth over 2 million yuan to its brigades for capital construction projects.

50. Rural Nanjing interview, 1981.

51. Chapter 5 discusses the excessive number of cadres drawing salaries from the brigade without performing labor. See also *RMRB*, 5 July 1978.

52. Middle-level officials in Nazi Germany did not care whether local Nazi leaders were corrupt, only whether they maintained tight control over the locality. Sheridan, *The Nazi Seizure of Power*.

53. Francis L. K. Hsu, "Chinese Kinship and Chinese Behavior," in Ping-ti Ho and Tang Tsou, eds., *China in Crisis*, vol. 1, *China's Heritage and the Communist Political System* (Chicago: University of Chicago Press, 1968), pp. 579–608.

54. Michel Oksenberg, "Local Leaders in Rural China."

55. After 1968, upward mobility at my research sites, particularly for brigade officials, increased with the expanding size and functions of the commune bureaucracy and the advancing age of its leadership.

56. One team leader described his brigade, which had only one factory, as "an empty shell." Rural Nanjing interview, 1981.

57. John P. Burns, "The Election of Production Team Cadres: 1958–1974," *CQ*, no. 74 (1978): 273–296.

58. Parish and Whyte, *Village and Family*, p. 107.

59. For a thorough discussion of the power that team leaders wielded over team members is see Jean C. Oi, "Communism and Clientelism: Rural Politics in China," *World Politics*, vol. 37, no. 2 (January 1985): 238–266.

60. Parish and Whyte argued that few peasants wanted to lead poor teams. The old peasant who led the poorest team at one of my research sites was unable to retire because no one would replace him.

61. For Townsend there is no "autonomous peasant participation," only "system-supportive" mobilization. James R. Townsend, *Political Participation in China* (Berkeley: University of California Press, 1969). Pye attributes a lack of participation to China's "subject" rather than "citizen" political culture. Lucian W. Pye, "Mass Participation in Communist China: Its Limitations and the Continuity of Culture," in John M. H. Lindbeck, ed., *China: Management of a Revolutionary Society* (Seattle: University of Washington Press, 1971), pp. 3–33. Advocates of the concept include Burns and Falkenheim. See Burns, "Chinese Peasant Interest Articulation," and Victor C. Falkenheim, "Political Participation in China," *Problems of Communism*, vol. 27, no. 3 (May–June 1978). Burns and Falkenheim looked at the pursuit of personal and economic interests, not merely at "political" behavior as understood in the West.

62. According to Blecher, middle peasants actively participated in local politics, while even rich peasants were involved in "apolitical issues" having to do with agriculture. Personal communication, 15 September 1986.

63. Falkenheim, "Political Participation."

64. Martin K. Whyte, *Small Groups and Political Rituals* (Berkeley: University of California Press, 1974).

65. Burns, "Chinese Peasant Interest Articulation."

66. According to one rural Nanjing interview, "in the years 1967–1976, we got burned [*chi kuile*] because we were beside the brigade. We had to do things well . . . If you are far away, they can't see what you are doing, but if you are close, they can see."

67. A rusticated youth who had lived in Yan'an District recalled that for her team "it seemed as if the brigade did not exist. The teams were at least five *li* [2.5 kms.] apart or more. Everything was run by the teams, so what the team leader said went." Another informant from Hunan said that his mountain village expanded its private plots while elsewhere in the province they were being restricted. Hong Kong interview, 1980. See also Gu Hua, *Pagoda Ridge and Other Stories* (Beijing: Panda Books, 1985).

68. Parish and Whyte, *Village and Family*, p. 67. However, 75 percent of all *RMRB* articles between 1968 and 1978 advocating Dazhai workpoints discussed them in relation to hilly areas, which are not necessarily wealthy.

69. Merilee S. Grindle, "Policy Content and Context in Implementation," in Merilee S. Grindle, ed., *Politics and Policy Implementation in the Third World* (Princeton: Princeton University Press, 1980), p. 6.

70. For one cadre's problems following his opposition to the Great Leap

see Liu Binyan, "Sound Is Better than Silence," in Link, ed., *People or Monsters*.

71. "How to be a Good Leader," in *Selected Works of Zhou Enlai*, vol. 1, p. 147, cited in David M. Lampton, "Introduction," in David M. Lampton, ed., *Policy Implementation in Post-Mao China* (Berkeley: University of California Press, 1987).

72. Mao Zedong, "The United Front in Cultural Work," 30 October 1945, *Selected Works*, vol. 3 (Peking: Foreign Languages Press 1968), pp. 236–237.

73. Chandler Morse, "Foreword," in Chandler Morse et al., *Modernization by Design: Social Change in the Twentieth Century* (Ithaca: Cornell University Press, 1969), pp. xii–xiii.

74. Lucian Pye, *The Dynamics of Chinese Politics* (Cambridge, Mass.: Oelgeschlager, Gunn and Hain, 1981), p. 16.

75. Richard H. Solomon, *Mao's Revolution and the Chinese Political Culture* (Berkeley: University of California Press, 1971), pp. 107–109.

76. Ibid., p. 116.

77. Susan Shirk, *Competitive Comrades* (Berkeley: University of California Press, 1982), pp. 1–20.

78. *Shanxi ribao* (Shanxi Daily), 27 July 1981, in *FBIS*, no. 164 (25 August 1981): R5.

79. A Nanjing brigade official admitted that after a visit to Dazhai he tried to work 300 days a year in the fields, as the Dazhai cadres did. Since he could not do this and also manage his brigade, he knew the Dazhai cadres had lied.

80. During the Great Leap, most rural bureaucrats knew that the grain statistics were false. See Thomas P. Bernstein, "Stalinism, Chinese Peasants and Famine: Grain Procurements during the Great Leap Forward," *Theory and Society* (May 1984): 1–39. Near Long Bow Village, county officials falsified grain statistics by purchasing team grain to meet the quota and then giving it back as food grain to avoid widespread starvation. William Hinton, *Shenfan* (New York: Random House, 1983), pp. 248–249.

81. Stephen A. Quick, "The Paradox of Popularity: 'Ideological' Program Implementation in Zambia," in Grindle, *Politics and Policy Implementation*, p. 50.

82. Philip Raikes, "Ujamaa Vijijini and Rural Socialist Development," cited in Goran Hyden, *Beyond Ujamaa in Tanzania* (Berkeley: University of California Press, 1980).

83. Hyden, *Beyond Ujamaa in Tanzania*.

84. During the Great Leap in Long Bow Village, cadres, responding to pressures for a 10,000-pig farm, felt compelled to "put up a gate, anything. Show that we are moving on it." Hinton, *Shenfan*, p. 244.

85. Two different Chinese officials, one a cadre in rural Nanjing and the other working in a university, described similar strategies.

86. Falkenheim outlined five strategies for local cadres which were not limited to unpopular policies. They were (1) procrastinate; (2) innovate—in order to implement the policy first; (3) tidewatch—implement the policy but don't be enthusiastic; (4) avoid risk—carry out all instructions: and (5) falsely report compliance. Falkenheim, "Decentralization and Control," p. 199.

87. In 1977, aware that all "Dazhai-type" counties in Hebei Province were frauds, Li Xiannian suppressed this information, as he had been closely tied to the Dazhai campaign run by Hua in 1976–1977 (Edward Friedman, personal communication).

88. Pye, "Mass Participation," p. 31.

89. Herbert Kaufman, *Administrative Feedback: Monitoring Subordinates' Behavior* (Washington, D.C.: The Brookings Institution, 1973).

90. Local cadres argued that the most successful brigade Party secretaries were those who regularly walked the entire brigade.

91. Indonesian peasants also planted official varieties of rice by the roadside, since local officials judged implementation from their passing cars, not from careful inspection. James C. Scott, personal communication.

92. Cadres in the Great Leap complained that demands for figures were always coming from upper levels. "It's figures here and figures there. No one goes to the fields to check." See Hinton, *Shenfan,* pp. 248–249.

93. Anthony Downs, *Inside Bureaucracy* (Boston: Little, Brown, 1967), pp. 132–136.

94. While "winds" may not "leak" (personal comment by Roderick MacFarquhar), county officials were often the bureaucratic actors who picked up on the winds and tried to force the brigade or team leaders to implement the radical policy; this left two layers between initiators and implementers. Given the limited opportunities for real investigations by these county officials, local leaders sometimes had room to adjust the policies.

95. A brigade in Jiangsu Province stopped using Dazahi workpoints in 1971, but when asked by visiting officials, the brigade Party secretary did not admit the change. "When the people came from the upper levels to ask if we were still doing it, we would nod. In the upper levels some people liked it and others didn't. If we knew that they liked it, we told them the benefits of it, how it was good. If they didn't like it, we told them that it was not good." Rural Nanjing interview, 1981.

96. In 1978 a brigade official outside Jinan, whom I interviewed in May 1978, reported that the brigade was still organizing labor assistance projects for the poorer brigades, a policy that had come out of the radical line. In 1976 the rich teams had contributed 30,000 labor days; in 1977 they had contributed 20,000 labor days; and in 1978 they planned to contribute 10,000 labor days. I suspect that this was only a verbal demonstration of adherence to a radical policy. The official knew I would be unable to ask to see any proof.

97. Carl Riskin, "Introduction," in Dorothy J. Solinger, ed., *Three Visions of Chinese Socialism* (Boulder: Westview Press, 1984), p. 6.

98. Theodore de Bary, Wing-tsit Chan and Burton Watson, eds., *Sources of Chinese Tradition, vol. 1* (New York: Columbia University Press, 1960), p. 19.

99. Hsu, "Chinese Kinship and Chinese Behavior," pp. 579–649.

5. Brigades and Higher Stages of Socialism

1. See "A Foot of Mud and a Pile of Shit," in B. Michael Frolic, *Mao's People* (Cambridge, Mass.: Harvard University Press, 1980).

2. Mao stressed the first two criteria. See Mao Zedong, "Du 'Zhengzhi jingjixue jiaoke shu,' shehuizhuyi bufen, disanben de biji," (Reading Notes on the Textbook on Political Economy, Socialist Section, Number 3, 1960), in

Yoshihiko Ogura, ed., *Mao Zedong sixiang wan sui* (Tokyo: Tashu-kan, 1967), p. 225. In 1981 cadres in a commune outside Nanjing had heard of this guideline but did not know that Mao had suggested it.

3. Thoughtful discussions of these criteria are Wang Fenglin, *Xin shiqi renmin gongshe jingji wenti* (Economic Problems of the People's Communes in the New Era) (Beijing: Nongye chubanshe, 1979), p. 119, and David Zweig, "Agrarian Radicalism in China, 1968–1978: The Search for a Social Base" (Ph.D. diss., University of Michigan, 1983), chap. 6.

4. According to Fei Xiaotong, "the simple enlargement of the operating unit without any corresponding change in the productive forces meant that the management problem was multiplied at least as many times as the unit was enlarged." Cited in Victor Nee, "Peasant Household Individualism: The Collective Economy and the State," paper presented at the Conference on Bureaucracy and Rural Development, SSRC-ACLS Joint Committee on Contemporary China, Chicago, 26–29 August 1981.

5. Information received during an interview at the Agricultural Economics Institute of the Chinese Academy of Social Sciences, 28 April 1981.

6. However, provincial leadership need not be the most important factor here, since Shandong Province was never seen to be very radical. Local characteristics particular to North China, such as cropping patterns, weaker lineage ties, or density of Party membership, may be equally important.

7. Rusticated youth interview, Beijing, 1981.

8. Rusticated youth interview, Beijing, 1981.

9. Any positive relationship may result from an "ecological fallacy." See Richard L. Merritt and Stein Rokkan, eds., *Comparing Nations: The Use of Quantative Data in Cross-National Research* (New Haven: Yale University Press, 1966).

10. I visited Xiyang County in the summer of 1981. On Sungchuang Brigade, see *RMRB*, 6 August 1973.

11. Interview at the Agricultural Economics Institute, Chinese Academy of Social Sciences, 28 April 1981.

12. M. Stiefel and W. F. Wertheim, *Production, Equality and Participation in China* (London: Zed Press, 1983), p. 61.

13. Edward Friedman, "The Politics of Local Models, Social Transformation and State Power Struggles in the People's Republic of China: Tachai and Teng Hsiao-p'ing," *CQ*, no. 76 (December 1978): 873–890.

14. *RMRB*, 4 April 1979.

15. *RMRB*, 28 November 1978.

16. Rusticated youth interview, Beijing, 1981.

17. Hong Kong interview, 1980.

18. The data, collected by Michel Oksenberg, were first used by Fredrick Teiwes in "Provincial Politics in China: Themes and Variations," in John M. H. Lindbeck, ed., *China: Management of a Revolutionary Society* (Seattle: University of Washington Press, 1971), pp. 116–189.

19. *RMRB*, 28 November 1978.

20. *Hubei Daily*, 21 January 1979.

21. Neville Maxwell, "The Fourth Mobilization: New Phase of the Tachai Movement," *World Development*, no. 6 (1978): 499–518.

22. Victor Nee, "Peasant Household Individualism."

23. *RMRB*, 20 March 1979, p. 3.

24. *RMRB*, 4 January 1979.

25. Hong Kong interview, 1980.

26. Rusticated youth interview, Beijing, 1981.

27. *Hubei Daily*, 21 January 1979, p. 1. The expression was *Biankai geming da bu, bu dang xiao tui nuren.*

28. Rural Nanjing interview, 1981.

29. Interview, Nanjing Municipality Rural Work Office, 1981.

30. See Victor Nee, "Peasant Household Individualism," in William L. Parish, ed., *Chinese Rural Development: The Great Transformation* (Armonk, N.Y.: M. E. Sharpe, 1985), p. 183.

31. Hong Kong interview, 1980.

32. Blecher interview.

33. *Wan sui* (1967), p. 192.

34. "Brigades and Teams: Survey of a Commune (iii)," *Peking Review*, no. 12 (18 March 1966).

35. Rural Nanjing interview, 1981.

36. Rural Nanjing interview, 1981.

37. Peter Bachrach and Morton Baratz, "The Two Faces of Power," *American Political Science Review*, no. 56 (December 1962): 947–952.

38. Rusticated youth interview, Beijing, 1981.

39. Information supplied by Marc Blecher who, with Vivienne Shue and Steve and Phyllis Andors, visited this brigade in 1979. It was also the focus of a *BR* report on 14 April 1980.

40. Dazhai had limited the value of a workpoint to 0.25 yuan and per capita distribution to 150 yuan, no matter how much the brigade earned. Many hilly units all over China were forbidden to distribute more than 150 yuan per person, while units not in the hills were often limited to 180 yuan. The slogan was "If you surpass Dazhai, how can you learn from Dazhai?" (*Chaoguo Dazhai, zenme xue Dazhai*).

41. Hong Kong interview, 1980.

42. This was also an issue in the Soviet Union, where collective farms were merged in 1949, forming larger units with five to eight villages in each. The number of kolkhozes decreased nationwide by almost two-thirds. See Roy A. Medvedev and Zhores Medvedev, *Khrushchev: The Years in Power* (New York: W. W. Norton, 1978), pp. 33–37.

43. Rural Nanjing interview, 1981.

44. Xu Dixin, "Lun qiong guodu" (On the Transition through Poverty), *JJYJ*, no. 4 (1979): 2–7.

45. The data on systemic explanations of brigade accounting support this latter point. In a locality where brigade accounting had occurred, a county official explained that "these two brigades had only three and four teams each which makes amalgamating easier than if there are lots of teams." Blecher interview.

46. Some teams in China alternately amalgamated and split as many as six times between 1962 and 1980. John P. Burns, "Peasant Interest Articula-

tion: 1949–1974" (Ph.D. diss., Columbia University, 1978), and *RMRB*, 14 November 1979, p. 2.

47. "Fazhan dadui jiti jingji, cujin nongye da shang kuai shang," (Develop the Brigade's Collective Economy, Promote the Rapid Development of Agriculture), in *Renmin gongshe zai yuejin* (People's Communes are Advancing) (Shanghai: People's Publishing House, 1974), pp. 57–64, and *XXYPP*, no. 10 (1975): 7–11, emphasized how brigade development could narrow interteam inequality.

48. Hong Kong interview, 1980.

49. Ibid.

50. Zhang Chunqiao, *On Exercising All-Round Dictatorship over the Bourgeoisie* (Peking: Foreign Languages Press, 1975).

51. See "Here Lies the Hope," *RMRB*, 17 October 1975.

52. The two levels possessing nothing were the brigade and the commune. Hua's remarks were reported by Long Yulan to the December 1976 Second Conference on Learning from Dazhai in Agriculture and were cited in Jurgen Domes, *Socialism in the Chinese Countryside* (Montreal: McGill-Queen's University Press, 1980), p. 99.

53. In a 1981 interview with Lee Travers, Wang Fenglin recalled that Zhou had supported brigade and commune enterprises at this conference. Lee Travers, personal communication.

54. These posts could include a brigade Party secretary, one or two vice-Party secretaries, a brigade leader and several vice-brigade leaders responsible for production, a political study leader, a women's representative, agricultural and industrial accountants, a cashier (*chu na*), a militia head, a leader of the Young Communist League, a radio broadcaster, and so forth. Alley discovered a brigade of 15 teams in Bolo County, Guangdong Province, which had 89 full-time brigade cadres. Rewi Alley, *Travels in China, 1966–1971*, cited in China Group.

55. See "Regulations on the Work in the Rural People's Communes (Revised Draft) (Sixty Articles on Agriculture)," in *Issues and Studies* (December 1979): 106–115. The same point was made in article 38 of the *New Sixty Articles*.

56. David Zweig, "Peasants, Ideology, and the New Incentive Systems," in Parish, *Chinese Rural Development*, p. 150n13.

57. *Wan sui*, p. 192.

58. John B. Starr, *Continuing the Revolution: The Political Thought of Mao* (Princeton: Princeton University Press, 1979), p. 277, and Samuel Huntington, *Political Order in Changing Societies* (New Haven: Yale University Press, 1968).

59. Jonathan Unger, "Collective Incentives in the Chinese Countryside: Lessons from Chen Village," *World Development*, no. 6 (1978): 588.

60. William L. Parish, "China—Team, Brigade, or Commune," *Problems of Communism*, vol. 25, no. 2 (March-April 1976): 51–65.

61. Findings based on interviews in Hong Kong and rural Nanjing.

62. Theodore Lowi, "American Business, Public Policy, Case Studies and Political Theory," *World Politics*, vol. 16, no. 4 (July 1964): 677.

63. Ralf Dahrendorf, *Class and Class Conflict in Industrial Society* (Stanford: Stanford University Press, 1959). For an application of this theory to Cultural Revolutionary China see Tang Tsou, "The Cultural Revolution and the Chinese Political System," *CQ*, no. 38 (April-June 1969): 63–91.

64. Rusticated youth interview, Nanjing, 1981.

65. David Lane, *Politics and Society in the USSR* (New York: New York University Press, 1980), p. 409.

66. Rusticated youth interview, Beijing, 1981.

67. Rusticated youth interview, Beijing, 1981.

68. *Zhejiang Daily*, 29 November 1978.

69. Hong Kong interview, 1980.

6. Restricting Private Plots

1. Liao Luyen, "Guzu ganjin lizheng fengshou" (Go all out and aim high for a bountiful harvest), *HQ*, nos. 3–4 (1961): 28.

2. The impact and content of this radical wind varied with factional struggles in Beijing. In 1968–1970, under the influence of Chen Boda and Lin Biao, units collectivized their private plots, while during the 1975–1977 debate over bourgeois rights some units prevented peasants from producing marketable commodities in their private plots. See Chapter 3.

3. The Appendix describes each type of private plot.

4. Data for this table come from interviews and *RMRB* articles. I also used data from *FB*, but as a district newspaper it is more detailed and contains many examples of restrictions. Therefore I counted each type of restriction mentioned in *FB* only once. The finding of only three incidents of moving of plots does not reflect the frequency of this phenomenon. At one research site, this transpired almost every time land was leveled. While this table is in no way representative of the population of restrictions at large, it suggests the variety of restrictions that occurred during the period and shows the distribution of the type of restrictions that I found.

5. These locations were drawn from my interviews (in both Hong Kong and China), Han Ke-chuan's article, and reports in *RMRB*. No doubt restrictions happened in other places as well. See Han Ke-chuan, "Recent Developments in Rural Communes on the Chinese Mainland," *Issues and Studies*, vol. 5, no. 8 (May 1969): 4–11.

6. Hong Kong interview, 1980.

7. Rusticated youth interview, Beijing, 1981.

8. Rusticated youth interview, Beijing, 1981.

9. In another brigade in Dinghuan County they did set a limit of 1.2 sq. m. on the size of the cultivated area within the yard. This way officials felt they were "cutting the tail of capitalism." Rusticated youth interview, Beijing, 1981.

10. Interviews in Hong Kong, 1980, and rural Nanjing, 1981.

11. In Chinese the poem went, *Shengjiang, yangcong, dabaicai, yi nian gaoguo jibai kuai, na you xingsi xue Dazhai?*

12. Rural Nanjing interview, 1981.

13. Hong Kong interview, 1980.

14. Rusticated youth interview, Nanjing, 1981.

15. Rusticated youth interview, Nanjing, 1981.

16. Rusticated youth interview, Nanjing, 1981.

17. Hong Kong interview, 1980.

18. It is important to recall that the average annual cash distribution to commune members for all of China in 1974–1978 never reached 14 yuan. Nicholas Lardy, personal communication.

19. Rusticated youth interview, Beijing, 1981.

20. Hong Kong interview, 1980.

21. A Nanjing peasant made 200 yuan in 1980 from a tiny plot of .01 *mu* (.00067 hectare), raising chili peppers which he sold to the collective.

22. Hong Kong interview, 1980.

23. Although one could not assume this to be a representative sample, the fact that data, based on combining 1978 *RMRB* articles and interviews, mirror findings based on the 1968–1977 *RMRB* articles suggests that *RMRB* may have reflected the true distribution of the restrictions.

24. In 1970 all brigades in a suburban Nanjing commune reduced their private plots from .04 to .02 mu per person, while the brigade closest to the city—the one under the most intense pressure for land—lost an additional .01 mu per person. A commune official in this locality attributed the smaller plots to proximity to the city.

25. Rural Nanjing interview, 1981.

26. Rusticated youth interview, Nanjing, 1981.

27. Rural Nanjing interview, 1981.

28. Rural Nanjing interview, 1981.

29. Jonathan Unger, "Collective Incentives in the Chinese Countryside: Lessons from Chen Village," *World Development*, no. 6 (1978): 583–601.

30. Interviews with commune, brigade, and team leaders in rural Nanjing, 1981.

31. Rural Nanjing interview, 1981.

32. Hong Kong interview, 1980.

33. See George Foster, "Peasant Society and the Image of the Limited Good," in May N. Diaz, George M. Foster, and Jack M. Potter, eds., *Peasant Society: A Reader* (Boston: Little, Brown, 1967).

34. Rural Nanjing interview, 1981.

35. Hong Kong interview, 1980.

36. Rural Nanjing interview, 1981.

37. Rural Nanjing interview, 1981.

38. Hong Kong interview, 1980.

39. Hong Kong interview, 1980.

40. Hong Kong interview, 1980.

41. *RMRB*, 22 July 1979.

42. Interviews in Hong Kong, 1980, and rural Nanjing, 1981.

43. Hong Kong interview, 1980.

44. Rural Nanjing interview, 1981.

45. Rusticated youth interview, Beijing, 1981. See also *RMRB*, 24 January 1979.

46. Marc Blecher, personal communication, 15 September 1986.

47. See Shahid J. Burki, *A Study of Chinese Communes, 1965* (Cambridge, Mass.: Harvard East Asian Monographs, no. 29, 1970), p. 41, and Kenneth R. Walker, *Planning in Chinese Agriculture: Socialization and the Private Sector, 1956–1962* (Chicago: Aldine Publishing Co., 1967).

48. Walker, *Planning in Chinese Agriculture*, pp. 33–36.

49. I am indebted to Vikram Seth of Stanford University, who kindly shared his data on the Four Families Brigade. The income from private plots in these teams was about average for the areas of China visited by foreigners. See William L. Parish and Martin K. Whyte, *Village and Family in Contemporary China* (Chicago: University of Chicago Press, 1978), p. 119. Also, the 5 to 10 percent figure for direct income meets the national average. See Fredrick Crook, "The Commune System in the People's Republic of China, 1963–1974," in Joint Economic Committee, U.S. Congress, *China: A Reassessment of the Economy* (Washington, D.C.: Government Printing Office, July 1975), p. 404.

50. The data were collected during field research in this brigade, April-May 1981. In 1980 peasants averaged 250 yuan per household from all private sidelines, including 85.43 yuan per household from raising tree seedlings. Per capita income was 110 yuan in 1980, and each household averaged 4.2 people. Therefore, average household income from the collective was 457.66 yuan, with private income constituting 36 percent of total household income. See David Zweig, "Prosperity and Conflict in Post-Mao Rural China," *CQ*, no. 105 (March 1986): 1–18.

51. Walker, *Planning in Chinese Agriculture*, p. 10.

52. Hong Kong interview, 1980.

53. See *RMRB*, 18 January 1979, for a similar story in 1976.

54. Hong Kong interview, 1980.

55. Hong Kong interview, 1980.

56. Hong Kong interview, 1980.

57. Hong Kong interview, 1980.

58. Hong Kong interview, 1980.

59. Rural Nanjing interview, 1981.

60. Rural Nanjing interview, 1981.

61. Rusticated youth interview, Beijing, 1981.

62. Hong Kong interview, 1980.

63. Overdrawn households either lacked workpoints or funds to pay for grain they had received from the team, or could not repay money they had borrowed.

64. Rural Nanjing interview, 1981.

65. Rural Nanjing interview, 1981.

66. Hong Kong interview, 1980.

67. Rural Nanjing interview, 1981.

68. According to Burns, peasants were best able to pursue their interests when they were cloaked in economic rather than political terms. See John P. Burns, "Chinese Peasant Interest Articulation: 1949–1974." (Ph.D. diss., Columbia University, 1978).

69. Hong Kong interview, 1980.

70. Rusticated youth interview, Nanjing, 1981.

71. Hong Kong interview, 1980.

72. Rural Nanjing interview, 1981.

73. Hong Kong interview, 1980.

74. Informants in China and Hong Kong suggested that peasants felt less inclined to complain when private plot restrictions occurred on a brigade-wide basis; their sensibilities were upset less when everyone in their immediate reference group suffered a similar fate. "Sure some people complained, but it was a policy carried out by the brigade, across the whole brigade, so peasants couldn't really complain." Rural Nanjing interview, 1981.

75. Hong Kong interview, 1980.

76. Under political reforms of the mid-1980s, and as a reward for protecting peasant interests and resisting radical winds, this brigade secretary was promoted.

77. Rural Nanjing interview, 1981.

7. Resource Expropriation and Equalization

1. For a discussion of this problem during the Great Leap see Roderick MacFarquhar, *The Origins of the Cultural Revolution,* vol. 2, *The Great Leap Forward, 1958–1960* (New York: Columbia University Press, 1983), pp. 146–150.

2. On high tides in rural capital construction projects see Michel Oksenberg, "Policy Formulation in Communist China: The Case of the Mass Irrigation Campaign, 1957–1958" (Ph.D. diss., Columbia University, 1969).

3. For examples of this communist spirit, where units helped their neighbors without proper compensation, see *RMRB*, 29 December 1968, p. 2; 22 November 1969, p. 4; 17 May 1972, p. 4; and 9 March 1975, p. 2.

4. *FBIS*, no. 97 (18 May 1978): H2.

5. Xu Lu, *Renmin gongshede zizhuquan he suoyouzhi* (The Rights of Sovereignty and Ownership in the People's Communes) (Guangzhou: Guangdong renmin chubanshe, 1979), pp. 12–13.

6. State investment in agriculture never exceeded 10 percent of the state budget after 1949.

7. Marx discussed his concept of objectified labor in "The Grundrisse." Robert C. Tucker, ed., *The Marx-Engels Reader,* 2nd ed. (New York: W. W. Norton, 1978), p. 259.

8. James E. Nickum, "Labour Accumulation in Rural China and Its Role since the Cultural Revolution," *Cambridge Journal of Economics,* no. 2 (1978): 277.

9. State Council Directive, 24 October 1959, in *Fagui huibian* (Compilation of Legal Documents), no. 10 (1959), p. 388.

10. See Richard Levy, "New Light on Mao," *CQ*, no. 61 (March 1975): 95–117, and Mao Tse-tung, "Speech at the Lushan Conference," in Stuart R. Schram, ed., *Mao Tse-tung Unrehearsed: Talks and Letters, 1956–1971* (Harmondsworth: Penguin Books, 1975), p. 134.

11. "Regulation on the Work in the Rural People's Communes (Revised Draft)," in *Issues and Studies* (Taipei) (October 1979): 96.

12. Examples where peasants who did not benefit did not work hard are *RMRB*, 10 January 1972, p. 1; 18 March 1972, p. 2; and 14 July 1972, p. 4.

13. Nickum, "Labour Accumulation," pp. 283–284.

14. Team leaders did not really expect "voluntariness" to be an important consideration for participating in these projects. They only hoped they would be paid something or receive some benefit for contributing, in which case they did not see it as equalization and transfer. Rural Nanjing interview, 1981.

15. Rusticated youth interview, Beijing, 1981, and *RMRB*, 6 November 1978, p. 3.

16. *RMRB* editorial, 28 July 1978. In the Great Leap the third slogan referred to "recalling loans." MacFarqhuar, *Origins of the Cultural Revolution, vol. 2*, p. 146.

17. Interviews with commune leader and county water conservation officials, rural Nanjing, 1981.

18. "Piedmont counties" were most supportive of capital construction projects in the 1957–58 irrigation movement. Oksenberg, "Policy Formulation in Communist China," chap. 13.

19. Rural Nanjing interview, 1981.

20. Rural Nanjing interview, 1981.

21. Rural Nanjing interview, 1981.

22. Personal visit by the author in July 1981. Like a county official, I never discovered whether land away from the road had been improved.

23. Hong Kong interview, 1980.

24. See Point 6 in Hua Guofeng's Dazhai Conference speech, entitled *Let the Whole Party Mobilize for a Vast Effort to Develop Agriculture and Build Tachai-type Counties throughout the Country* (Peking: Foreign Languages Press, 1975), p. 24.

25. I visited this Jinan brigade and the two of the following discussion in Qingdao and Shanghai municipalities in May-June 1978.

26. *RMRB*, 2 April 1978.

27. *RMRB*, 2 April 1978.

28. Rural Nanjing interview, 1981.

29. Two interviews in rural Nanjing, 1981, *FBIS* (8 September 1972): C2–3, and Hong Kong interview, 1980.

30. They usually paid 30 yuan per month to the collective; since buying grain in the cities was either expensive or impossible, it was a fair price.

31. Rural Nanjing interview, 1981.

32. Teams with many outside workers did not support these projects, so the radicals tried to get outside workers to return to their villages permanently.

33. Vivienne Shue, *Peasant China in Transition* (Berkeley: University of California Press, 1980).

34. According to a northside official, southern leaders knew that labor investment in the northside yielded faster returns than similar investments in the south, thereby increasing overall brigade welfare. They also knew that since they were richer, the north would not have to give them the same amount of help.

35. Rural Nanjing interview, 1981.

36. James E. Nickum, "A Collective Approach to Water Resource Development: The Chinese Commune System, 1962–1972" (Ph.D. diss., University of California, 1974).

37. Rural Nanjing interview, 1981.

38. Rural Nanjing interview, 1981.

39. John P. Burns, "Chinese Peasant Interest Articulation," (Ph.D. diss., Columbia University, 1978), pp. 42–43, and *RMRB*, 21 February 1973.

40. Hong Kong interview, 1980.

41. Interviews in rural Nanjing, 1981, and Hong Kong, 1980.

42. Rusticated youth interview, Nanjing, 1981.

43. Whyte's interviews found a "spouse-prospecting" motive for participating in these projects. Martin K. Whyte, personal communication. Jack Chen, in *A Year in Upper Felicity* (New York: Macmillan, 1973), argues that young men volunteered for a railway project to learn new things and to contribute funds to the family budget. Blecher's interviews show that young people of both sexes enjoyed these projects because they were fun. Marc Blecher, personal communication. But according to one informant, only young bachelors wanted to go. Hong Kong interview, 1980.

44. Nickum, "A Collective Approach," p. 208.

45. Hong Kong interview, 1980.

46. Hong Kong interview, 1980.

47. Military control of counties in Guangdong and Jiangsu provinces is documented in Blecher interview and my own interview with county water conservation officials, rural Nanjing, 1981. Gao Yuan, *Born Red* (Stanford: Stanford University Press, 1987), also describes the military takeover of a north China county during the Cultural Revolution.

48. Blecher interview.

49. Interview with county water conservation officials, rural Nanjing, 1981.

50. *FBIS* (6 September 1972): C4, cited in Nickum, "A Collective Approach," p. 252.

51. Rural Nanjing interview, 1981.

52. Rural Nanjing interview, 1981.

53. Hong Kong interview, 1980.

54. Rural Nanjing interview, 1981.

55. Hong Kong interview, 1980.

56. Hong Kong interview, 1980.

57. Rusticated youth interview, Nanjing, 1981.

58. Interview, Nanjing Municipality Agricultural Work Office, 1981. The Chinese was *Shuji diaodong, shuili chongnong.*

59. Edward Friedman, personal communication.

60. Blecher interview.

61. Peter Nolan and Gorden White, "Socialist Development and Rural Inequality: The Chinese Countryside in the 1970s," *Journal of Peasant Studies,* vol. 7, no. 1 (October 1979): 17, and Blecher interview.

62. James C. Scott, "Revolution in the Revolution: Peasants and Com-

missars," *Theory and Society*, vol. 7, nos. 1–2 (January-March 1979): 97–134.

63. Rural Nanjing interview, 1981.

64. *RMRB*, 5 July 1978, p. 1.

65. Vivienne Shue, "Beyond the Budget: Finance Organization and Reform in a Chinese County," *Modern China*, vol. 10, no. 2 (April 1984): 147–186.

66. T'ung-tsu Ch'u, *Local Government in China under the Ch'ing* (Stanford: Stanford University Press, 1969), p. 155.

67. Philip A. Kuhn, "Local Taxation and Finance in Republican China," in Susan Mann Jones, ed., *Select Papers from the Center for Far Eastern Studies*, no. 3 (University of Chicago, 1978–79), pp. 115–116.

68. Ibid., pp. 120–121, 128–129.

69. Interview with county water conservation officials, rural Nanjing, 1981.

70. Rural Nanjing interview, 1981.

71. Blecher interview.

72. Hong Kong interview, 1980.

73. *RMRB*, 14 July 1972, p. 4. While the article claims that the county rectified the problem, six years later, almost to the day, this county became notorious as one of the worst examples of county and commune expropriation. Interviews in Beijing with the Ministry of Water Conservation in 1981 attest to the 1976 inflation of quotas.

74. Rural Nanjing interview, 1981.

75. Ibid.

76. Ibid.

77. Ibid.

78. Ibid.

79. Siu also argues that commune enterprises expanded during leftist periods. See Helen Siu, "Ethnographic Fieldwork in Rural Guangdong," in Anne F. Thurston and Burton Pasternak, eds., *The Social Sciences and Fieldwork in China: Views from the Field* (Boulder: Westview Press, 1984), p. 153.

80. Rural Nanjing interview, 1981.

8. The Making of a New Rural Order

1. Throughout this chapter the policies of the *Sixty Articles on Agriculture* refer to respect for production team "sovereignty" (*zizhuquan*), as compared to brigade accounting and interference by upper-level officials; a more liberal grain and income distribution policy; remuneration based on labor, not politics; and peasant rights to private plots, household sidelines, and rural trade fairs. This package of policies also includes criticism of long-term borrowing of team labor—as in Hua's field and water conservation construction corps—and equalization and transfer of labor, capital, and material. In the late 1970s reformers also criticized workpoint supplements for an ever-increasing pool of collective cadres.

2. *RMRB*, 9 August 1977, 29 August 1977, 12 October 1977, and 22 October 1977.

3. *RMRB*, 9 July 1981, p. 2, in *FBIS*, no. 141 (23 July 1981): K11–18.

4. *RMRB*, 31 January 1978 and 22 February 1978.

5. *RMRB*, 20 December 1977.

6. *FBIS*, no. 27 (8 February 1978): E14–15, and *RMRB*, 2 April 1978.

7. *MECE*, p. 595.

8. Wan Li, "Energetically Carry Out the Party's Rural Economic Policy," *HQ*, no. 3 (1978): 92–97.

9. *MECE*, p. 598. See also *Deng Xiaoping wenxuan* (Selected Works of Deng Xiaoping) (Hong Kong: People's Publishing House, 1983), p. 98, for his critique of political workpoints.

10. *RMRB*, 12 April 1978, p. 1; 13 May 1978, p. 2; and 5 June 1978, p. 1. Such a conference was held in Jiangxi between 12 and 19 May. See *RMRB*, 5 June 1978, p. 1.

11. *MECE*, p. 603, and *Zhongguo baike nianjian, 1980* (Chinese Yearbook) (Beijing: Zhongguo da baike quanshu chubanshe, 1981), p. 337.

12. *MECE*, p. 603.

13. Twenty six of 28 provinces and the municipalities of Beijing and Shanghai reported public support. See *RMRB*, 8 July 1978, 10 July 1978, 11 July 1978, 14 July 1978, and 16 July 1978.

14. *MECA*, p. 161.

15. In October 1978 some cadres accused peasants who cut grass in their spare time of following the "capitalist road." Xu Lu, *Renmin gongshede zizhuquan he suoyouzhi* (The Rights of Sovereignty and Ownership of People's Communes) (Guangzhou: Guangdong renmin chubanshe, 1979), pp. 19–20.

16. For an analysis of the criticism of the radical's line in this period, see William A. Joseph, *The Critique of Ultra-Leftism in China, 1958–1981* (Stanford: Stanford University Press, 1984), chap. 6.

17. Stuart R. Schram, *Ideology and Policy in China since the Third Plenum, 1978–1984* (London: Contemporary China Institute Research Notes and Studies, no. 6, 1984), p. 3.

18. Ibid., and Brantly Womack, "Politics and Epistemology in China since Mao," *CQ*, no. 80 (December 1979): 774–775.

19. Tang Tsou first linked the debate on the criteria of truth to the new rural reforms. See Tang Tsou, Marc Blecher, and Mitch Meisner, "Policy Change at the National Summit and Institutional Transformation at the Local Level: The Case of Tachai and Hsiyang County in the Post-Mao Era," *Select Papers from the Center for Far Eastern Studies*, no. 4 (Chicago: University of Chicago, 1979–1980), p. 274.

20. Zhou Cheng, "An Exploratory Discussion of the Transition of Rural People's Communes from Production Team Accounting to Brigade Level Accounting," *Zhongguo nongye jingji xuehui diyici xueshu taolunhui lunwen xuanluo* (Collection of Articles from the First Academic Conference of the Chinese Institute of Agricultural Economics) (Beijing: Nongye chubanshe, 1979), pp. 337–350.

21. Joseph, *Critique of Ultra-Leftism*, p. 202. Much of the following argument borrows from Joseph's excellent work.

22. Chin Wan, "On Transition in Poverty," *Jiefangjun bao* (Liberation Army Daily), 5 December 1978, in *FBIS*, no. 236 (7 December 1978): E9–12.

23. He Zhiping and Yang Jianbai, "Guanyu gongnong lianmeng de jige

wenti" (Several Questions Concerning the Worker-Peasant Alliance), *JJYJ*, no. 1 (January 1980): 46–53.

24. Su Shaozhi and Feng Lanrui, "Wuchanjieji qude zhengquan hou de shehui fazhan jieduan wenti" (The Problem of Stages in Socialist Development after the Proletariat has Taken Power), *JJYJ*, no. 5 (1979): 14–19. See also Stuart R. Schram, "To Utopia and Back," *CQ*, no. 87 (1981): 428–429.

25. See Hu Qiaomu's article, *RMRB*, 5 May 1978.

26. Joseph, *Critique of Ultra-Leftism*, p. 206, and his table on p. 204.

27. Stuart R. Schram, "Economics in Command: Ideology and Policy since the Third Plenum," *CQ*, no. 99 (September 1984): 417–461.

28. Mao and Marxism-Leninism gave equal status to three major "struggles"—scientific experiment, production, and class struggle. See Joseph, *Critique of Ultra-Leftism*, pp. 208–211.

29. Zou Jianming, "Some Views on the Criticism of 'Spontaneous Capitalist Tendencies'," *RMRB*, 16 May 1980.

30. *RMRB*, 16 May 1980.

31. *MECA*, pp. 172, 176, 182.

32. See Joseph, *Critique of Ultra-Leftism*, p. 212, and Hua Guofeng, "Report on the Work of the Government" at the second session of the Fifth National People's Congress, 18 June 1979, in *BR*, no. 27 (1979): 10.

33. An in-depth analysis of decollectivization is David Zweig, "Content and Context in Policy Implementation: Household Contracts and Decollectivization in China, 1977–1983," in David M. Lampton, ed., *Policy Implementation in Post-Mao China* (Berkeley: University of California Press, 1987): 255–283.

34. "Decision on Some Questions Concerning the Acceleration of Agricultural Development," in *Issues and Studies*, vol. 15, no. 7 (July 1979): 111.

35. *Guangming ribao* (Guangming Daily), 28 November 1982, in *Xinhua yuebao* (New China Monthly), no. 11 (1982): 91. With household quotas, the collective takes the output and pays peasants bonuses for overproduction; with household quotas with fixed levies the peasant pays all taxes directly, meets the compulsory sale, donates some money to the collective accumulation fund, but keeps the excess output, making the household the unit of management and account.

36. For opposition to the reforms see *RMRB*, 1 March 1979 and 15 March 1979; support for the reforms appeared on 7 March 1979.

37. Posters at Democracy Wall accused Deng of supporting Hu Yaobang's efforts to undermine Mao's policies, while Zhang Pinghua, director of the CC-CCP Propaganda Department, organized a provincial meeting to attack the economic reforms. *FBIS*, no. 160 (15 August 1980): U16. For the adverse current see *FBIS*, no. 83 (27 April 1979): O1.

38. *RMRB*, 20 May 1981. Because household quotas were accepted at the Fourth Plenum in September 1979, the speech must have occurred before that meeting.

39. *RMRB*, 9 April 1980.

40. *Banyue tan* (Fortnightly Chats), no. 8 (25 April 1981).

41. *RMRB*, 20 May 1981.

42. See Nicholas R. Lardy, *Agriculture in China's Modern Economic*

Development (Cambridge: Cambridge University Press, 1983), whose critique of this flaw in the development strategy is devastating.

43. Interview with a team accountant south of Nanjing. See also Thomas B. Wiens, "The Limits to Agricultural Intensification: The Suzhou Experience," Joint Economic Committee, U.S. Congress, *China under the Four Modernizations*, pt. 1 (Washington, D.C.: Government Printing Office, 1982), pp. 462–474.

44. Terry Sicular, "Market Restrictions in Chinese Agriculture: A Micro-Economic Analysis" (Ph.D. diss., Yale University, 1983).

45. Milton J. Esman and Norman T. Uphoff, *Local Organizations: Intermediaries in Rural Development* (Ithaca: Cornell University Press, 1984), pp. 151–153.

46. Victor Nee, "Peasant Household Individualism," in William L. Parish, ed., *Chinese Rural Development: The Great Transformation* (Armonk, N.Y.: M. E. Sharpe, 1985), p. 183.

47. Griffin and Saith found that "the higher the dependency ratio, the lower is collective income per head." Keith Griffin and Ashwani Saith, *Growth and Equality in Rural China* (Singapore: International Labour Office, 1981), p. 51. My thanks to Marty Whyte for this citation.

48. These data were collected in a wealthy area where brigade-run and commune-run industries greatly affected family income. In areas with strong collectives, then, restricting private plots might have increased the gap between rich and poor households, rather than decreasing it as the radicals had planned. I am grateful to Vikram Seth for this information.

49. For these households in the Four Families Brigade, the correlation between the number of laborers and noncollective income as a percentage of total income was $-.603$ ($p < .01$). Thus families with fewer laborers relied more on noncollective income. Using a slightly different measure, Griffin and Saith found a negative correlation of $-.62$ for collective income per household and outside income per household. Griffin and Saith, *Growth and Equality in Rural China*, p. 51. Thus those who made more from the collective relied less on outside income. Anita Chan and Jon Unger found that families with more laborers benefited more from private endeavors. Chan and Unger, personal communication. However, the importance of the collective sector to a family's income can vary across regions.

50. The low figure comes from William L. Parish, "Egalitarianism in Chinese Society," *Problems of Communism* (January-February 1981): 37–53; the higher figure comes from Thomas Rawski, "The Simple Arithmetic of Chinese Income Distribution," *Keizai kenkyu* (Economic Research, Tokyo), vol. 33, no. 1 (1982): 12–26. See also Martin K. Whyte, "The End to Inequality?" in A. Doak Barnett and Ralph Clough, eds., *Modernizing China* (Boulder: Westview Press, 1985), and David Zweig, "From Village to City: Reforming Urban-Rural Relations in China," *International Regional Science Review*, vol. 11, no. 1 (1987): 43–58.

51. Dwight Perkins, "China's Economic Policy and Performance during the Cultural Revolution and Its Aftermath," in John K. Fairbank and Roderick L. MacFarquhar, eds., *Cambridge History of China*, vol. 15 (Cambridge: Cambridge University Press, forthcoming). While Perkins shows that there was development in some directions, he does not discuss important aspects of the rural economy where there was no development.

52. Dwight Perkins and Shahid Yusuf, *Rural Development in China* (Baltimore: Johns Hopkins University Press, 1984), p. 69.

53. The figure for 1978 was given in a lecture at the Economics Department of Nanjing University in 1981.

54. *Zhongguo tongji nianjian, 1981* (Chinese Statistical Yearbook) (Beijing: Zhongguo tongji chubanshe, 1981), p. 132. While the number of units with brigade accounting decreased, the number of brigades increased by 4 percent, from 690,000 in 1978 to 718,020 by 1981.

55. *FBIS* (26 August 1981): K1.

56. Zweig, "Content and Context."

57. David Zweig, "Peasants, Ideology and the New Incentive Systems: Jiangsu Province, 1978–1981," in Parish, *Chinese Rural Development*, pp. 141–163.

58. Christine Wong, "Material Allocation and Decentralization: Impact of the Local Sector on the Industrial Reform," in Elizabeth J. Perry and Christine Wong, eds., *The Political Economy of Reform in Post-Mao China* (Cambridge, Mass.: Council on East Asian Studies, Harvard University, 1984), pp. 253–278.

59. Robert Delfs, "Rural Output Rises Further," in *Far Eastern Economic Review*, vol. 131, no. 3 (18 January 1986): 104–105.

60. *RMRB*, 31 March 1978, 20 April 1978, and 26 August 1978. Article 5 of the *New Sixty Articles* criticized equalization and transfer, while Article 19 outlined the proper manner for organizing farmland capital construction projects. See *Issues and Studies* (August 1979): 101, 106.

61. *MECA*, p. 181.

62. Wang Fenglin, *Xin shiqi renmin gongshe jingji wenti* (Economic Problems of the People's Communes in the New Era) (Beijing: Nongye chubanshe, 1979), p. 159. Translated by the author.

63. *Nongye jingji wenti* (Problems in Agricultural Economics), no. 10 (1980): 36–37. In spring 1981 a commune water conservation official in Nanjing's suburbs was notified that he was forbidden to start new projects.

64. *Issues and Studies* (August 1979): 110.

65. For total area in Sichuan see Li Bingkun, "China's Local Commune Member Sideline Occupations," in *Almanac of China's Economy* (1982), in *JPRS—Economic Affairs*, no. 370 (8 August 1983). For the provincial guidelines see *Zhongguo nongye nianjian, 1981* (Chinese Agricultural Yearbook) (Beijing: Nongye chubanshe, 1983), p. 90.

66. *FBIS* (9 April 1981): K8–11.

67. *Xinhua ribao*, 16 January 1979, p. 2. In a commune in suburban Fuzhou, Fujian Province, peasant income from household sidelines doubled from 1977 to 1978. *RMRB*, 2 January 1979, p. 2.

68. Li Bingkun, "Sideline Occupations."

69. *Zhongguo tongji nianjian, 1984* (Chinese Statistical Yearbook), p. 363.

70. Calculations are based on State Statistical Bureau, *Statistical Yearbook of China, 1983*, English ed. (Hong Kong: Economic Information and Agency, 1984), pp. 152–155.

71. *RMRB*, 22 October 1979, p. 2. Measured in 1977 yuan, total peasant per capita income rose from 102.8 yuan in 1957 to 113 yuan in 1977, or 0.5

percent per year. See S. Lee Travers, "Getting Rich through Diligence: Peasant Income after the Reforms," in Perry and Wong, *The Political Economy of Reform*, p. 111.

72. Shi San, "The Current Situation in the Rural Areas and the New Problems," *Jingji wenti* (Economic Problems) (December 1982): 4. This report may not have controlled for the significant inflation that occurred during the period.

73. S. Lee Travers, "Post-1978 Rural Economic Policy and Peasant Income in China," *CQ*, no. 98 (June 1984): 241–259.

74. *Statistical Yearbook of China, 1983*, p. 210.

75. *Cunzhong* (The Masses), no. 13 (1979): 14–16.

76. Mu Qing, "In Two Decades," *Liaowang* (20 August 1981): 6–9, in *FBIS* (27 October 1981): K11–18. See also Vivienne Shue, "The Fate of the Commune," *Modern China*, vol. 10, no. 3 (July 1984): 259–284.

77. *Nongye jingji wenti* (Problems in Agricultural Economics) no. 11 (1980): 2–4. For an excellent early critique see *RMRB*, editorial, 2 June 1980.

78. David Zweig, "Prosperity and Conflict in Post-Mao Rural China," *CQ*, no. 105 (March 1986): 1–18.

79. Jean C. Oi, "Commercializing China's Rural Cadres," *Problems of Communism*, vol. 25 (September-October 1986): 1–15; and Jean C. Oi, "Peasant Households between Plan and Market," *Modern China*, vol. 12, no. 2 (April 1986): 230–251.

80. Richard Latham, "The Political, Social and Economic Implications of the Household Production Responsibility System" (manuscript, 1983), p. 96.

81. *Xinhua ribao*, 6 February 1979.

82. Godwin C. Chu and Leonard L. Chu, "Parties in Conflict: Letters to the Editor of the People's Daily," *Journal of Communication* (Autumn 1981): 88.

83. A county in Gansu Province became a Xiyang County model in 1975 even though it could not feed itself. See *RMRB*, 12 February 1978. Dingyuan County, Anhui Province, another false model, was criticized very early in the reform process. See *RMRB*, 16 February 1978, p. 1.

84. Yin Ta-keng, "Will the Banner of Tachai [Dazhai] Fall?" *Dongxiang*, no. 1 (20 October 1978): 22–25, in *FBIS*, no. 208 (26 October 1978).

85. Report of the Party Committee of Puzhong District, Shanxi Province, where Dazhai is situated, in *MECA*, p. 189.

86. *RMRB*, 18 July 1980.

87. See *RMRB*, 15 June 1980, and Central Document No. 83 (1980), "Zhonggong zhongyang zhuanfa guanyu nongye xue Dazhai yundong zhong jingyan jiaoxun de jiancha baogao de piyu" (Central Committee Remarks on Transmitting the Shanxi Provincial Party Committee "Investigatory Report On the Experience and Lessons of the Movement to Learn from Dazhai in Agriculture") in *Nongcun jingji zhengce huibian, 1978–1981* (Compendium of Agricultural Economic Policies) (Beijing: Nongcun duwu chubanshe, 1982), p. 109–113.

88. *Liaowang*, no. 1 (1981).

89. David Zweig, "Dazhai Today: Myth and Reality" (manuscript, 1981).

90. The man who designed and supervised its construction gave me a guided tour by jeep of the entire project.

91. In 1981 a Nanjing official told me that thousands of peasants and cadres were visiting Fengyang every day.

92. For reports on famine see "Starving to Death in China," with an introduction by Thomas P. Bernstein and an anonymous coauthor, *New York Review of Books*, vol. 30, no. 10 (16 June 1983): 36–38. For forced implementation of household contracts see Zweig, "Content and Context," and Jonathan Unger, "The Decollectivization of the Chinese Countryside: A Survey of Twenty-Eight Villages," *Pacific Affairs*, vol. 58, no. 4 (Winter 1985–86): 585–606.

93. Richard Latham, "The Implication of Rural Reforms for Grass-Roots Cadres," in Perry and Wong, *The Political Economy of Reform*, pp. 157–174.

94. *Hebei ribao*, 23 August 1981, in *FBIS*, no. 171 (3 September 1981): K7–9.

95. Anita Chan, Richard Madsen, and Jonathan Unger, *Chen Village: The Recent History of a Peasant Community in Mao's China* (Berkeley: University of California Press, 1984), p. 276.

96. Zweig, "Peasants, Ideology and the New Incentive Systems."

97. Dazhai peasants in 1980 received 20 kg of grain in lieu of private plots. In 1981, following the national policy to expand private plot acreage from 5 to 15 percent of collective land, peasants were offered 70 kg of grain. According to the brigade secretary at that time, peasants did not want their plots back, although pressure from above on the cadres to return the plots and on the peasants to accept them was intense. Zweig, "Dazhai Today: Myth and Reality."

98. Zweig, "Prosperity and Conflict," and *FBIS*, no. 96 (15 May 1980).

99. *FBIS*, (8 January 1980): Q2–3, and no. 112 (9 June 1980): Q2–3.

100. Rural Nanjing interview, 1981.

101. While I was hitchiking to Fuzhou, rural cadres gave me a ride on their bus, during which the conversation ensued.

102. *China Daily*, 19 January 1983, p. 4.

103. *RMRB*, 10 October 1978, p. 2.

104. Personal investigations. See also *Xinhua ribao*, 18 December 1980, p. 1.

105. According to William Hinton, a village in Shanxi Province still farmed collectively in 1985 because local cadres left town whenever the work team came. Hinton lecture, 24 February 1986, University of Toronto.

106. *FBIS*, no. 161 (20 August 1981): R1–6.

107. Zweig, "Content and Context."

108. Hinton lecture, 24 February 1986, University of Toronto. Agricultural officials in Nanjing agreed and expressed concern about the future of agriculture if small strips persisted. Interview, September 1987.

109. David Zweig, Kathleen Hartford, James Feinerman, and Deng Jianxu, "Law, Contracts and Economic Development: Lessons from Rural China under the Reforms," *Stanford Journal of International Law* (Summer 1987): 319–364.

Conclusion

1. Bertram Silverman, "Economic Organization and Social Consciousness: Some Dilemmas of Cuban Socialism," in June Nash, Juan Corradi, and

Hobart Spalding, Jr., eds., *Ideology and Social Change in Latin America* (New York: Gordon and Breach, 1977), pp. 237–266.

2. G. William Skinner, "Chinese Peasants and the Closed Community: An Open and Shut Case," *Comparative Studies in Society and History*, vol. 13, no. 3 (July 1971): 270–281.

3. Edgar Snow, *Red Star over China* (New York: Random House, 1938), pp. 66–67.

4. Louis Putterman, "Extrinsic versus Intrinsic Problems of Agricultural Cooperation: Anti-Incentivism in Tanzania and China," *Journal of Development Studies*, vol. 21, no. 2 (January 1985): 175–204.

5. Ibid.

Appendix

1. According to Walker, five percent of the land was the "minimum useful size" of a plot that could provide a family with the necessary vegetables, fodder, and cash to fulfill its needs. See Kenneth R. Walker, *Planning in Chinese Agriculture: Socialization and the Private Sector, 1956–1962* (Chicago: Aldine Publishing, 1967), p. 29.

2. Shahid Javed Burki, *A Study of Chinese Communes: 1965* (Cambridge, Mass.: Harvard University Press, 1970), p. 35.

3. *Issues and Studies* (December 1979): 107.

4. William L. Parish and Martin K. Whyte, *Village and Family in Contemporary China* (Chicago: University of Chicago Press, 1978), p. 118.

SELECT BIBLIOGRAPHY

Bowie, Robert, and John K. Fairbank, eds. *Communist China, 1955–1959: Policy Documents with Analysis*. Cambridge: Harvard University Press, 1962.

CCP Central Committee. "Directive Concerning the Question of Distribution in the Rural People's Communes, Zhongfa, 1971, No. 82 (26 December 1971)." In *Issues and Studies*, 9:2 (November 1972).

Chai, Winberg, ed. *Essential Works of Chinese Communism*. New York: Bantam Books, 1972.

Chen, Boda. *Chen Boda wenji, 1949–1967* (Collected Essays of Chen Boda). Hong Kong: Lishi ziliao chubanshe, 1971.

Chen, C. S., and Charles P. Ridley. *Rural People's Communes in Lien-chiang*. Stanford: Hoover Institution Press, 1969.

Chen, Yonggui. "Thoroughly Criticize the 'Gang of Four' and Bring about a New Upsurge in the Movement to Build Tachai-type Counties throughout the Country." Speech to the Second National Conference on Learning from Tachai [Dazhai] in Agriculture. 20 December 1976. *SPRCM-77-05*, 910 (7 February 1977), 64–82.

Chin, Wan. "On Transition in Poverty." *Liberation Daily* (5 December 1978) in *FBIS*, 236 (7 December 1978), E9–12.

"Decision on Some Questions Concerning the Acceleration of Agricultural Development." In *Issues and Studies*, 15:7 (1979), 102–119, and 15:8 (1979), 91–99.

Deng Xiaoping. *Deng Xiaoping wenxuan* (Selected Writings of Deng Xiaoping). Hong Kong: People's Publishing House, 1983.

Editor. "The Conflict between Mao Tse-t'ung and Liu Shao-ch'i over Agricultural Mechanization in Communist China." *Current Scene*, 6:17 (1 October 1968), 1–20.

Gu, Hua. *Pagoda Ridge and Other Stories*. Beijing: Panda Books, 1985.

He Zhiping and Yang Jianbai. "Guanyu gongnong lianmeng de jige wenti" (Several Questions Concerning the Worker Peasant Alliance). *Jingji yanjiu*, 1 (January 1980), 46–53.

Hua, Guofeng. *Let the Whole Party Mobilize for a Vast Effort to Develop Agriculture and Build Tachai-type Counties throughout the Country*. Peking: Foreign Languages Press, 1975.

——— "Report on the Work of the Government," at the Second Session of the Fifth National People's Congress, 18 June 1979, in *Beijing Review*, 27 (1979).

Jiang Qing. "Chiang Ch'ing's (2 July 1975) Letter to the Delegates Attending the CCP-CC All-China Conference on Professional Work in Agriculture." *Issues and Studies* 11:10 (October 1975), 86–87.

—— "Speech at the National Conference on Learning from Tachai in Agriculture (Summary)." *Chinese Law and Goverment*, 10:1 (Spring 1977), 12–16.

Li Bingkun. "China's Local Commune Member Sideline Occupations." *Almanac of China's Economy, 1982.* Translated in *JPRS–Economic Affairs*, 370 (8 August 1983).

Li Chengrui. "An Analysis of China's Economic Situation." *Jingji yanjiu*, 1 (1984), 23–31.

Liao Luyen. "Go All Out and Aim High for a Bountiful Harvest." *Hongqi*, 3:4 (1961).

Liu Bingyan. "Sound Is Better than Silence." In *People or Monsters*, ed. Perry Link. Bloomington: University of Indiana Press, 1983.

Ma Yanwen. "The Bureaucratic Class and the Dictatorship of the Proletariat." *Beijing daxue xuebao* (Peking University Journal), 4 (September 1976) translated in *SPRCM*, 895 (26 October 1976).

Mao Zedong. *Mao Zedong sixiang wansui* (Long Live Mao Zedong Thought), ed. Yoshihko Ogura. Tokyo: Tashu-kan, 1967.

—— *Miscellany of Mao Tse-tung Thought (1949–1968)*. Vols. I and II, in *JPRS*, 61269:1 and 2 (20 February 1974).

—— *On the Correct Handling of Contradictions among the People*. Beijing: Foreign Language Press, 1957.

—— *Selected Works*. Beijing: Foreign Languages Press, 1969.

—— "Speech at Zhengzhou." (27 February 1959). Translated by Pierre Perrolle. *Chinese Law and Government*, 9:4 (Winter 1976–1977).

Ministry of Agriculture and Forestry Mass Criticism Group. "Two Line Struggle around the First National Conference on Learning from Dazhai in Agriculture." *Hongqi*, 1 (January 1977).

"Minutes of the Yunnan Provincial Conference on Rural Work (Draft)." *Issues and Studies*, 7:2 (November 1971).

Mu Qing. "In Two Decades." *Liaowang*, (20 August 1981), 6–9. Translated in *FBIS* (27 October 1981), K11–18.

Nongcun jingji zhengce huibian, 1978–1981 (Compendium of Agricultural Economic Policies). Vols. I and II. Beijing: Nongcun duwu chubanshe, 1982.

Renmin gongshe zai yuejin (People's Communes Are Advancing). Shanghai: Shanghai renmin chubanshe, 1974.

"Regulations on the Work in the Rural People's Communes (Revised Draft, 60 Articles)." In *Issues and Studies*, 15:10 (October 1979), 93–111; 15:12 (December 1979), 106–115.

Resolution on Certain Questions in the History of Our Party since the Founding of the People's Republic of China. Beijing: Foreign Languages Press, 1981.

"Resolution on the Question of Cooperativization." *Xinhua yuebao*, 73:11 (11 October 1955), 9–13.

Selden, Mark, ed. *The People's Republic of China: A Documentary History of Revolutionary Change*. New York: Monthly Review Press, 1979.

Shi San. "The Current Situation in the Rural Areas and the New Problems." *Jingji wenti* (December 1982).

Ssumao District Party Committee. "Ssumao District Party Committee's

Opinion about the Implementation of the CCP Central Committee Directive Concerning the Question of Distribution in the Rural People's Communes, Zong Dangfa, 1972, No. 22 (26 March 1972)." *Issues and Studies,* 9:6 (March 1973).

State Statistical Bureau. *Statistical Yearbook of China, 1983.* Hong Kong: Economic Information and Agency, 1984.

"The Opinion Concerning the Government Purchase and Distribution of Food and Oil in 1969, Issued by the Revolutionary Committee of Mung-Lien County in Yunnan." *Issues and Studies,* 7:4 (January 1971).

Thomas, Hugh, ed. *Comrade Editor: Letters to the People's Daily.* Hong Kong: Joint Publishing Co., 1980.

Union Research Institute. *CCP Documents of the Great Proletarian Cultural Revolution, 1966–1967.* Hong Kong: Union Research Publication, 1968.

—— *The Case of P'eng Te-huai.* Hong Kong: Union Research Publication, 1968.

Wan Li. "Energetically Carry Out the Party's Agricultural Policy." *Hongqi,* 3 (1978), 92–97.

Wang Enmao. "Thoroughly Expose and Criticize the Gang of Four, Conscientiously Learn from Tachai [Dazhai] and Strive to Develop Agriculture in Our Province at High Speed." Report to the Second Jilin Learn from Tachai [Dazhai] in Agriculture Conference, 28 January 1978. Translated in *FBIS,* (23 February 1978).

Wang Fenglin. *Xinshiqi renmin gongshe jingji wenti* (Economic Problems of the People's Communes in the New Era). Beijing: Nongye chubanshe, 1979.

—— "We Must Certainly Handle Carefully the Problem of the Transition of the Basic Accounting Unit of the Rural People's Communes." *Zhongguo nongye jingji xuehuide yici xueshu taolunhui lunwen xuanluo* (Collection of Articles from the First Academic Conferences of the Chinese Institute of Agricultural Economics), pp. 351–364. Beijing: Nongye chubanshe, 1979.

Xu Dixin. "Lun qiong guodu" (On Transition through Poverty). *Jingji yanjiu,* 4 (1979), 2–7.

Xu Lu. *Renmin gongshede zizhuquan he suoyouzhi* (The Rights of Sovereignty and Ownership in the People's Communes). Guangzhou: Guangdong renmin chubanshe, 1979.

Yao Wenyuan. "On the Social Basis of the Lin Piao Anti-Party Clique." *Hongqi,* 3 (1975). Translated in *Peking Review,* 10 (7 March 1975), 5–10.

Yin Ta-keng. "Will the Banner of Tachai Fall?" *Dongxiang,* 1 (20 October 1978), 22–25. Translated in *FBIS,* 208 (26 October 1978).

Yu Guoyao. "Understanding Some Problems in Our Country's Agricultural Policy." *Hongqi,* 5 (1980).

Yu Lin County Theoretical Group. *Shehuizhuyi jiti suoyouzhi* (The Socialist Collective Ownership System). Nanning: Guangxi renmin chubanshe, 1976.

Zeng Qixian. "Comments on Consumption and Savings." *Social Sciences in China,* 4 (1983), 137–163.

Zhang Chunqiao. *On Exercising All-Round Dictatorship Over the Bourgeoisie.* Peking: Foreign Language Press, 1975.

Zhongguo baike nianjian, 1980 (Chinese Encyclopedia). Beijing: Zhongguo dabaike quanshu chubanshe, 1981.

Zhongguo nongye dashiji, 1949–1980. (Major Events in Chinese Agriculture). Beijing: Nongye chubanshe, 1982.

Zhongguo nongye nianjian, 1980, 1981, 1983 (Chinese Agriculture Yearbook). Beijing: Nongye chubanshe, 1981, 1982, 1984.

Zhongguo renmin daxue shubao ziliao, baokan ziliao, nongye jingji (Chinese People's University Materials Room. Materials Republished from the Press, Agricultural Economics). 1979. (Source for most provincial newspaper reports from 1978 and 1979.)

Zhongguo renmin gongheguo jingji dashiji, 1949–1980 (Major Economic Events in the PRC). Beijing: Zhongguo shehui kexue chubanshe, 1984.

Zhongguo tongji nianjian, 1984 (Chinese Statistical Yearbook). Beijing: Zhongguo tongji chubanshe, 1984.

Zhou Cheng. "An Exploratory Discussion of the Transition of Rural People's Communes from Production Team Accounting to Brigade Level Accounting." *Zhongguo nongye jingji xuehuide yici xueshu taolunhui lunwen xuanluo* (Collection of Articles from the First Academic Conference of the Chinese Institute of Agricultural Economics), pp. 337–350. Beijing: Nongye chubanshe, 1979,

Zou Jianming. "Some Views on the Criticism of 'Spontaneous Capitalist Tendencies'." *RMRB*, 16 May 1980.

INDEX

HARVARD EAST ASIAN SERIES

83. *Folk Buddhist Religion: Dissenting Sects in Late Traditional China.* Daniel L. Overmyer.

84. *The Limits of Change: Essays on Conservative Alternatives in Republican China.* Ed. Charlotte Furth.

85. *Yenching University and Sino-Western Relations, 1916–1952.* Philip West.

86. *Japanese Marxist: A Portrait of Kawakami Hajime, 1879–1946.* Gail Lee Bernstein.

87. *China's Forty Millions: Minority Nationalities and National Integration in the People's Republic of China.* June Teufel Dreyer.

88. *Japanese Colonial Education in Taiwan, 1895–1945.* E. Patricia Tsurumi.

89. *Modern Chinese Literature in the May Fourth Era.* Ed. Merle Goldman.

90. *The Broken Wave: The Chinese Communist Peasant Movement, 1922–1928.* Roy Hofheinz, Jr.

91. *Passage to Power: K'ang-hsi and His Heir Apparent, 1661–1722.* Silas H. L. Wu.

92. *Chinese Communism and the Rise of Mao.* Benjamin I. Schwartz.

93. *China's Development Experience in Comparative Perspective.* Ed. Robert F. Dernberger.

94. *The Chinese Vernacular Story.* Patrick Hanan.

95. *Chinese Village Politics in the Malaysian State.* Judith Strauch.

96. *Chinese Elites and Political Change: Zhejiang Province in the Early Twentieth Century.* R. Keith Schoppa.

97. *Hideyoshi.* Mary Elizabeth Berry.

98. *Ding Ling's Fiction: Ideology and Narrative in Modern Chinese Literature.* Yi-tsi Mei Feuerwerker.

99. *Millenarianism and Peasant Politics in Vietnam.* Hue-Tam Ho Tai.

100. *Long Lives: Chinese Elderly and the Communist Revolution.* Deborah Davis Friedmann.

101. *Wang Kuo-wei: An Intellectual Biography.* Joey Bonner.

102. *Agrarian Radicalism in China, 1968–1981.* David Zweig.

(Some of these titles may be out of print in a given year. Write to Harvard University Press for information and ordering.)